HULK

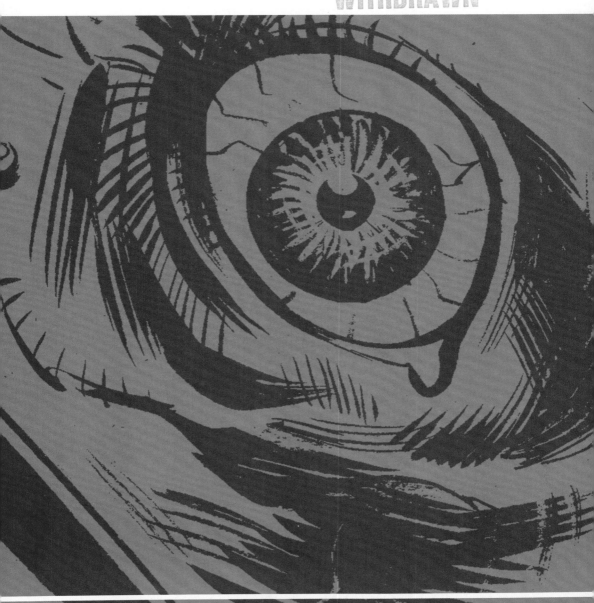

COLLECTION EDITOR: **JENNIFER GRÜNWALD**
ASSISTANT EDITOR: **CAITLIN O'CONNELL**
ASSOCIATE MANAGING EDITOR: **KATERI WOODY**
EDITOR, SPECIAL PROJECTS: **MARK D. BEAZLEY**
VP PRODUCTION & SPECIAL PROJECTS: **JEFF YOUNGQUIST**
BOOK DESIGN: **JEFF POWELL**

SVP PRINT, SALES & MARKETING: **DAVID GABRIEL**
DIRECTOR, LICENSED PUBLISHING: **SVEN LARSEN**
EDITOR IN CHIEF: **C.B. CEBULSKI**
CHIEF CREATIVE OFFICER: **JOE QUESADA**
PRESIDENT: **DAN BUCKLEY**
EXECUTIVE PRODUCER: **ALAN FINE**

HULK: INCREDIBLE ORIGINS. Contains material originally published in magazine form as HULK: SEASON ONE and IMMORTAL HULK #1. First printing 2019. ISBN 978-0-7851-6392-3. Published by MARVEL WORLD INC., a subsidiary of MARVEL ENTERTAINMENT, LLC. OFFICE OF PUBLICATION: 135 West 50th Street, New York, NY 10020. **Printed in Canada.** DAN BUCKLEY, President, Marvel Entertai JOHN NEE, Publisher; JOE QUESADA, Chief Creative Officer; TOM BREVOORT, SVP of Publishing; DAVID BOGART, Associate Publisher & SVP of Talent Affairs; DAVID GABRIEL, SVP of Sales & Marketing, Publishing YOUNGQUIST, VP of Production & Special Projects; DAN CARR, Executive Director of Publishing Technology; ALEX MORALES, Director of Publishing Operations; DAN EDINGTON, Managing Editor; SUSAN CRESPI, Proc Manager; STAN LEE, Chairman Emeritus. For information regarding advertising in Marvel Comics or on Marvel.com, please contact Vit DeBellis, Custom Solutions & Integrated Advertising Manager, at vdebellis@m com. For Marvel subscription inquiries, please call 888-511-5480. **Manufactured between 8/16/2019 and 9/17/2019 by SOLISCO PRINTERS, SCOTT, QC, CANADA.**

10 9 8 7 6 5 4 3 2 1

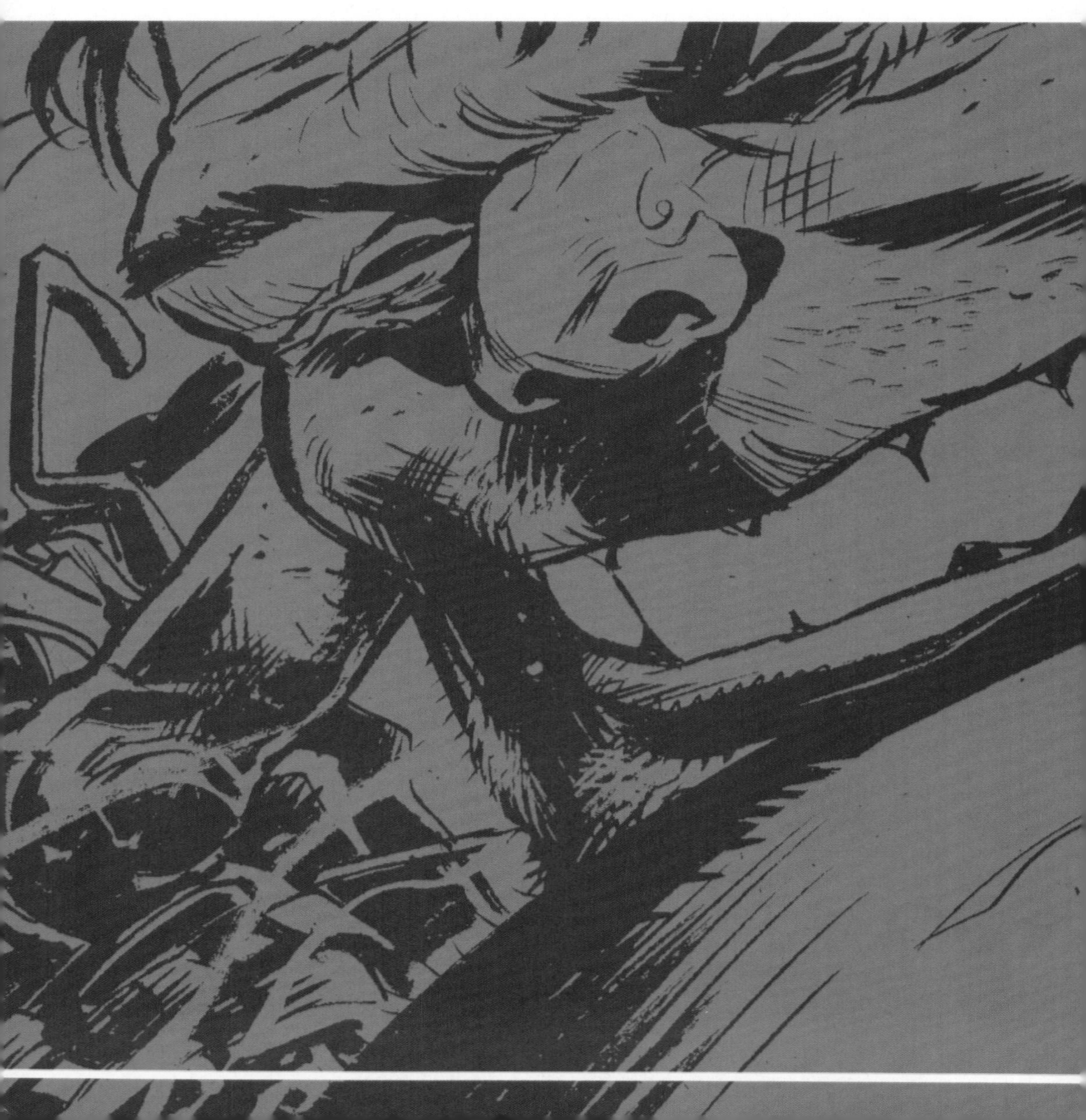

HULK

WRITER
FRED VAN LENTE

ARTIST
TOM FOWLER

COLOR ARTIST
JORDIE BELLAIRE

LETTERERS
**VC'S CHRIS ELIOPOULOS
& JOE SABINO**

COVER ART
JULIAN TOTINO TEDESCO

EDITORS
**TOM BRENNAN
& JAKE THOMAS**

SENIOR EDITOR
MARK PANICCIA

HULK CREATED BY STAN LEE & JACK KIRBY

INCREDIBLE ORIGINS

AIR FORCE RESEARCH LABORATORY GAMMA BASE. 25 MILES SE OF LAS CRUCES, NM. T-MINUS 2 MINUTES, BANNERBOMB TEST "A"

CLEAR DAY. *STILL DAY.*

NOTHING OUT OF THE *ORDINARY.*

OPTIMAL CONDITIONS.

THE SO-CALLED "*BANNERBOMB*"--THE *BEAUTY* OF IT--

--IF SUCH A WORD CAN EVEN BE *USED* IN THIS CONTEXT--

--IS THAT IT DELIVERS AN ENORMOUS BURST OF HIGH-ENERGY *GAMMA RAYS.*

ITS EXTRAORDINARY *ENERGY DENSITY* COMES NOT FROM FISSION OR FUSION BUT *RADIOACTIVE DECAY.*

YOU GET THE *POWER* OF A NUKE WITHOUT THE ACCOMPANYING *FALLOUT.*

ITS WIDESPRE... ADOPTION WOU... *END* THE THRE... OF ARMAGEDD... AT LEAST *TH...* VERSION--FO... ALL TIME.

LITTLE GREEN MAN

THAT'S BEEN MY *DREAM.* SINCE I WAS OLD ENOUGH TO KNOW WHAT NUCLEAR WAR *WAS.*

AND I WAS SO CLOSE TO *ACHIEVING* THAT DREAM AT LAST.

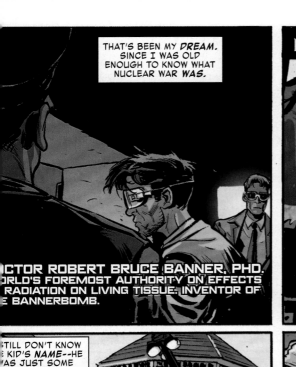

CTOR ROBERT BRUCE BANNER, PHD. ORLD'S FOREMOST AUTHORITY ON EFFECTS RADIATION ON LIVING TISSUE. INVENTOR OF E BANNERBOMB.

TILL DON'T KNOW E KID'S *NAME*--HE AS JUST SOME *ORPHAN*--

THE MINUTE I SAW HIM--THE TEST WAS FULLY AUTOMATED-- WE'D PASSED THE SHUTDOWN LIMIT--

KNEW HE WOULD E INCINERATED *INSTANTLY.*

I KNEW I HAD TO--

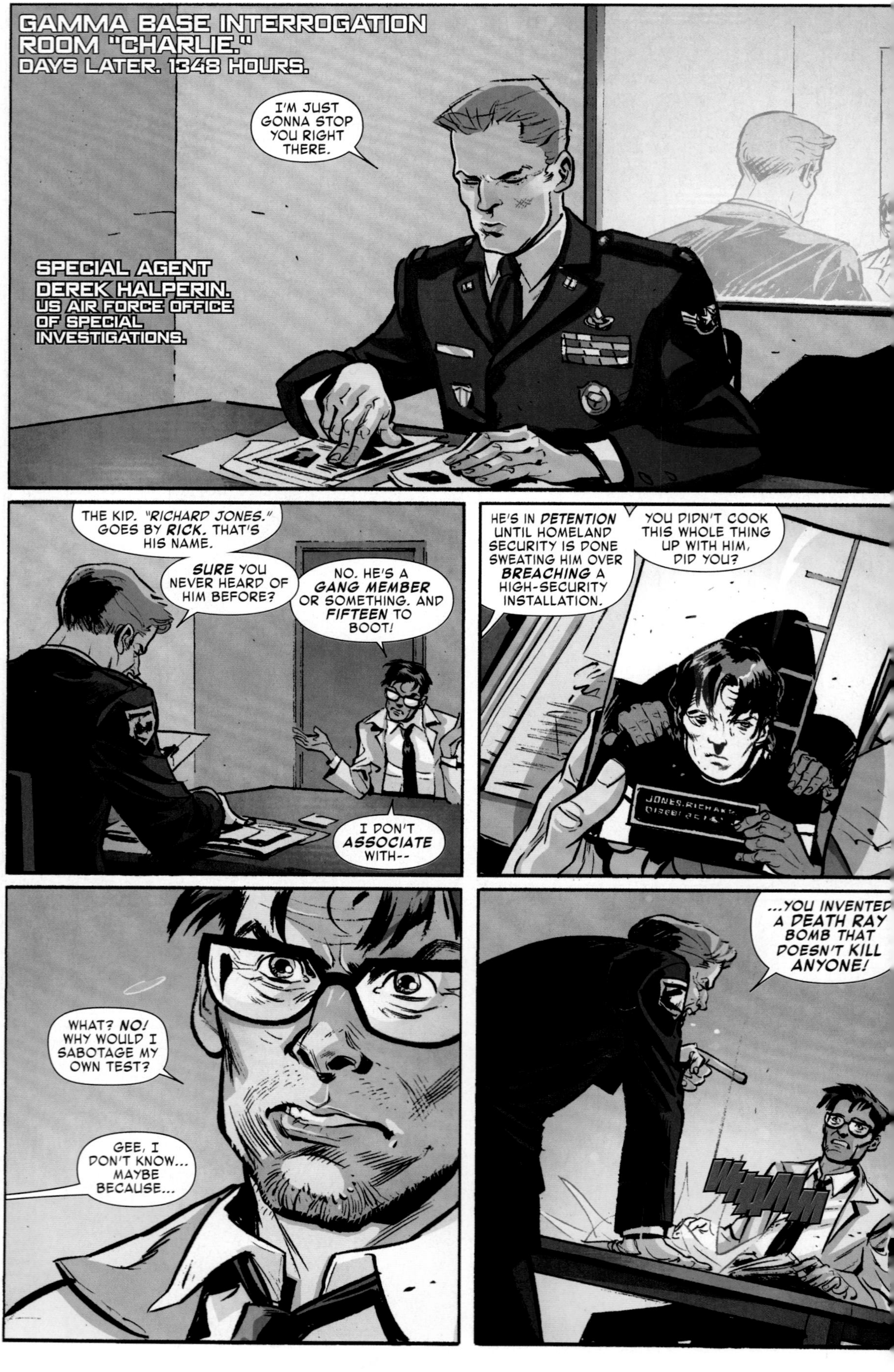
GAMMA BASE INTERROGATION ROOM "CHARLIE."
DAYS LATER. 1348 HOURS.
I'M JUST GONNA STOP YOU RIGHT THERE.
SPECIAL AGENT DEREK HALPERIN.
US AIR FORCE OFFICE OF SPECIAL INVESTIGATIONS.
THE KID. "RICHARD JONES." GOES BY RICK. THAT'S HIS NAME.
SURE YOU NEVER HEARD OF HIM BEFORE?
NO. HE'S A GANG MEMBER OR SOMETHING. AND FIFTEEN TO BOOT!
I DON'T ASSOCIATE WITH--
HE'S IN DETENTION UNTIL HOMELAND SECURITY IS DONE SWEATING HIM OVER BREACHING A HIGH-SECURITY INSTALLATION.
YOU DIDN'T COOK THIS WHOLE THING UP WITH HIM, DID YOU?
WHAT? NO! WHY WOULD I SABOTAGE MY OWN TEST?
GEE, I DON'T KNOW... MAYBE BECAUSE...
...YOU INVENTED A DEATH RAY BOMB THAT DOESN'T KILL ANYONE!

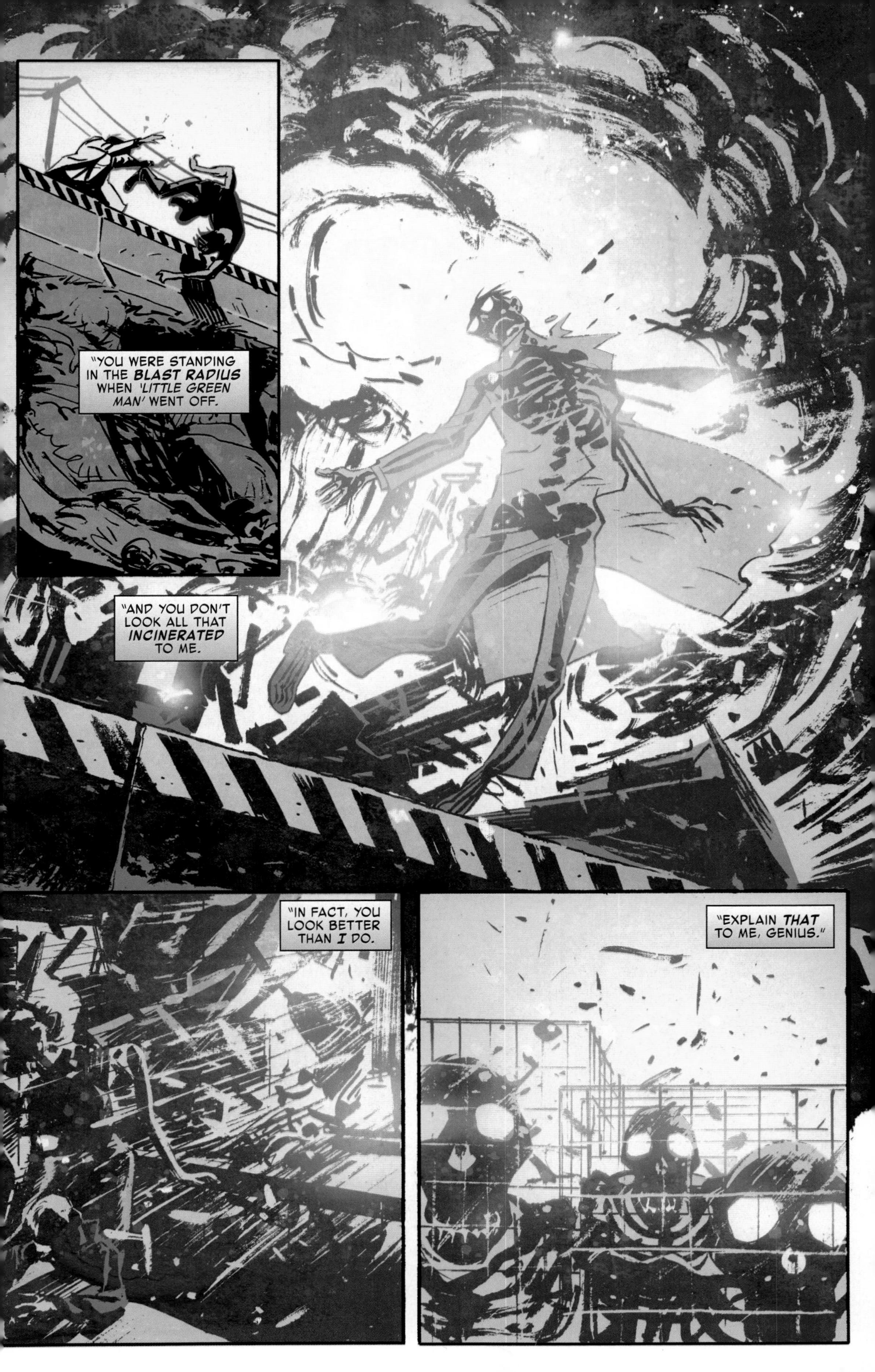
"YOU WERE STANDING IN THE BLAST RADIUS WHEN 'LITTLE GREEN MAN' WENT OFF.
"AND YOU DON'T LOOK ALL THAT INCINERATED TO ME.
"IN FACT, YOU LOOK BETTER THAN I DO.
"EXPLAIN THAT TO ME, GENIUS."

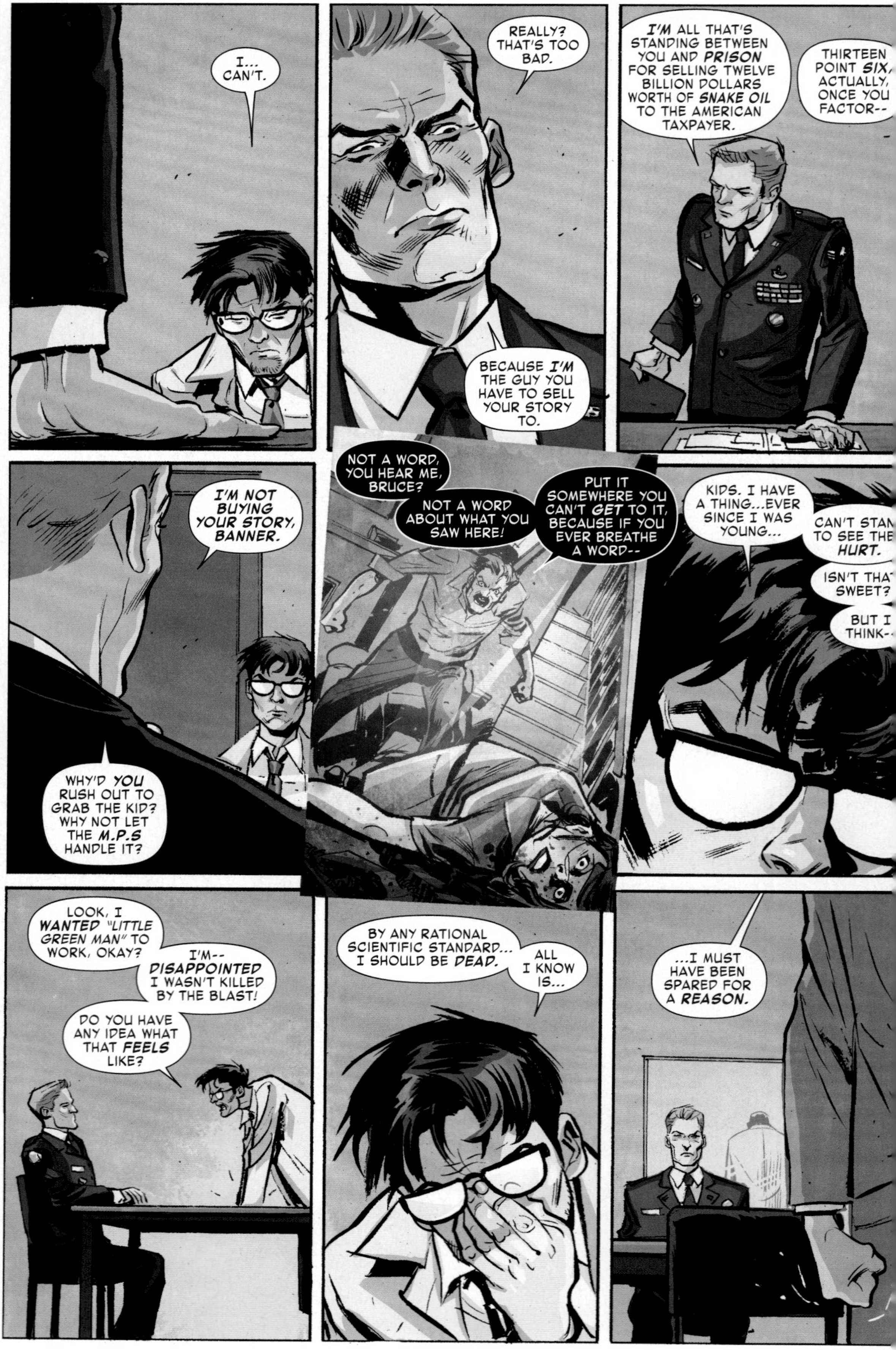
I... CAN'T.
REALLY? THAT'S TOO BAD.
BECAUSE I'M THE GUY YOU HAVE TO SELL YOUR STORY TO.
I'M ALL THAT'S STANDING BETWEEN YOU AND PRISON FOR SELLING TWELVE BILLION DOLLARS WORTH OF SNAKE OIL TO THE AMERICAN TAXPAYER.
THIRTEEN POINT SIX, ACTUALLY, ONCE YOU FACTOR--
I'M NOT BUYING YOUR STORY, BANNER.
WHY'D YOU RUSH OUT TO GRAB THE KID? WHY NOT LET THE M.P.S HANDLE IT?
NOT A WORD, YOU HEAR ME, BRUCE?
NOT A WORD ABOUT WHAT YOU SAW HERE!
PUT IT SOMEWHERE YOU CAN'T GET TO IT, BECAUSE IF YOU EVER BREATHE A WORD--
KIDS. I HAVE A THING...EVER SINCE I WAS YOUNG...
LOOK, I WANTED "LITTLE GREEN MAN" TO WORK, OKAY?
I'M-- DISAPPOINTED I WASN'T KILLED BY THE BLAST!
DO YOU HAVE ANY IDEA WHAT THAT FEELS LIKE?
BY ANY RATIONAL SCIENTIFIC STANDARD... I SHOULD BE DEAD.
ALL I KNOW IS...
...I MUST HAVE BEEN SPARED FOR A REASON.

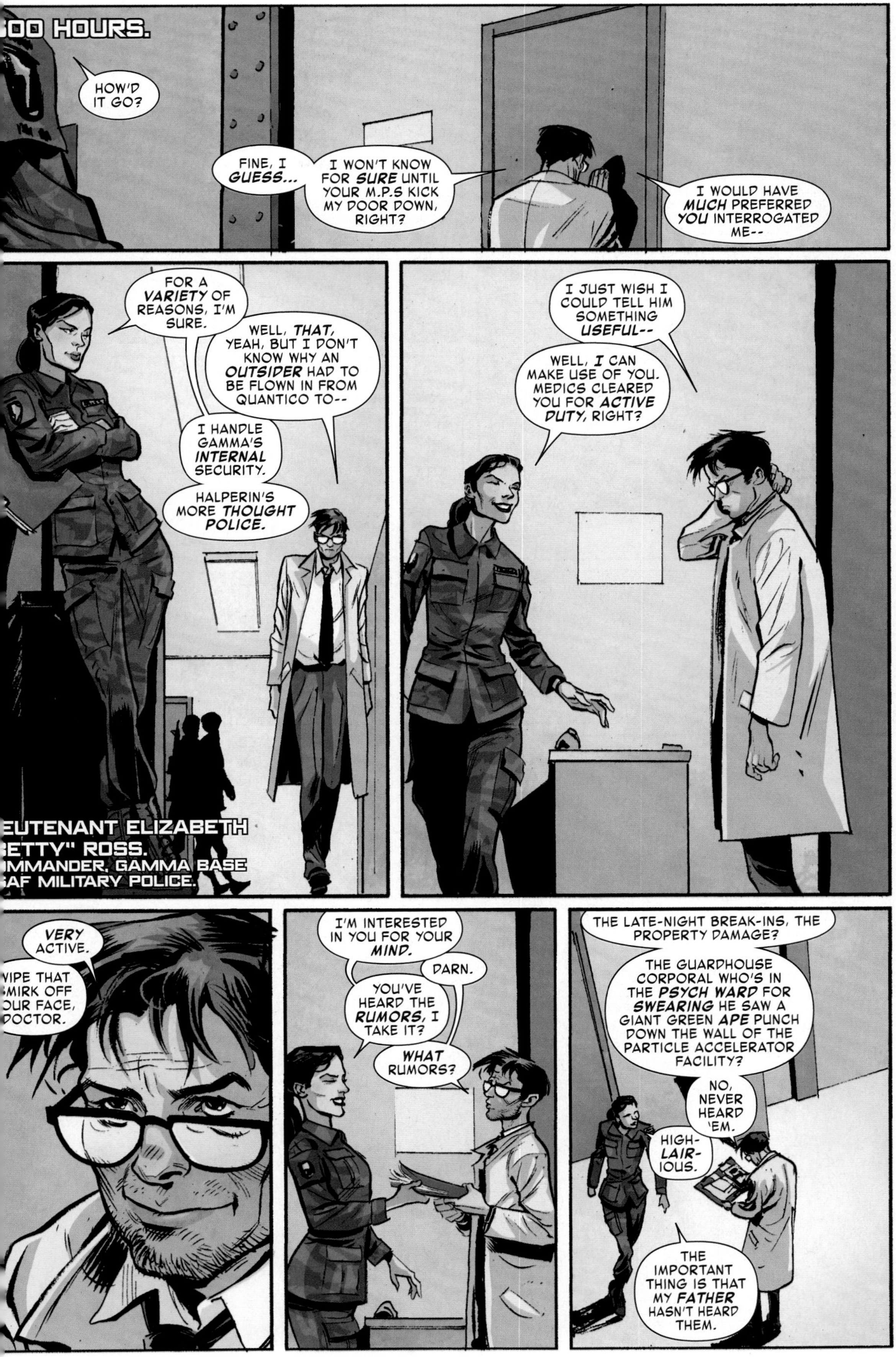

00 HOURS.
HOW'D IT GO?
FINE, I GUESS...
I WON'T KNOW FOR SURE UNTIL YOUR M.P.S KICK MY DOOR DOWN, RIGHT?
I WOULD HAVE MUCH PREFERRED YOU INTERROGATED ME--
FOR A VARIETY OF REASONS, I'M SURE.
WELL, THAT, YEAH, BUT I DON'T KNOW WHY AN OUTSIDER HAD TO BE FLOWN IN FROM QUANTICO TO--
I HANDLE GAMMA'S INTERNAL SECURITY.
HALPERIN'S MORE THOUGHT POLICE.
EUTENANT ELIZABETH
ETTY" ROSS.
MMANDER, GAMMA BASE
AF MILITARY POLICE.
I JUST WISH I COULD TELL HIM SOMETHING USEFUL--
WELL, I CAN MAKE USE OF YOU. MEDICS CLEARED YOU FOR ACTIVE DUTY, RIGHT?
VERY ACTIVE.
VIPE THAT SMIRK OFF OUR FACE, DOCTOR.
I'M INTERESTED IN YOU FOR YOUR MIND.
DARN.
YOU'VE HEARD THE RUMORS, I TAKE IT?
WHAT RUMORS?
THE LATE-NIGHT BREAK-INS, THE PROPERTY DAMAGE?
THE GUARDHOUSE CORPORAL WHO'S IN THE PSYCH WARD FOR SWEARING HE SAW A GIANT GREEN APE PUNCH DOWN THE WALL OF THE PARTICLE ACCELERATOR FACILITY?
NO, NEVER HEARD 'EM.
HIGH-LAIR-IOUS.
THE IMPORTANT THING IS THAT MY FATHER HASN'T HEARD THEM.

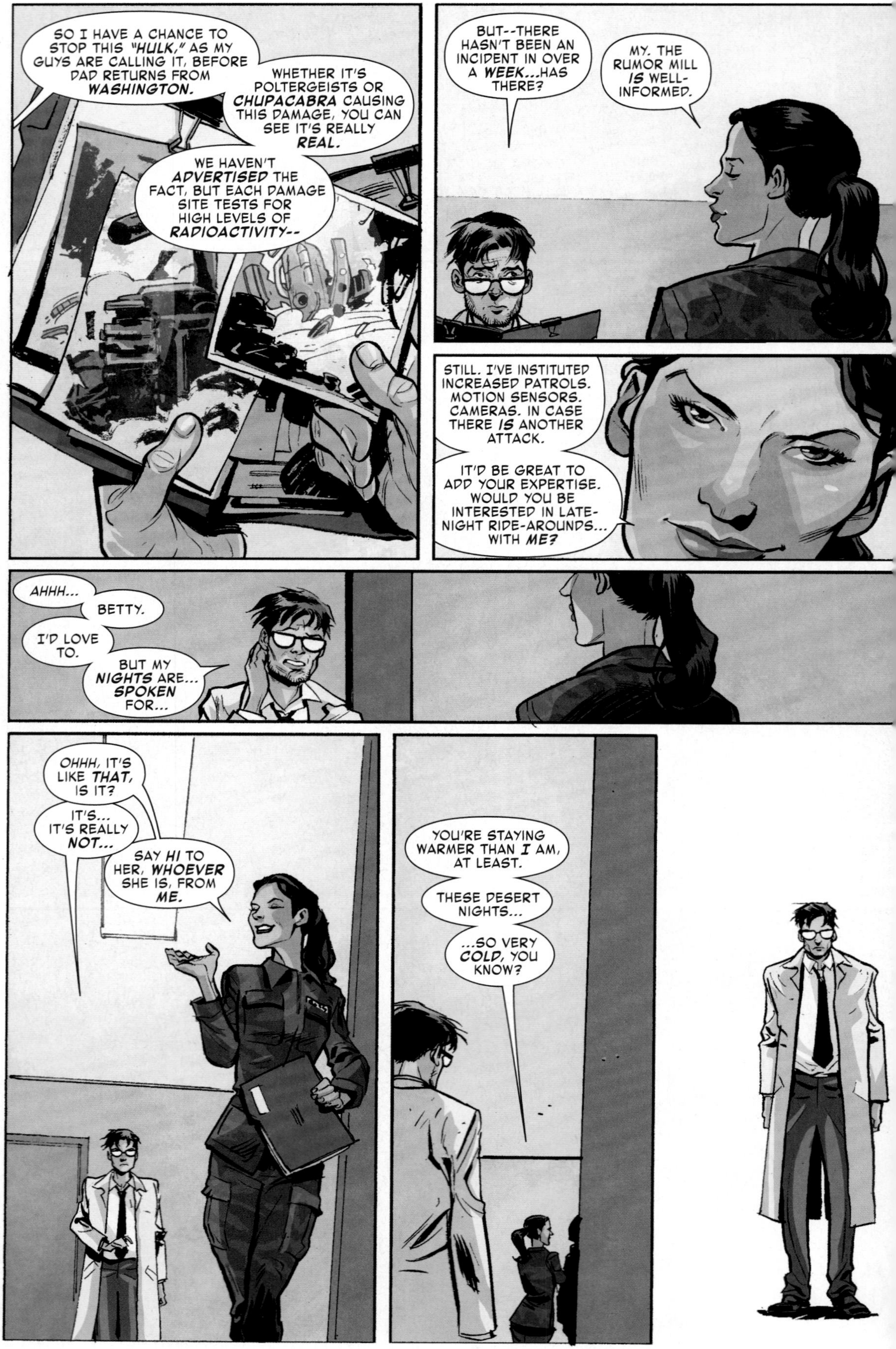
SO I HAVE A CHANCE TO STOP THIS "HULK," AS MY GUYS ARE CALLING IT, BEFORE DAD RETURNS FROM WASHINGTON.
WHETHER IT'S POLTERGEISTS OR CHUPACABRA CAUSING THIS DAMAGE, YOU CAN SEE IT'S REALLY REAL.
WE HAVEN'T ADVERTISED THE FACT, BUT EACH DAMAGE SITE TESTS FOR HIGH LEVELS OF RADIOACTIVITY--
BUT--THERE HASN'T BEEN AN INCIDENT IN OVER A WEEK...HAS THERE?
MY. THE RUMOR MILL IS WELL-INFORMED.
STILL. I'VE INSTITUTED INCREASED PATROLS. MOTION SENSORS. CAMERAS. IN CASE THERE IS ANOTHER ATTACK.
IT'D BE GREAT TO ADD YOUR EXPERTISE. WOULD YOU BE INTERESTED IN LATE-NIGHT RIDE-AROUNDS... WITH ME?
AHHH...
BETTY.
I'D LOVE TO.
BUT MY NIGHTS ARE... SPOKEN FOR...
OHHH, IT'S LIKE THAT, IS IT?
IT'S... IT'S REALLY NOT...
SAY HI TO HER, WHOEVER SHE IS, FROM ME.
YOU'RE STAYING WARMER THAN I AM, AT LEAST.
THESE DESERT NIGHTS...
...SO VERY COLD, YOU KNOW?

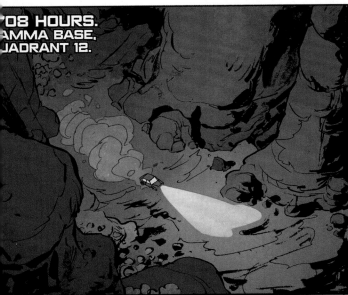

08 HOURS.
AMMA BASE,
JADRANT 12.

COLD FUSION FUEL
ROD LAB.
[DECOMMISSIONED 1991]

Bannerbomb
Survivor's Log.
Day 12 Since
Exposure.

Observation:

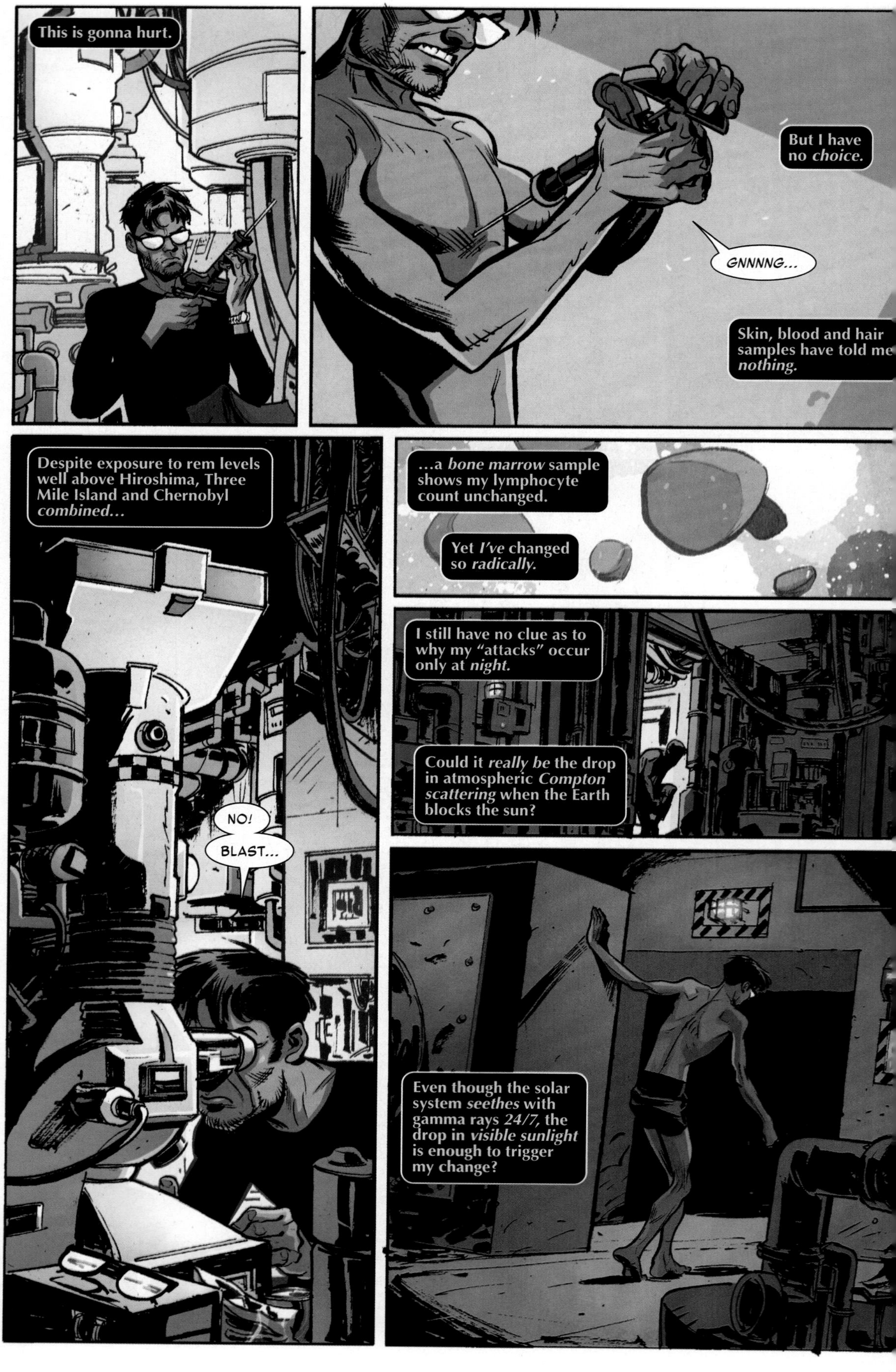

This is gonna hurt.
But I have no *choice.*
GNNNNG...
Skin, blood and hair samples have told me *nothing.*
Despite exposure to rem levels well above Hiroshima, Three Mile Island and Chernobyl *combined...*
NO!
BLAST...
...a *bone marrow* sample shows my lymphocyte count unchanged.
Yet *I've* changed so *radically.*
I still have no clue as to why my "attacks" occur only at *night.*
Could it *really be* the drop in atmospheric *Compton scattering* when the Earth blocks the sun?
Even though the solar system *seethes* with gamma rays *24/7,* the drop in *visible sunlight* is enough to trigger my change?

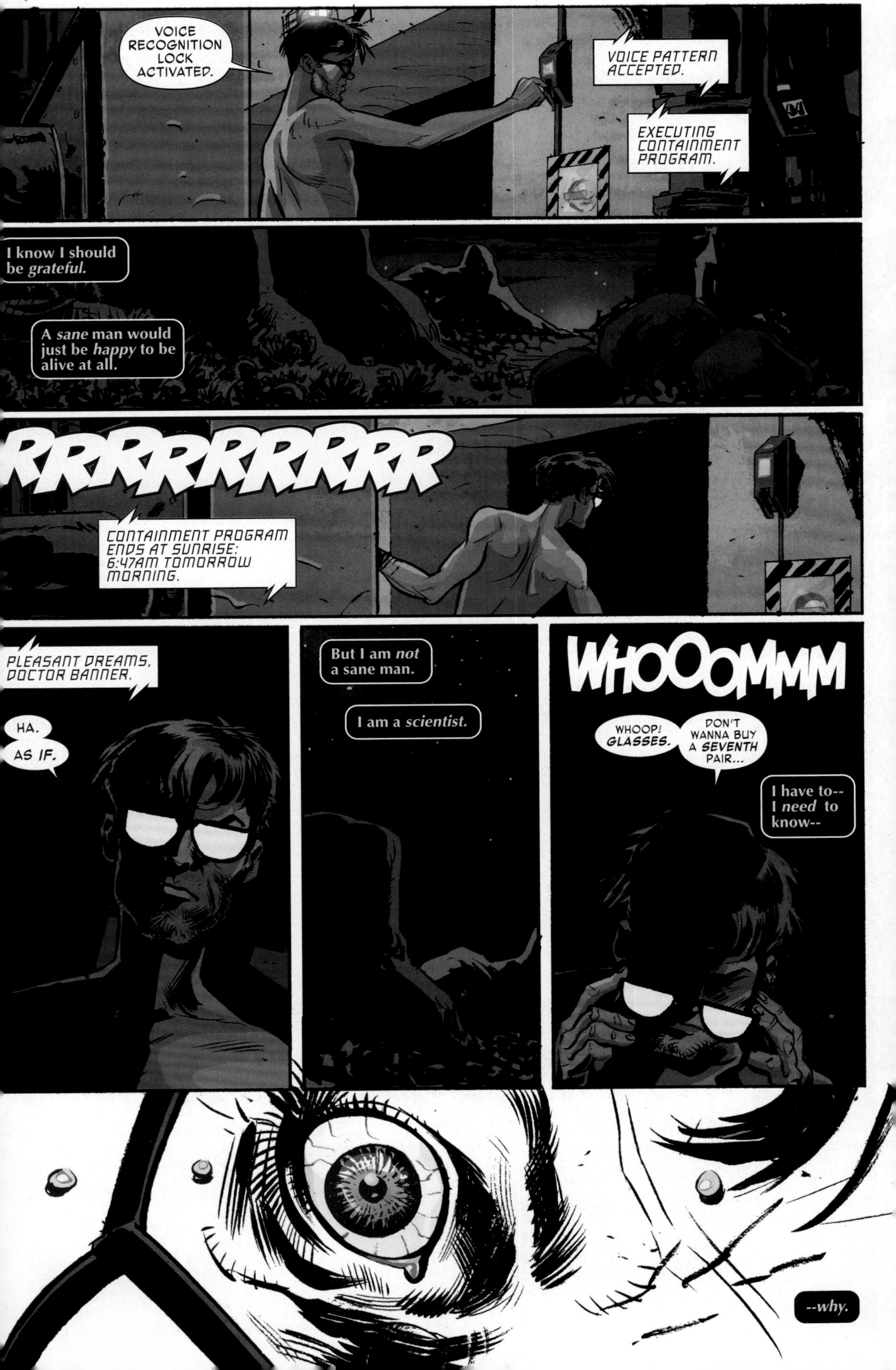
VOICE RECOGNITION LOCK ACTIVATED.
VOICE PATTERN ACCEPTED.
EXECUTING CONTAINMENT PROGRAM.
I know I should be *grateful.*
A *sane* man would just be *happy* to be alive at all.
RRRRRRRRRR
CONTAINMENT PROGRAM ENDS AT SUNRISE: 6:47AM TOMORROW MORNING.
PLEASANT DREAMS, DOCTOR BANNER.
HA.
AS IF.
But I am *not* a sane man.
I am a *scientist.*
WHOOOMMM
WHOOP! GLASSES.
DON'T WANNA BUY A SEVENTH PAIR...
I have to-- I *need* to know--
--*why.*

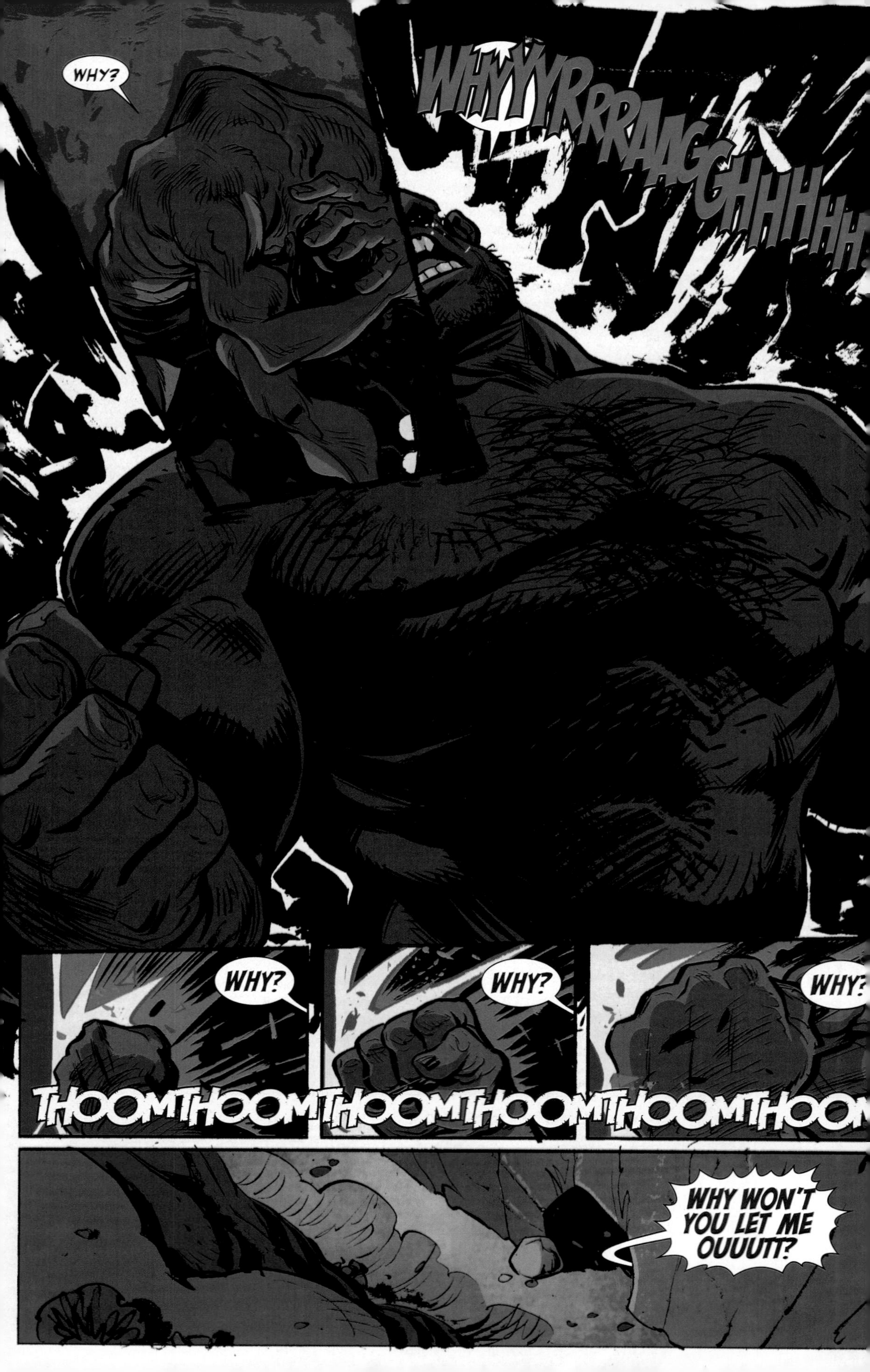
WHY?
WHYYYRRRAAGGHHHHH
WHY?
WHY?
WHY?
THOOMTHOOMTHOOMTHOOMTHOOMTHOOM
WHY WON'T YOU LET ME OUUUTT?

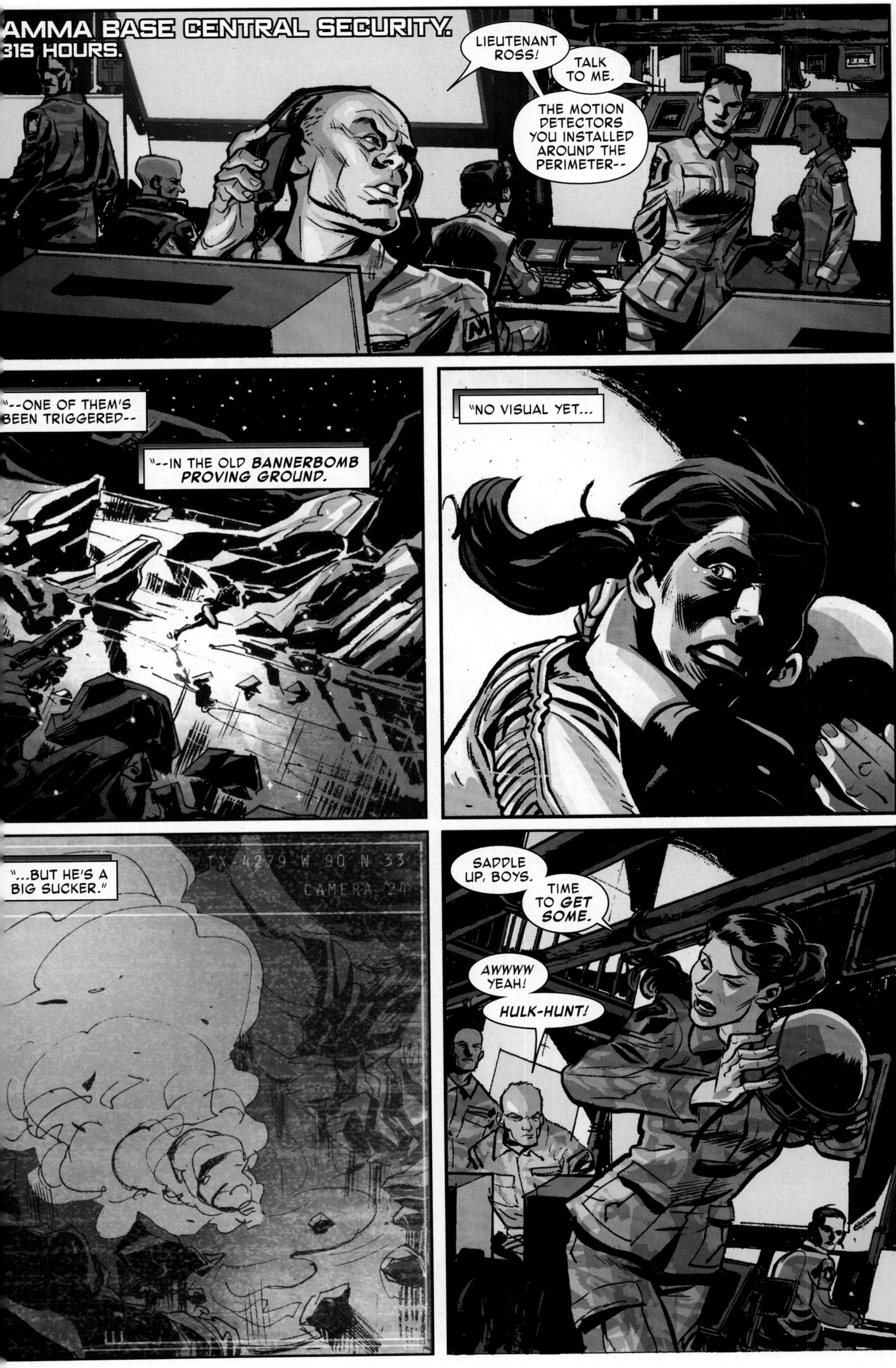
AMMA BASE CENTRAL SECURITY.
315 HOURS.
LIEUTENANT ROSS!
TALK TO ME.
THE MOTION DETECTORS YOU INSTALLED AROUND THE PERIMETER--
"--ONE OF THEM'S BEEN TRIGGERED--
"--IN THE OLD BANNERBOMB PROVING GROUND.
"NO VISUAL YET...
"...BUT HE'S A BIG SUCKER."
TX-4279-W 90 N 33
CAMERA 24
SADDLE UP, BOYS.
TIME TO GET SOME.
AWWWW YEAH!
HULK-HUNT!

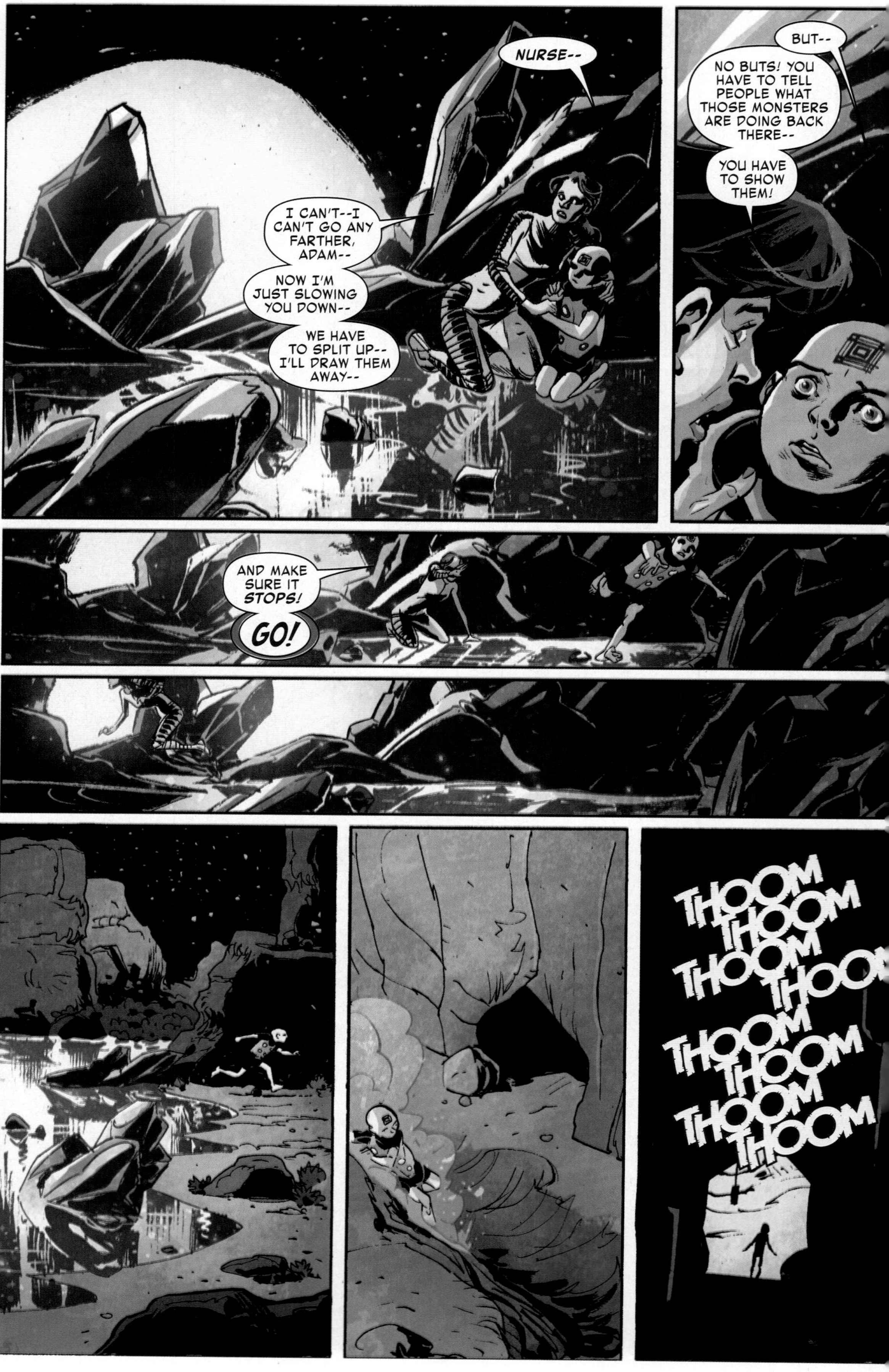
NURSE--
I CAN'T--I CAN'T GO ANY FARTHER, ADAM--
NOW I'M JUST SLOWING YOU DOWN--
WE HAVE TO SPLIT UP-- I'LL DRAW THEM AWAY--
BUT--
NO BUTS! YOU HAVE TO TELL PEOPLE WHAT THOSE MONSTERS ARE DOING BACK THERE--
YOU HAVE TO SHOW THEM!
AND MAKE SURE IT STOPS!
GO!
THOOM THOOM THOOM THOOM THOOM THOOM THOOM THOOM THOOM

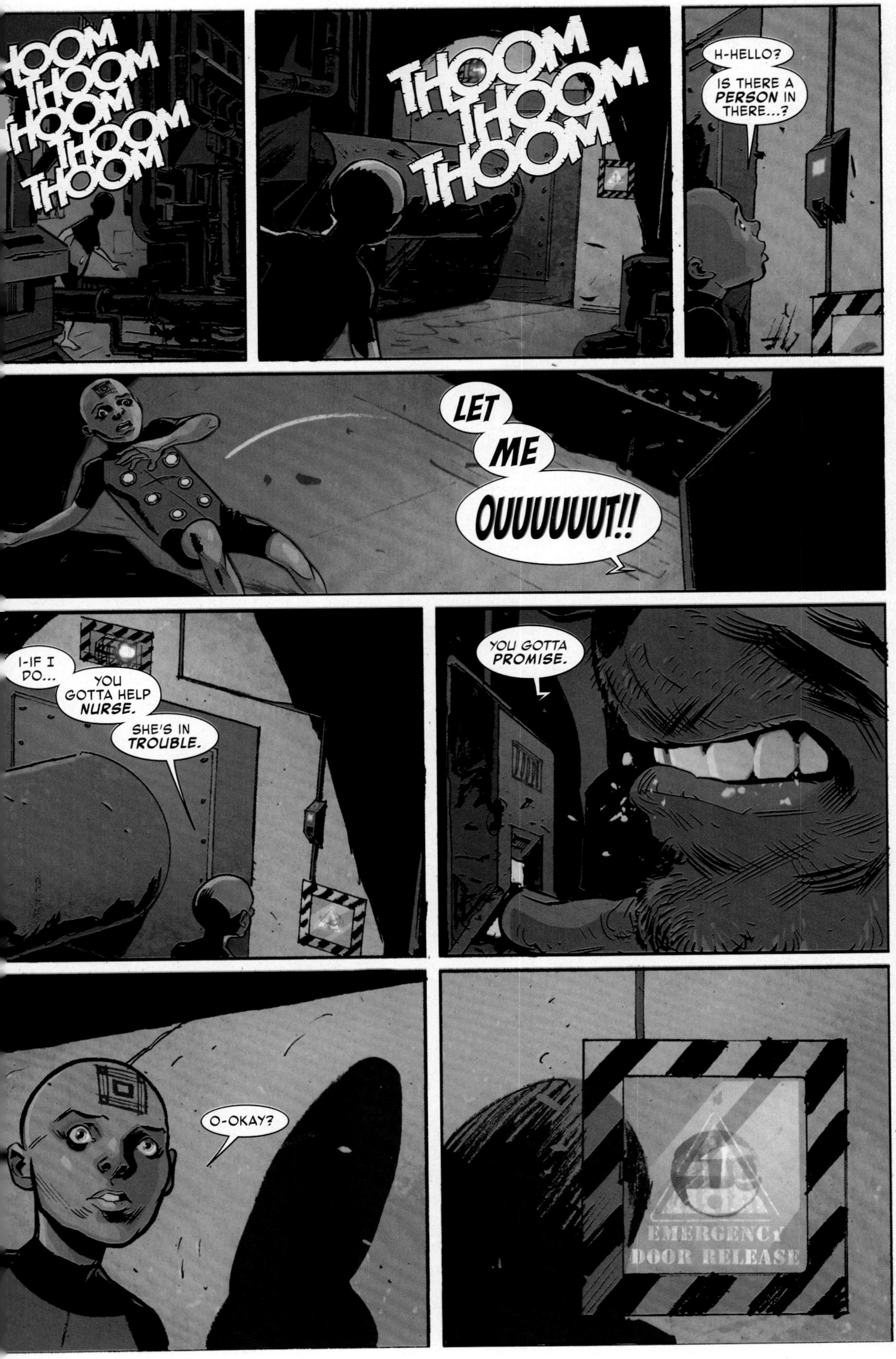
OOM
THOOM
HOOM
THOOM
THOOM
THOOM
THOOM
THOOM
H-HELLO?
IS THERE A PERSON IN THERE...?
LET
ME
OUUUUUUT!!
I-IF I DO...
YOU GOTTA HELP NURSE.
SHE'S IN TROUBLE.
YOU GOTTA PROMISE.
O-OKAY?
EMERGENCY
DOOR RELEASE

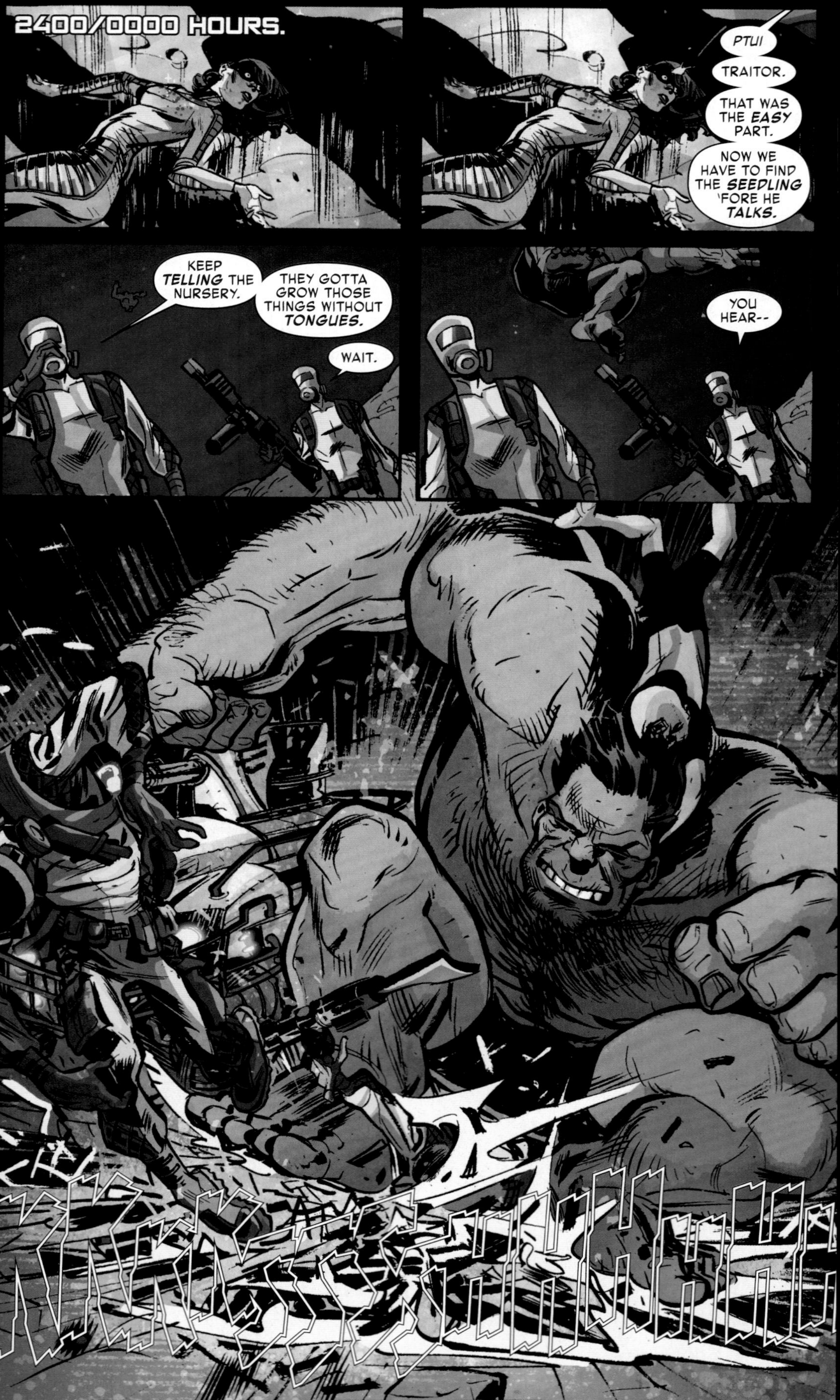
2400/0000 HOURS.
PTUI
TRAITOR.
THAT WAS THE EASY PART.
NOW WE HAVE TO FIND THE SEEDLING 'FORE HE TALKS.
KEEP TELLING THE NURSERY.
THEY GOTTA GROW THOSE THINGS WITHOUT TONGUES.
WAIT.
YOU HEAR--

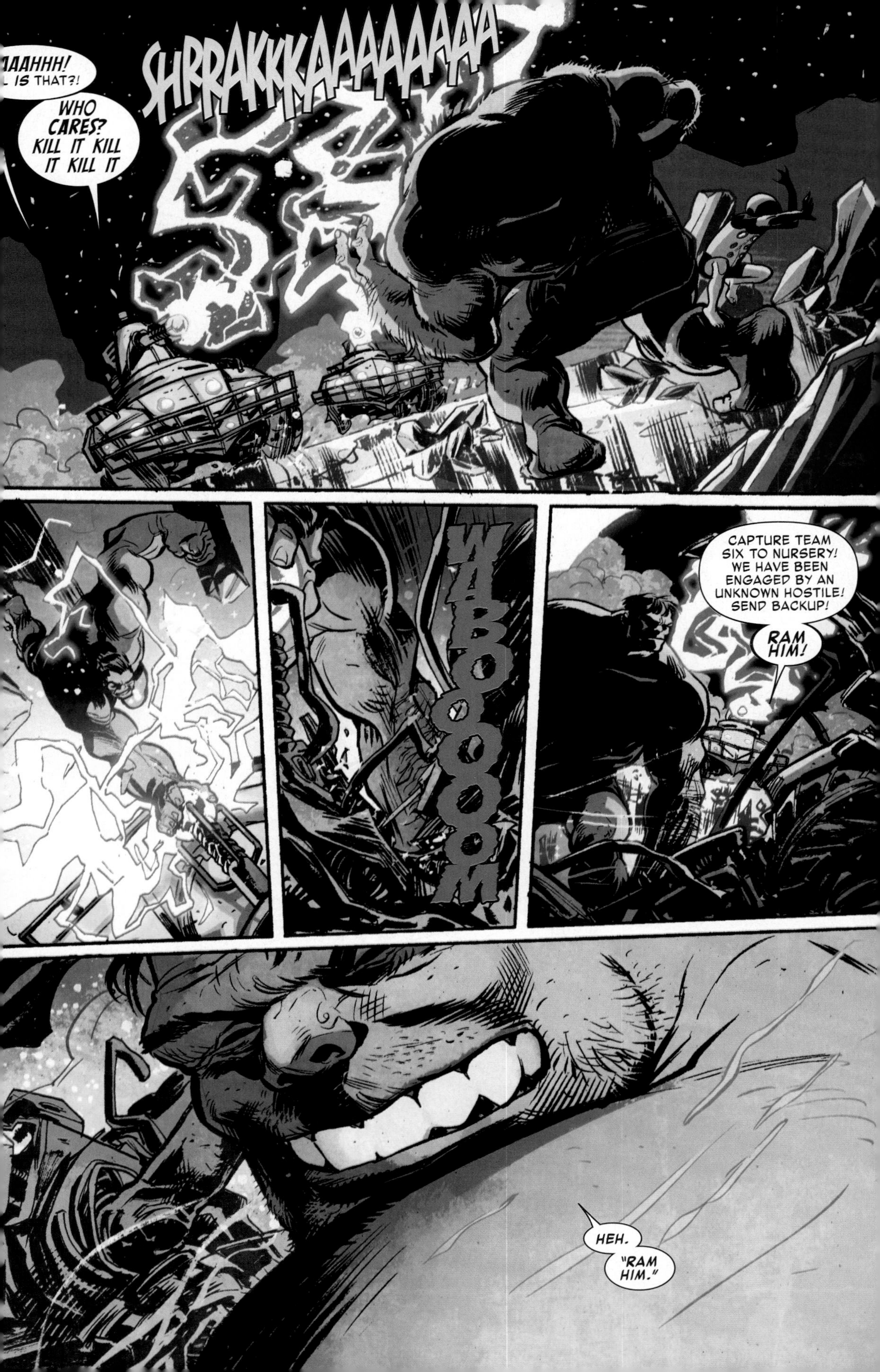
AAAHHH!
L IS THAT?!
WHO CARES? KILL IT KILL IT KILL IT
SHRRAKKKAAAAAAAA
WABOOOOOM
CAPTURE TEAM SIX TO NURSERY! WE HAVE BEEN ENGAGED BY AN UNKNOWN HOSTILE! SEND BACKUP!
RAM HIM!
HEH.
"RAM HIM."

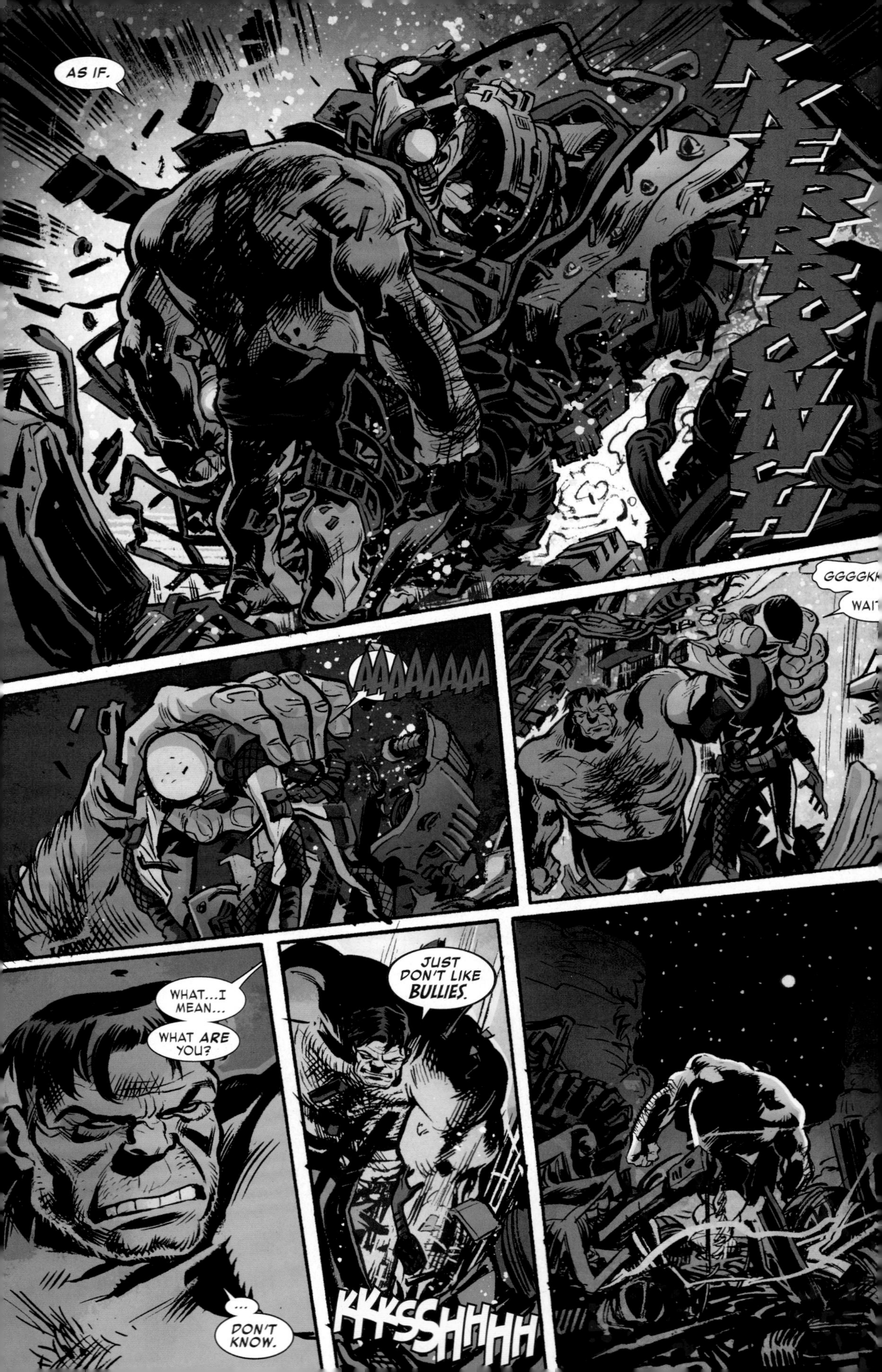
AS IF.
AAAAAAAA
GGGGKK
WAIT
WHAT...I MEAN...
WHAT ARE YOU?
...
DON'T KNOW.
JUST DON'T LIKE BULLIES.
KKKSSHHHH

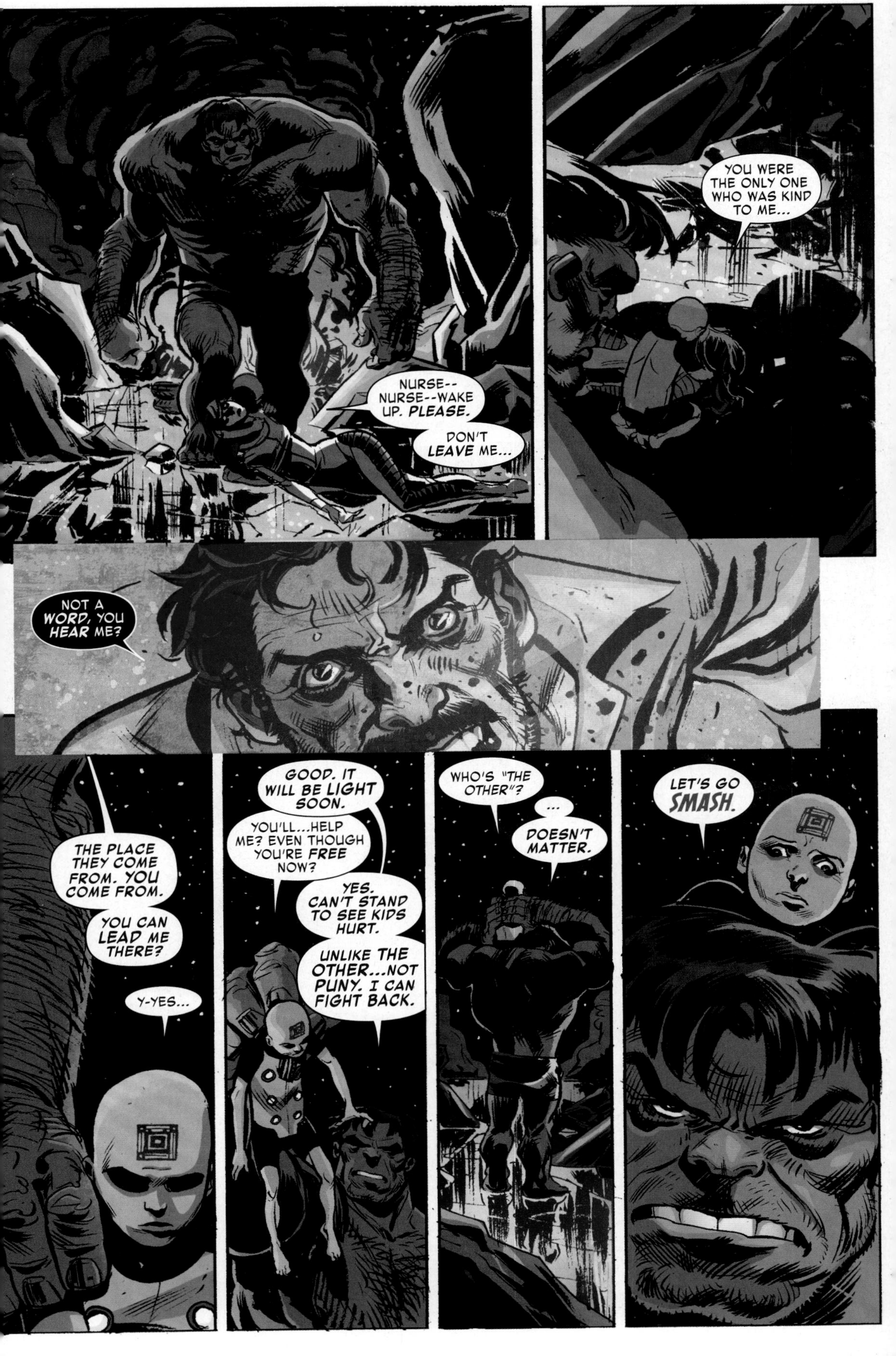
NURSE--
NURSE--WAKE UP. PLEASE.
DON'T LEAVE ME...
YOU WERE THE ONLY ONE WHO WAS KIND TO ME...
NOT A WORD, YOU HEAR ME?
THE PLACE THEY COME FROM. YOU COME FROM.
YOU CAN LEAD ME THERE?
Y-YES...
GOOD. IT WILL BE LIGHT SOON.
YOU'LL...HELP ME? EVEN THOUGH YOU'RE FREE NOW?
YES. CAN'T STAND TO SEE KIDS HURT.
UNLIKE THE OTHER...NOT PUNY. I CAN FIGHT BACK.
WHO'S "THE OTHER"?
...
DOESN'T MATTER.
LET'S GO SMASH.

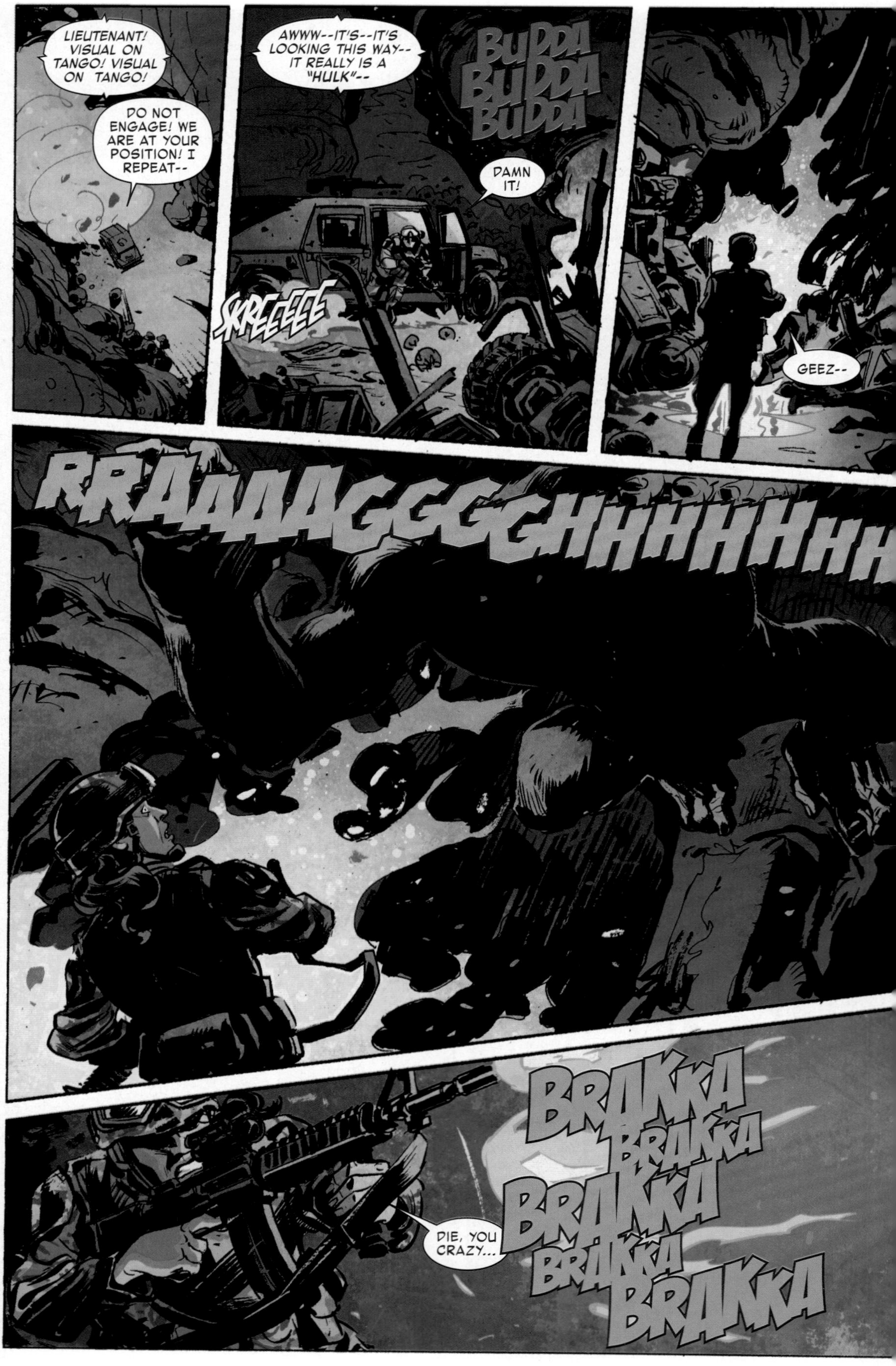
LIEUTENANT! VISUAL ON TANGO! VISUAL ON TANGO!
DO NOT ENGAGE! WE ARE AT YOUR POSITION! I REPEAT--
AWWW--IT'S--IT'S LOOKING THIS WAY-- IT REALLY IS A "HULK"--
BUDDA BUDDA BUDDA
DAMN IT!
SKREEEEEE
GEEZ--
RRAAAAGGGGHHHHHHHH
BRAKKA BRAKKA BRAKKA BRAKKA BRAKKA
DIE, YOU CRAZY...

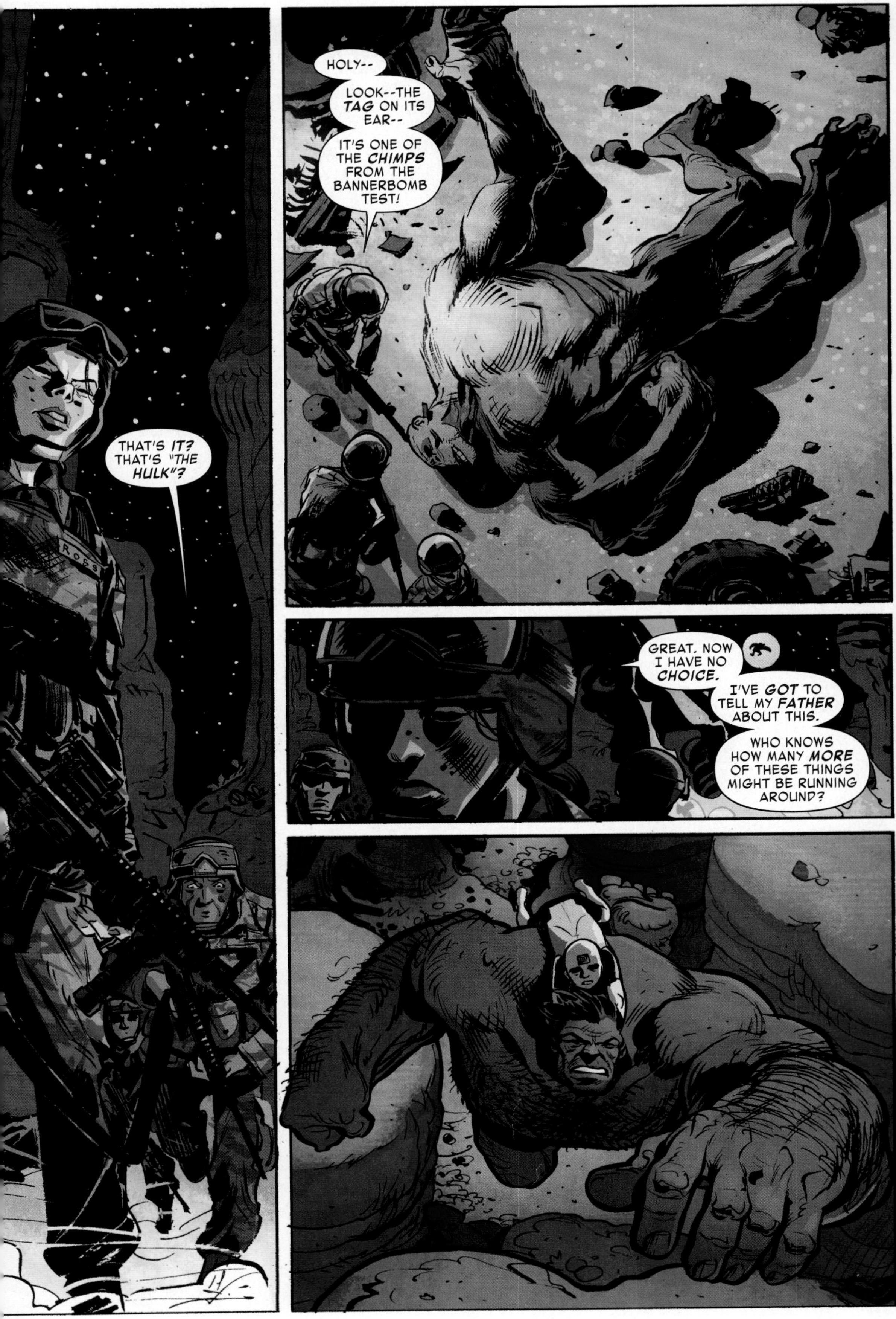
HOLY--
LOOK--THE TAG ON ITS EAR--
IT'S ONE OF THE CHIMPS FROM THE BANNERBOMB TEST!
THAT'S IT? THAT'S "THE HULK"?
GREAT. NOW I HAVE NO CHOICE.
I'VE GOT TO TELL MY FATHER ABOUT THIS.
WHO KNOWS HOW MANY MORE OF THESE THINGS MIGHT BE RUNNING AROUND?

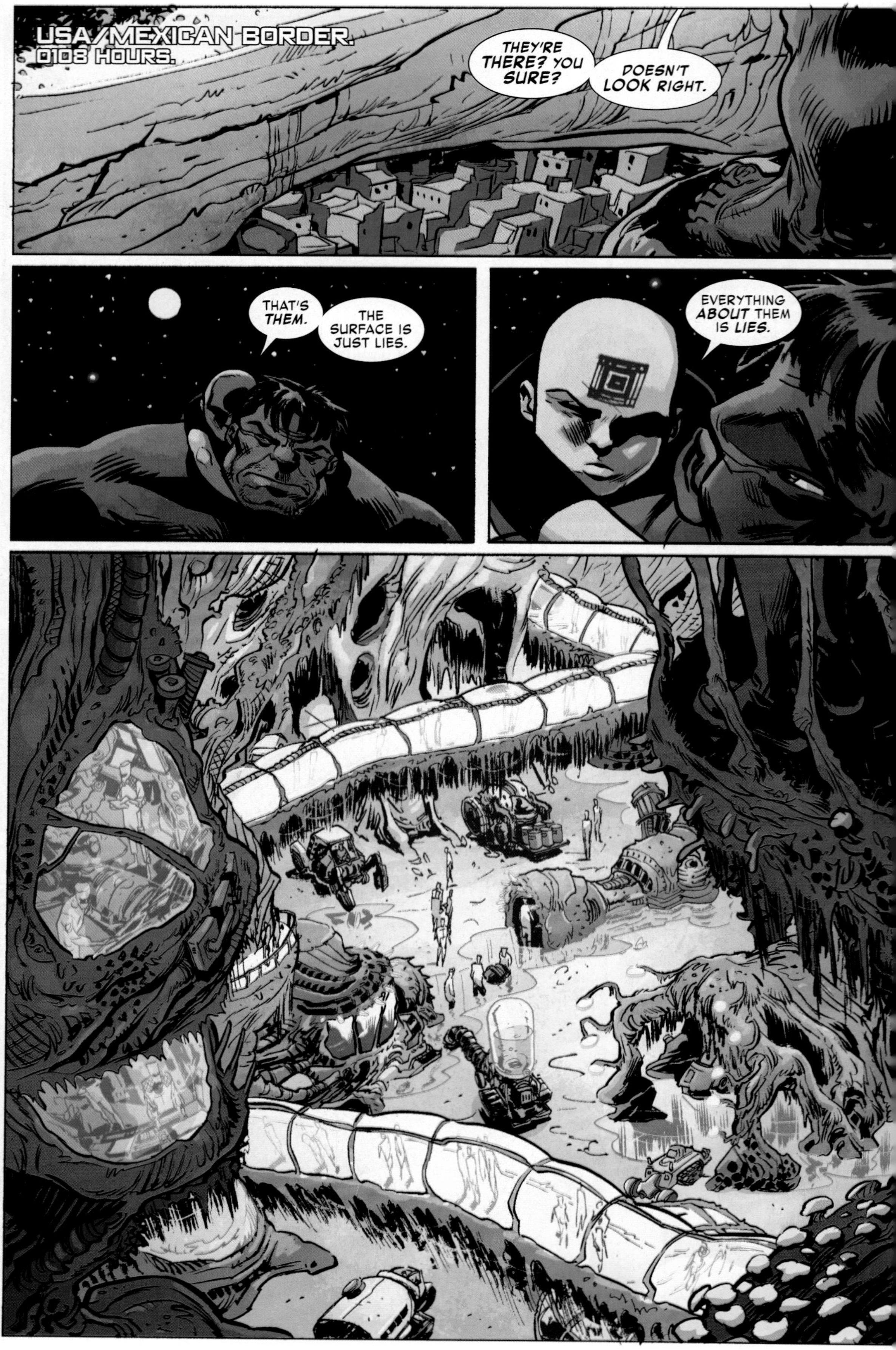
USA/MEXICAN BORDER.
0108 HOURS.
THEY'RE THERE? YOU SURE?
DOESN'T LOOK RIGHT.
THAT'S THEM.
THE SURFACE IS JUST LIES.
EVERYTHING ABOUT THEM IS LIES.

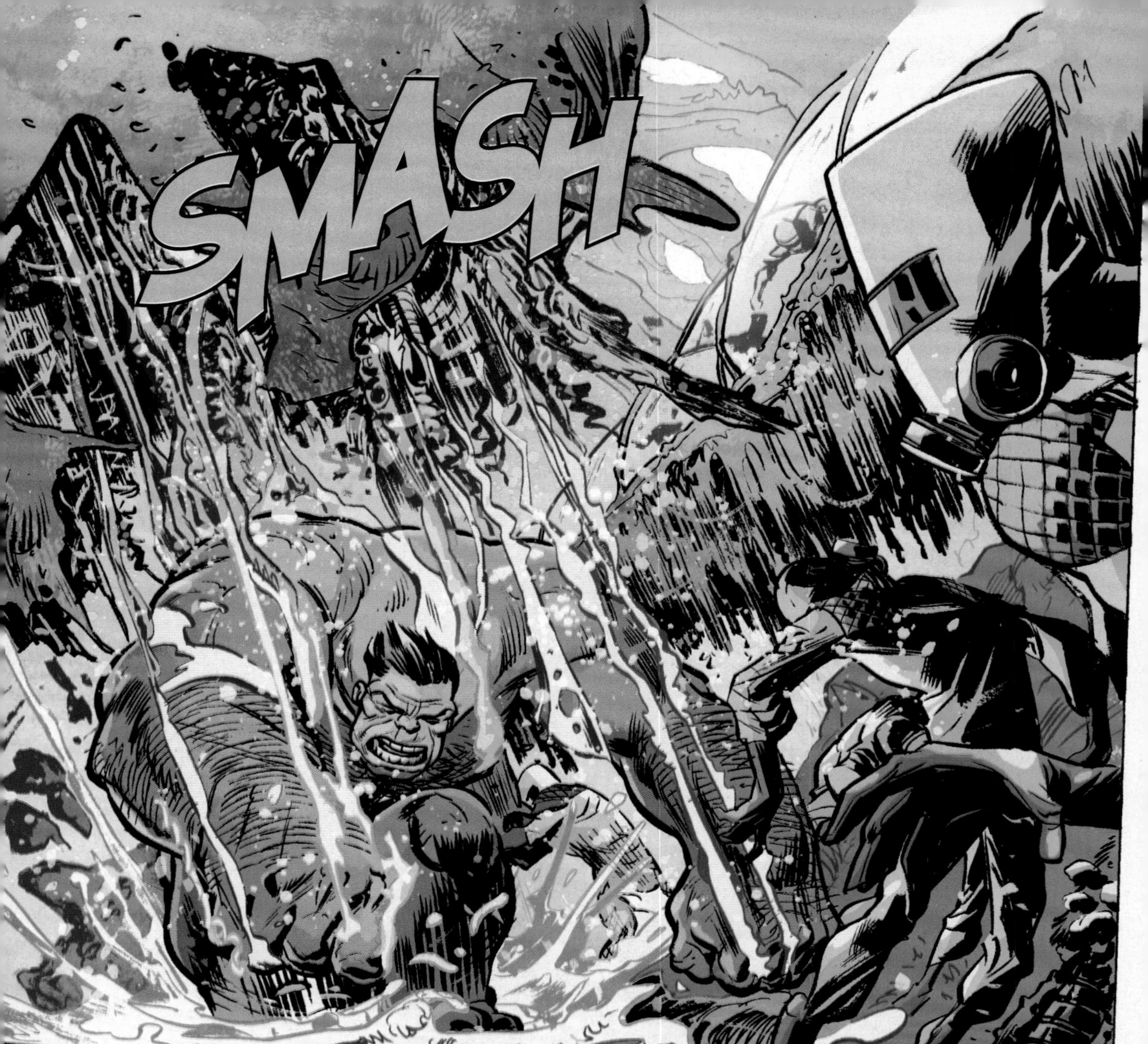
SMASH

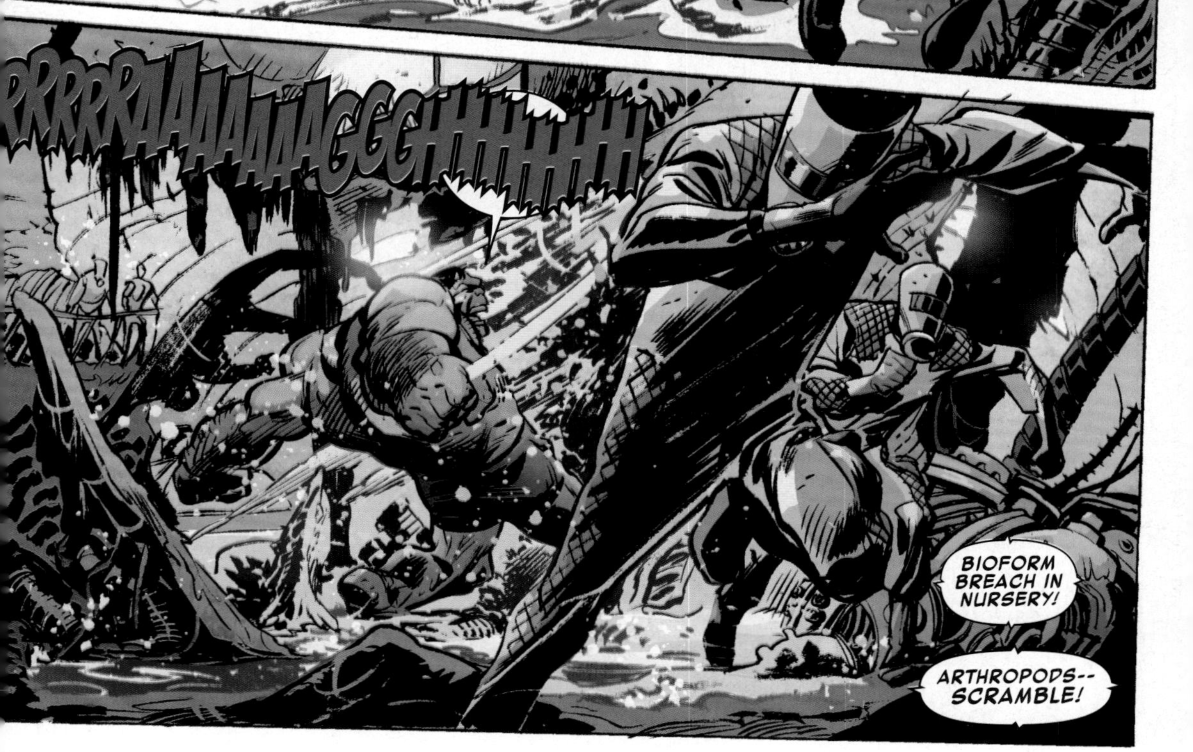
RRRRAAAAAAAGGGHHHHHHH
BIOFORM BREACH IN NURSERY!
ARTHROPODS-- SCRAMBLE!

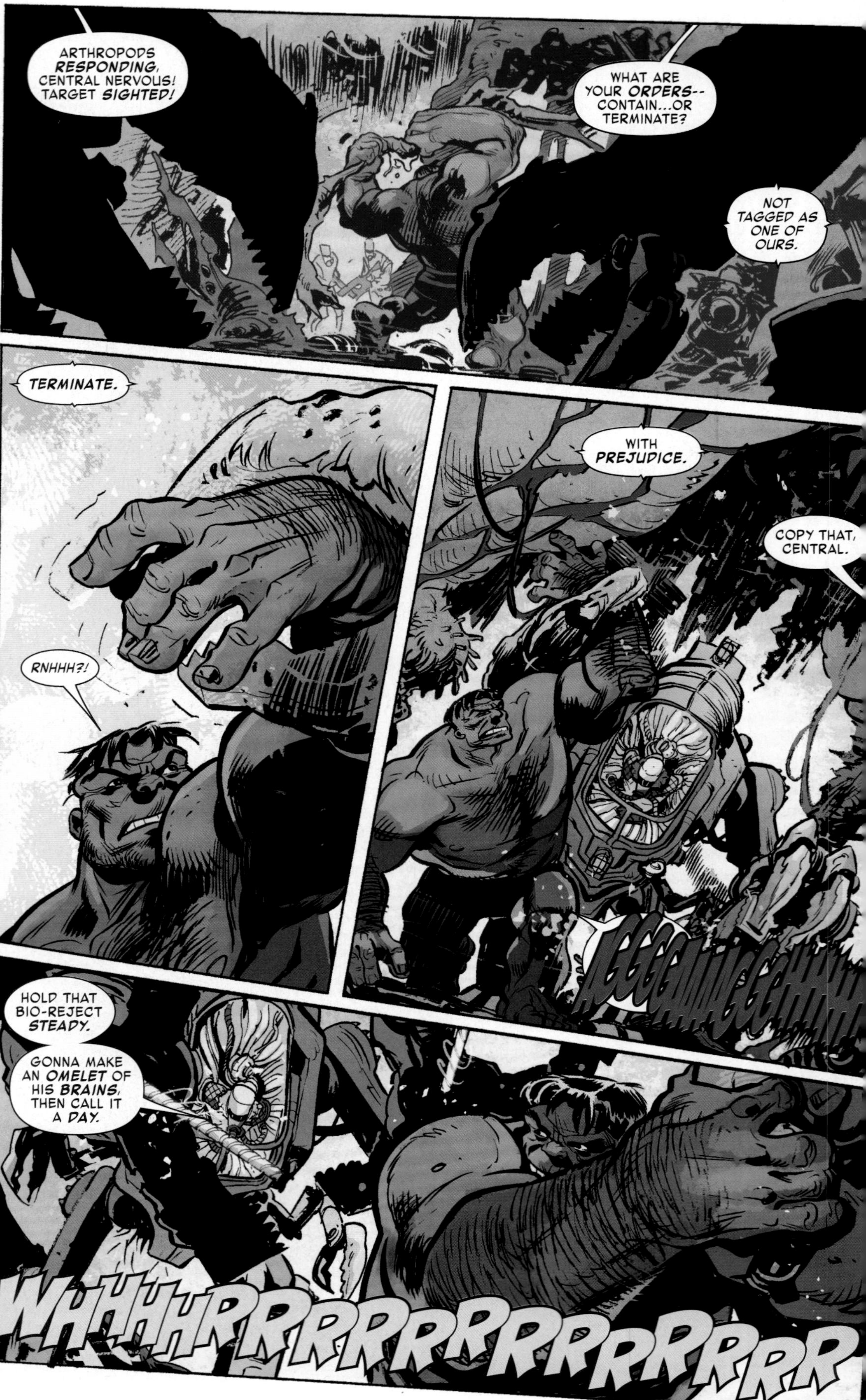
ARTHROPODS RESPONDING, CENTRAL NERVOUS! TARGET SIGHTED!
WHAT ARE YOUR ORDERS-- CONTAIN...OR TERMINATE?
NOT TAGGED AS ONE OF OURS.
TERMINATE.
RNHHH?!
WITH PREJUDICE.
COPY THAT, CENTRAL.
HOLD THAT BIO-REJECT STEADY.
GONNA MAKE AN OMELET OF HIS BRAINS, THEN CALL IT A DAY.
WHHHHRRRRRRRRRRRRRRRRR

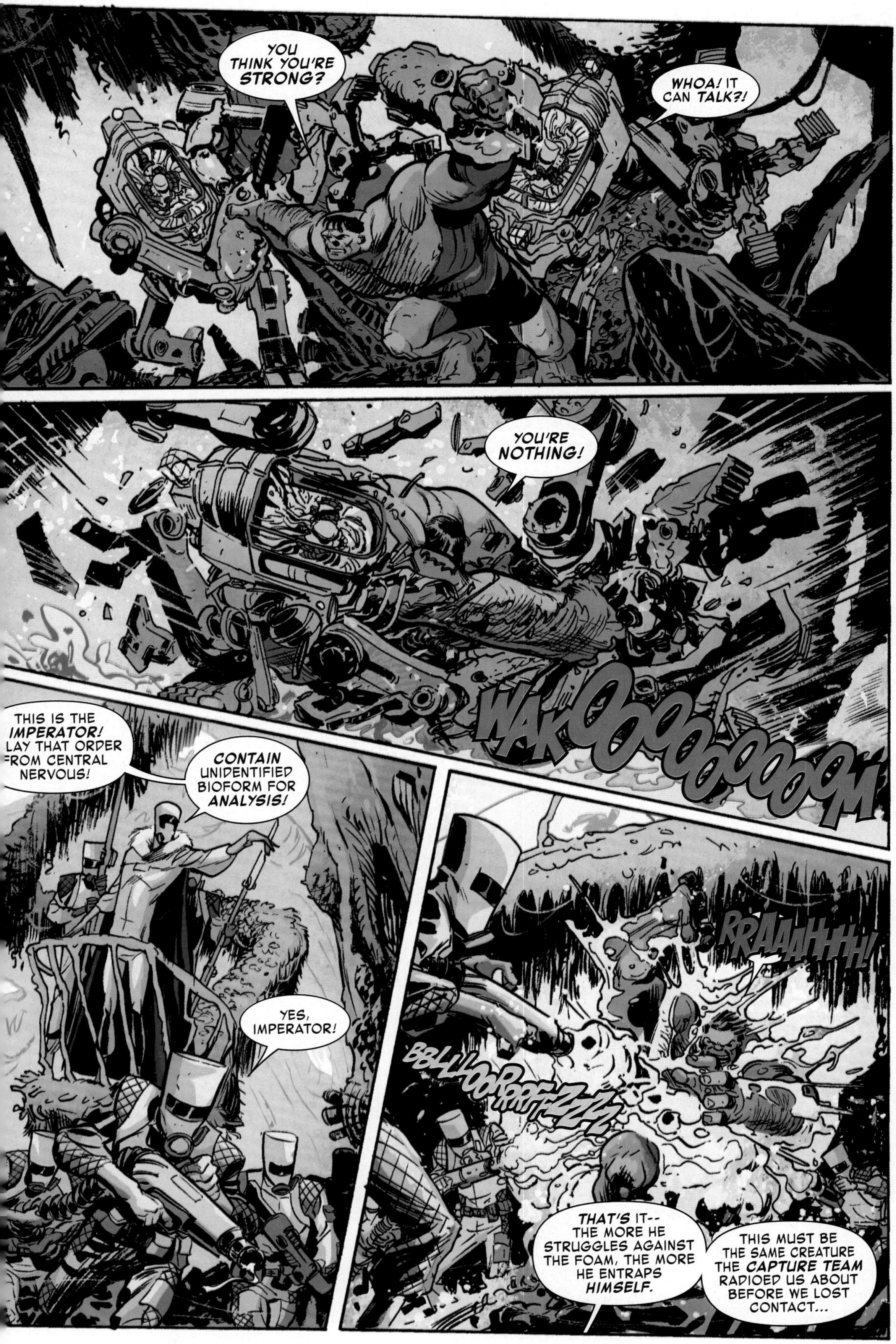
YOU THINK YOU'RE STRONG?
WHOA! IT CAN TALK?!
YOU'RE NOTHING!
WAKOOOOOOOOOOM
THIS IS THE IMPERATOR! LAY THAT ORDER FROM CENTRAL NERVOUS!
CONTAIN UNIDENTIFIED BIOFORM FOR ANALYSIS!
YES, IMPERATOR!
RRAAAHHHH!
BBLLLOORRRFFZZZZ
THAT'S IT-- THE MORE HE STRUGGLES AGAINST THE FOAM, THE MORE HE ENTRAPS HIMSELF.
THIS MUST BE THE SAME CREATURE THE CAPTURE TEAM RADIOED US ABOUT BEFORE WE LOST CONTACT...

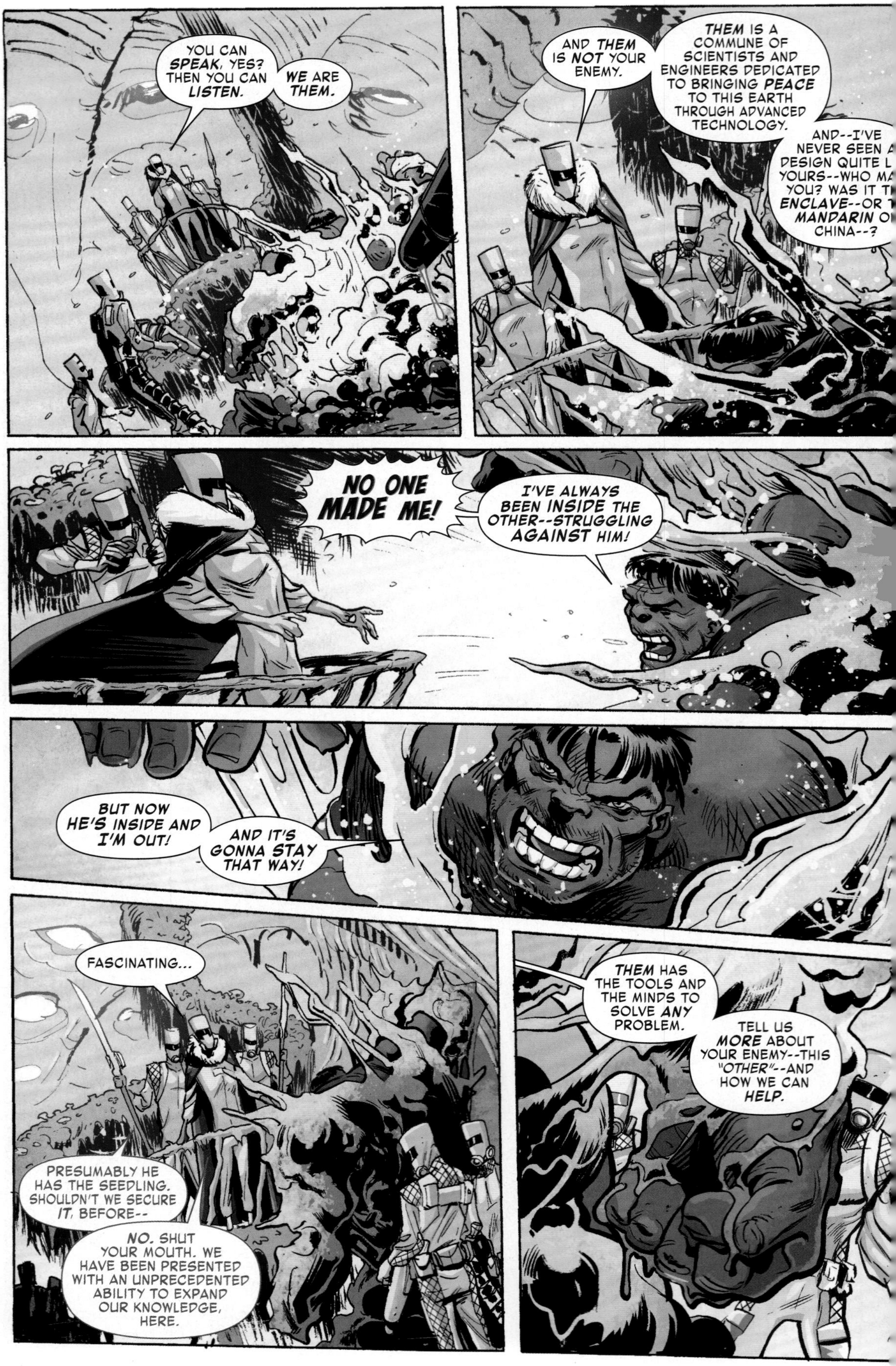

YOU CAN SPEAK, YES? THEN YOU CAN LISTEN.
WE ARE THEM.
AND THEM IS NOT YOUR ENEMY.
THEM IS A COMMUNE OF SCIENTISTS AND ENGINEERS DEDICATED TO BRINGING PEACE TO THIS EARTH THROUGH ADVANCED TECHNOLOGY.
NO ONE MADE ME!
I'VE ALWAYS BEEN INSIDE THE OTHER--STRUGGLING AGAINST HIM!
BUT NOW HE'S INSIDE AND I'M OUT!
AND IT'S GONNA STAY THAT WAY!
FASCINATING...
PRESUMABLY HE HAS THE SEEDLING. SHOULDN'T WE SECURE IT, BEFORE--
NO. SHUT YOUR MOUTH. WE HAVE BEEN PRESENTED WITH AN UNPRECEDENTED ABILITY TO EXPAND OUR KNOWLEDGE, HERE.
THEM HAS THE TOOLS AND THE MINDS TO SOLVE ANY PROBLEM.
TELL US MORE ABOUT YOUR ENEMY--THIS "OTHER"--AND HOW WE CAN HELP.

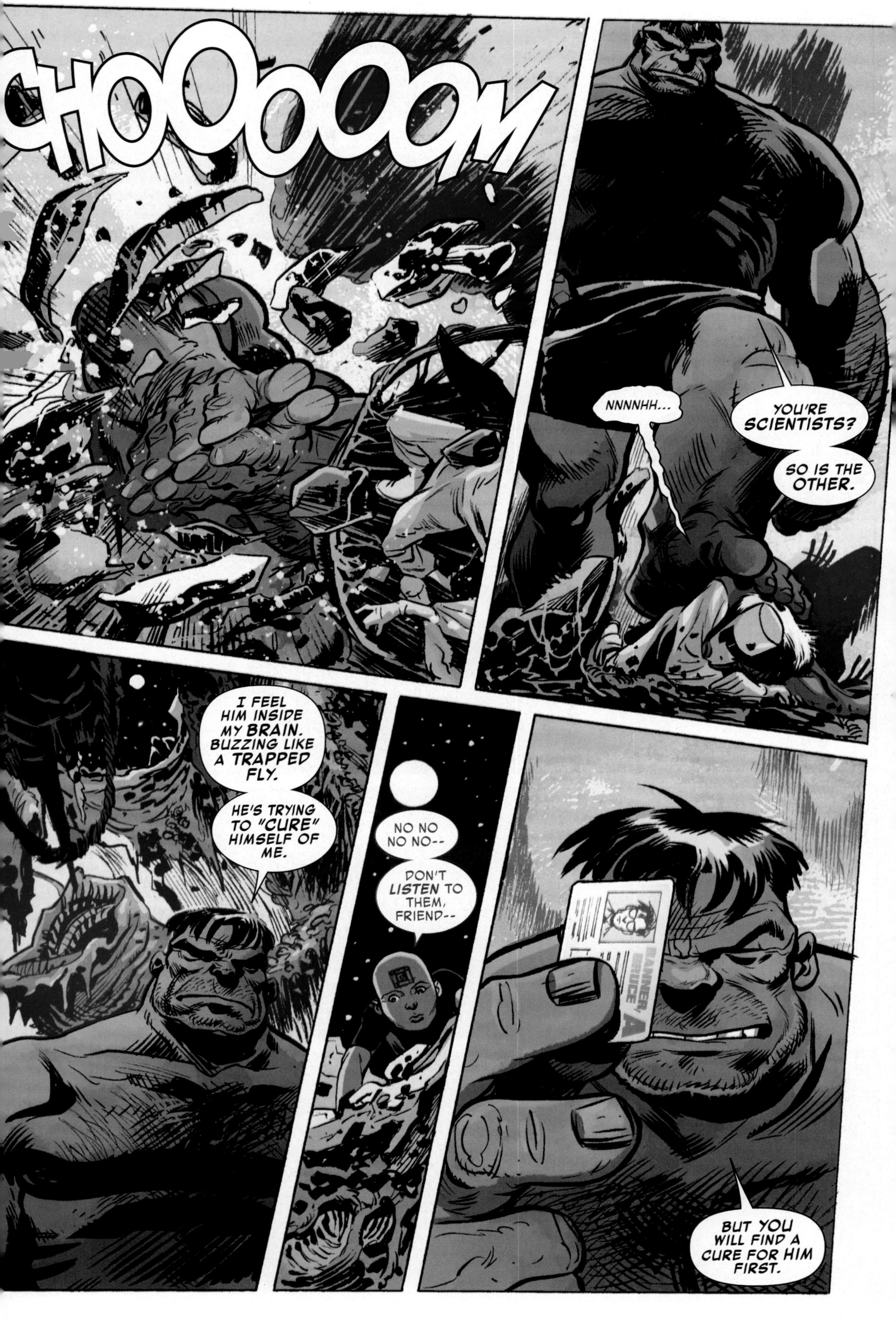
CHOOOOOOM
NNNNHH...
YOU'RE SCIENTISTS?
SO IS THE OTHER.
I FEEL HIM INSIDE MY BRAIN. BUZZING LIKE A TRAPPED FLY.
HE'S TRYING TO "CURE" HIMSELF OF ME.
NO NO NO NO--
DON'T LISTEN TO THEM, FRIEND--
BANNER, BRUCE
A
BUT YOU WILL FIND A CURE FOR HIM FIRST.

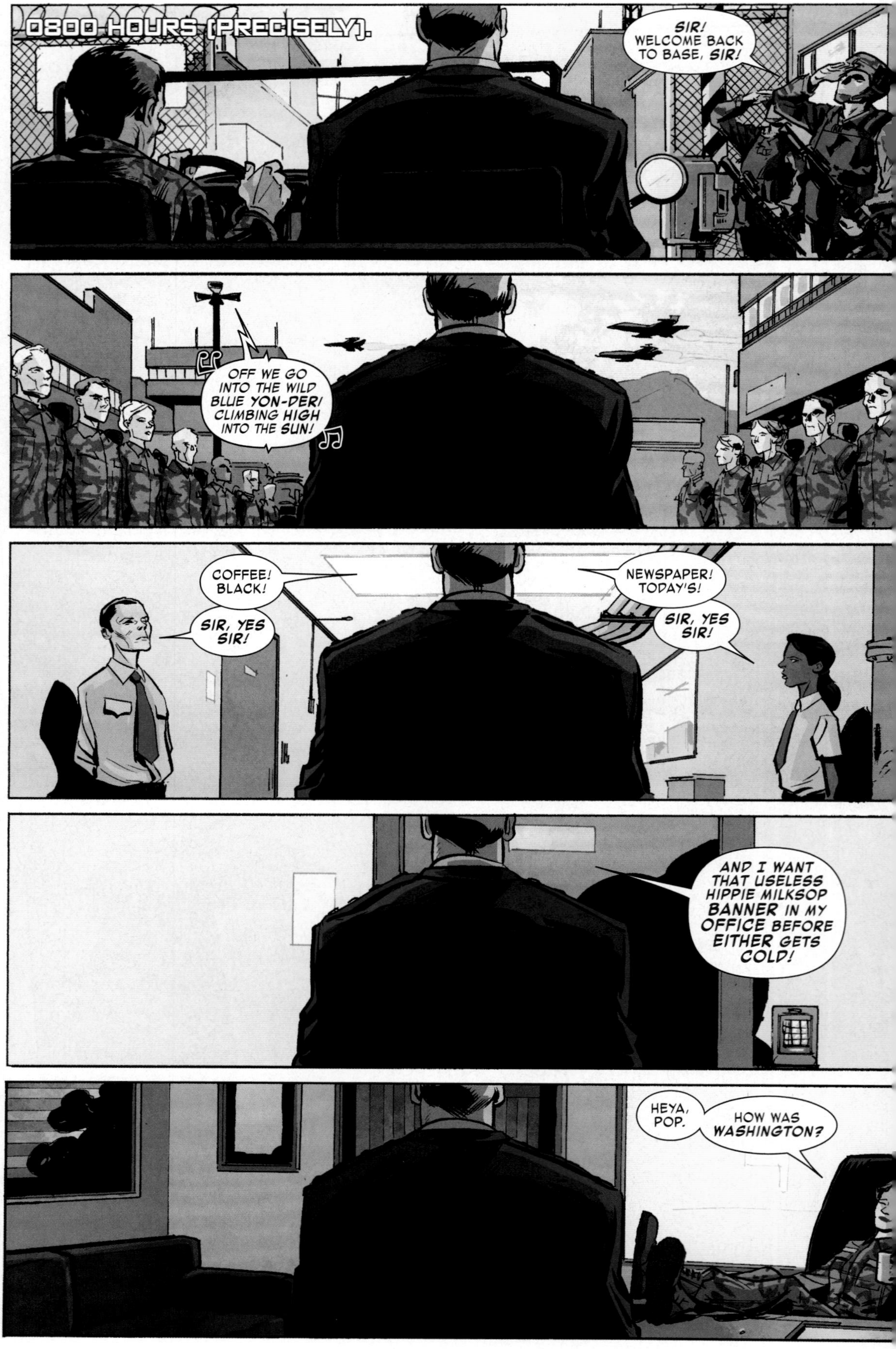
0800 HOURS (PRECISELY).
SIR! WELCOME BACK TO BASE, SIR!
OFF WE GO INTO THE WILD BLUE YON-DER! CLIMBING HIGH INTO THE SUN!
COFFEE! BLACK!
SIR, YES SIR!
NEWSPAPER! TODAY'S!
SIR, YES SIR!
AND I WANT THAT USELESS HIPPIE MILKSOP BANNER IN MY OFFICE BEFORE EITHER GETS COLD!
HEYA, POP.
HOW WAS WASHINGTON?

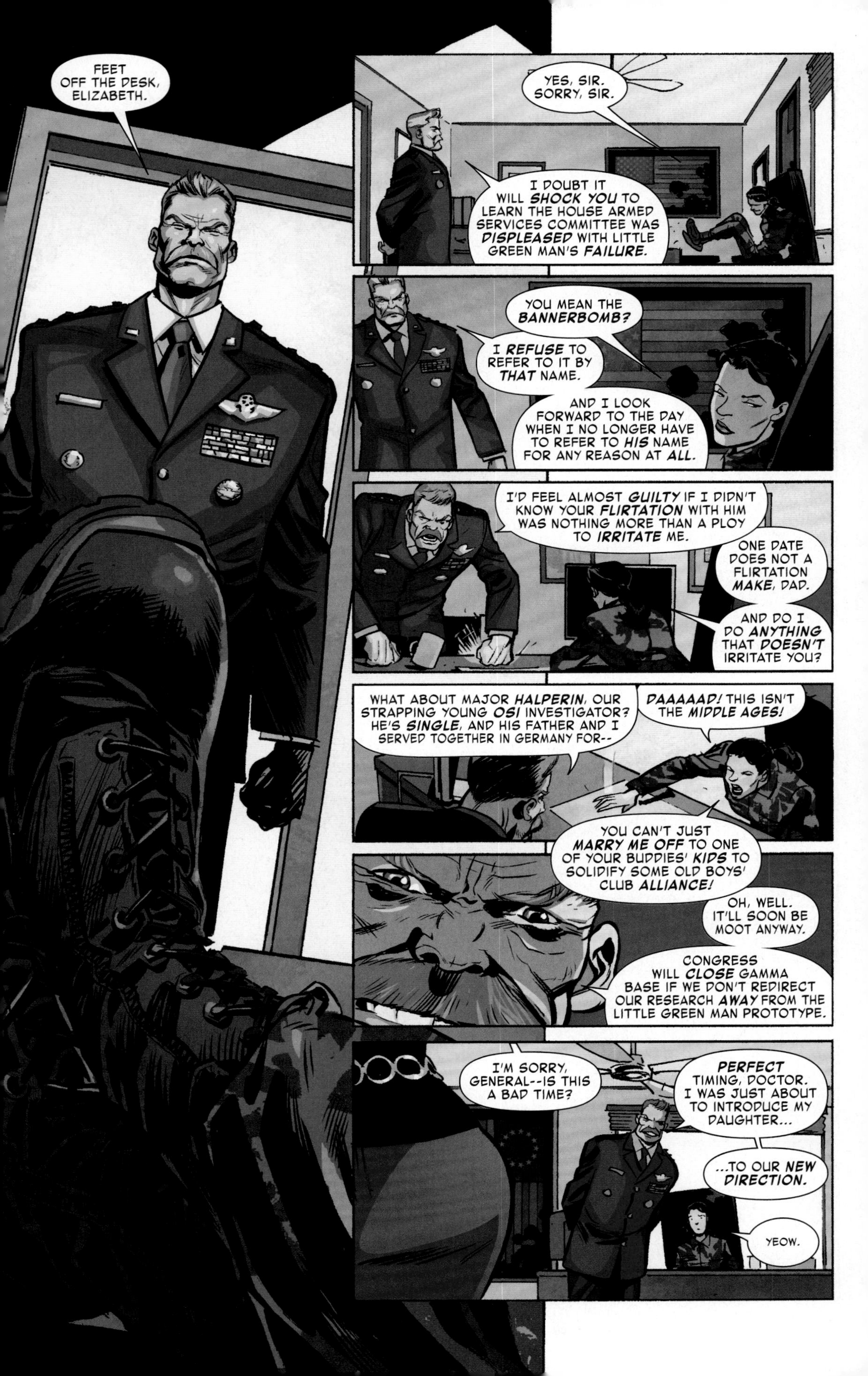
FEET OFF THE DESK, ELIZABETH.
YES, SIR. SORRY, SIR.
I DOUBT IT WILL SHOCK YOU TO LEARN THE HOUSE ARMED SERVICES COMMITTEE WAS DISPLEASED WITH LITTLE GREEN MAN'S FAILURE.
YOU MEAN THE BANNERBOMB?
I REFUSE TO REFER TO IT BY THAT NAME.
AND I LOOK FORWARD TO THE DAY WHEN I NO LONGER HAVE TO REFER TO HIS NAME FOR ANY REASON AT ALL.
I'D FEEL ALMOST GUILTY IF I DIDN'T KNOW YOUR FLIRTATION WITH HIM WAS NOTHING MORE THAN A PLOY TO IRRITATE ME.
ONE DATE DOES NOT A FLIRTATION MAKE, DAD.
AND DO I DO ANYTHING THAT DOESN'T IRRITATE YOU?
WHAT ABOUT MAJOR HALPERIN, OUR STRAPPING YOUNG OSI INVESTIGATOR? HE'S SINGLE, AND HIS FATHER AND I SERVED TOGETHER IN GERMANY FOR--
DAAAAAD! THIS ISN'T THE MIDDLE AGES!
YOU CAN'T JUST MARRY ME OFF TO ONE OF YOUR BUDDIES' KIDS TO SOLIDIFY SOME OLD BOYS' CLUB ALLIANCE!
OH, WELL. IT'LL SOON BE MOOT ANYWAY.
CONGRESS WILL CLOSE GAMMA BASE IF WE DON'T REDIRECT OUR RESEARCH AWAY FROM THE LITTLE GREEN MAN PROTOTYPE.
I'M SORRY, GENERAL--IS THIS A BAD TIME?
PERFECT TIMING, DOCTOR. I WAS JUST ABOUT TO INTRODUCE MY DAUGHTER...
...TO OUR NEW DIRECTION.
YEOW.

NGUF.

ALL RIGHT... WE WILL *AID* YOU. GIVE US SKIN AND BLOOD SAMPLES.

BUT AS A SHOW OF GOOD FAITH, YOU NEED TO DO SOMETHING FOR *THEM'S* CAUSE, AS WELL.

THEM HAS *ENEMIES* IN THIS PART OF THE WORLD. *BAD* MEN.

A RUSSI. *CRIMINA* WORKING (OF EL PA

WORSE THAN A HANGOVER...

CRAZIEST *DREAMS*...

DESTROY HIS OPERATION.

FREE THE IMPOVERISHED OF THIS REGION FROM HIS YOKE.

AND THEM SHALL DO *WHATEVER* YOU ASK.

COMPUTER. OPEN VAULT.

VOICE PRINT: RECOGNIZE. BANNER, BRUCE.

VAULT: OPENING.

RRRRRRRRR

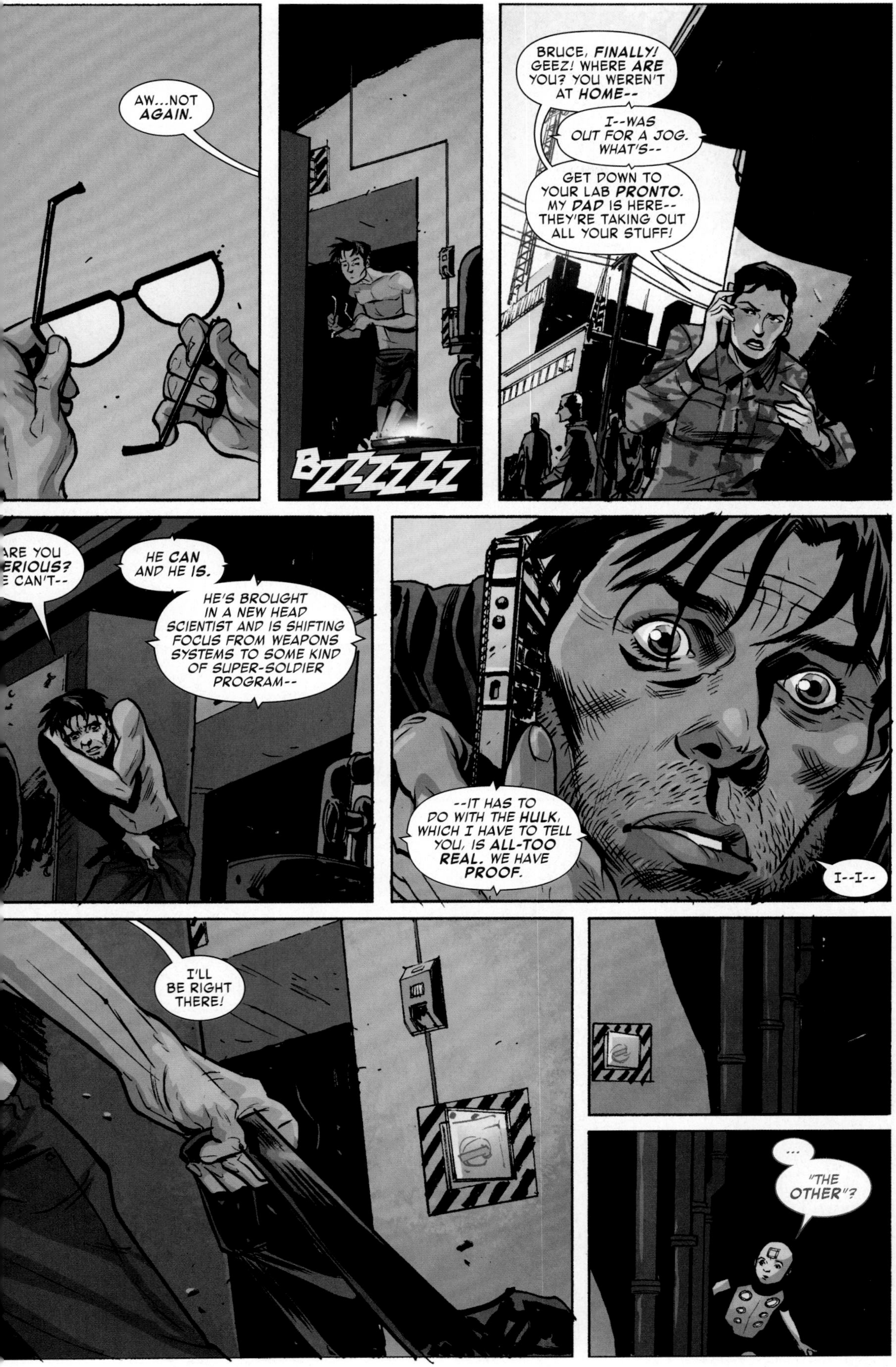
AW...NOT AGAIN.
BZZZZZZZ
BRUCE, FINALLY! GEEZ! WHERE ARE YOU? YOU WEREN'T AT HOME--
I--WAS OUT FOR A JOG. WHAT'S--
GET DOWN TO YOUR LAB PRONTO. MY DAD IS HERE-- THEY'RE TAKING OUT ALL YOUR STUFF!
ARE YOU ERIOUS? E CAN'T--
HE CAN AND HE IS.
HE'S BROUGHT IN A NEW HEAD SCIENTIST AND IS SHIFTING FOCUS FROM WEAPONS SYSTEMS TO SOME KIND OF SUPER-SOLDIER PROGRAM--
--IT HAS TO DO WITH THE HULK, WHICH I HAVE TO TELL YOU, IS ALL-TOO REAL. WE HAVE PROOF.
I--I--
I'LL BE RIGHT THERE!
...
"THE OTHER"?

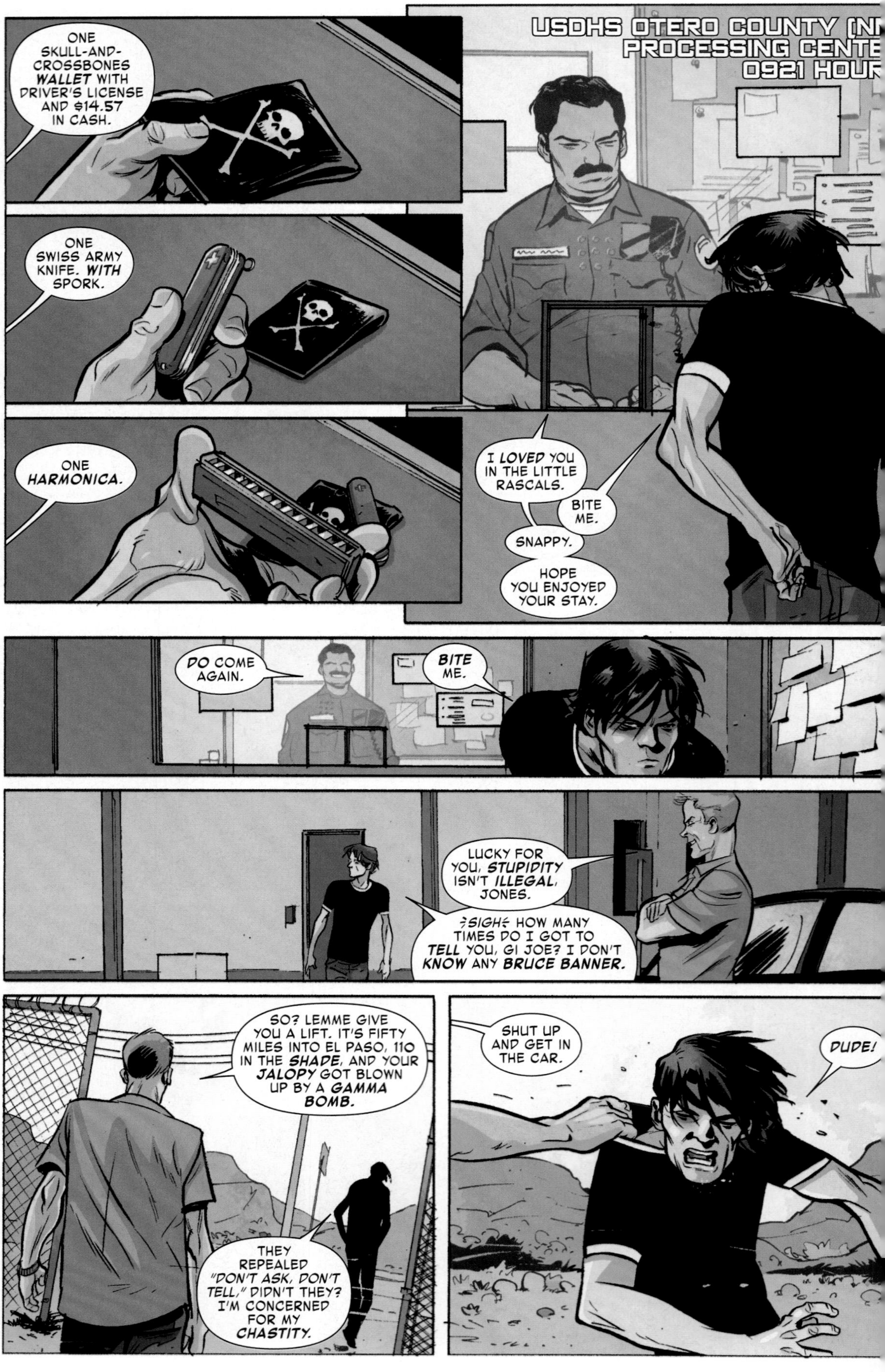
USDHS OTERO COUNTY (N
PROCESSING CENTE
0921 HOUR
ONE SKULL-AND-CROSSBONES WALLET WITH DRIVER'S LICENSE AND $14.57 IN CASH.
ONE SWISS ARMY KNIFE. WITH SPORK.
ONE HARMONICA.
I LOVED YOU IN THE LITTLE RASCALS.
BITE ME.
SNAPPY.
HOPE YOU ENJOYED YOUR STAY.
DO COME AGAIN.
BITE ME.
LUCKY FOR YOU, STUPIDITY ISN'T ILLEGAL, JONES.
SIGH HOW MANY TIMES DO I GOT TO TELL YOU, GI JOE? I DON'T KNOW ANY BRUCE BANNER.
SO? LEMME GIVE YOU A LIFT. IT'S FIFTY MILES INTO EL PASO, 110 IN THE SHADE, AND YOUR JALOPY GOT BLOWN UP BY A GAMMA BOMB.
THEY REPEALED "DON'T ASK, DON'T TELL," DIDN'T THEY? I'M CONCERNED FOR MY CHASTITY.
SHUT UP AND GET IN THE CAR.
DUDE!

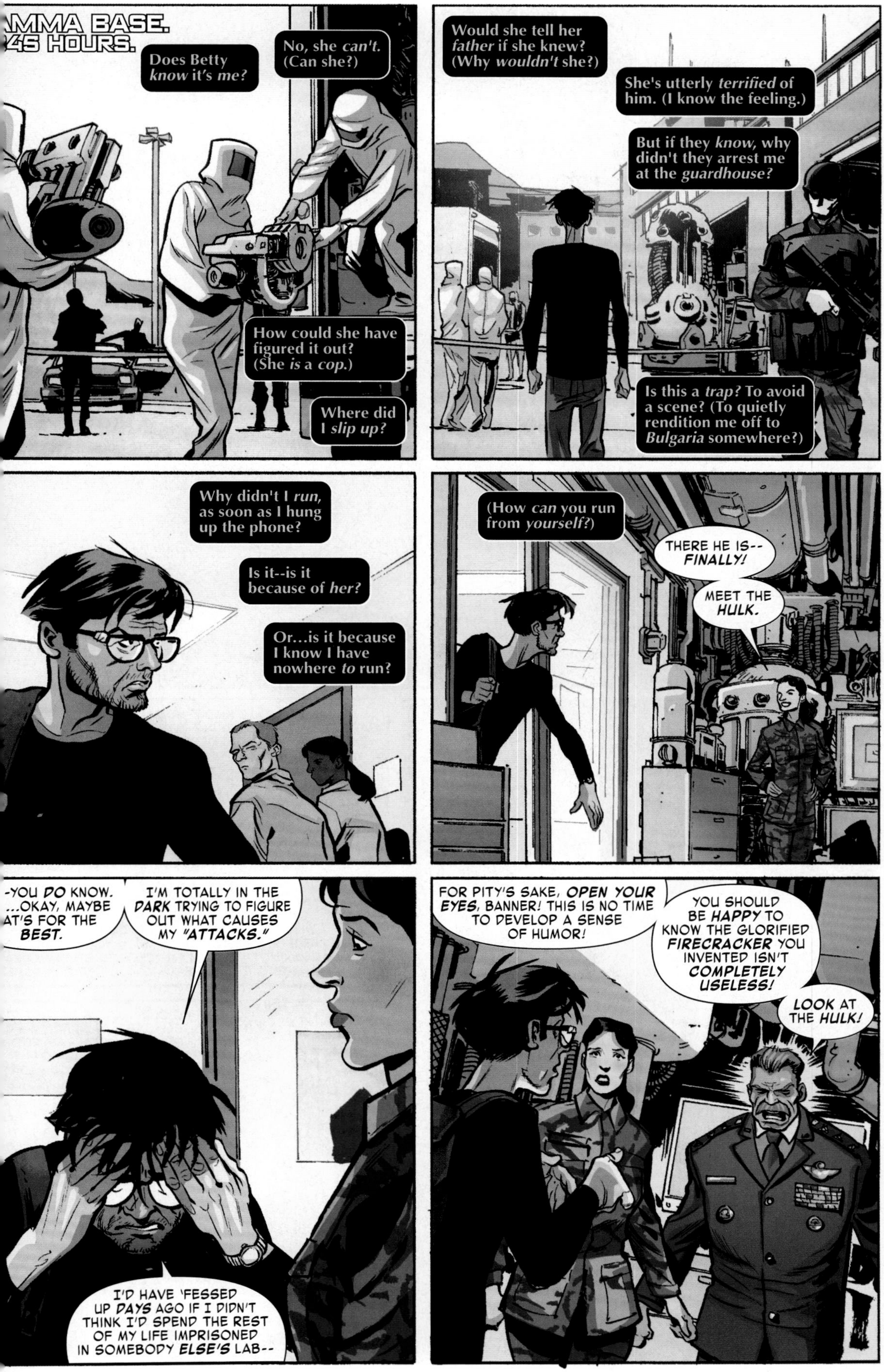
MMA BASE.
45 HOURS.
Does Betty *know* it's *me?*
No, she *can't.* (Can she?)
How could she have figured it out? (She *is* a *cop.*)
Where did I *slip up?*
Would she tell her *father* if she knew? (Why *wouldn't* she?)
She's utterly *terrified* of him. (I know the feeling.)
But if they *know,* why didn't they arrest me at the *guardhouse?*
Is this a *trap?* To avoid a scene? (To quietly rendition me off to *Bulgaria* somewhere?)
Why didn't I *run,* as soon as I hung up the phone?
Is it--is it because of *her?*
Or...is it because I know I have nowhere *to* run?
(How *can* you run from *yourself?*)
THERE HE IS-- *FINALLY!*
MEET THE *HULK.*
-YOU *DO* KNOW. ...OKAY, MAYBE AT'S FOR THE *BEST.*
I'M TOTALLY IN THE *DARK* TRYING TO FIGURE OUT WHAT CAUSES MY *"ATTACKS."*
I'D HAVE 'FESSED UP *DAYS* AGO IF I DIDN'T THINK I'D SPEND THE REST OF MY LIFE IMPRISONED IN SOMEBODY *ELSE'S* LAB--
FOR PITY'S SAKE, *OPEN YOUR EYES,* BANNER! THIS IS NO TIME TO DEVELOP A SENSE OF HUMOR!
YOU SHOULD BE *HAPPY* TO KNOW THE GLORIFIED *FIRECRACKER* YOU INVENTED ISN'T *COMPLETELY USELESS!*
LOOK AT THE *HULK!*

WHAT-- OH!

THIS IS-- NO...REALLY?

PROMETHEUS, ONE OF OUR TEST CHIMPS...?

HOW DID THIS HAPPEN?

THAT'S WHAT OUR NEW *HEAD SCIENTIST* IS TASKED WITH FINDING *OUT.*

SENATOR MANTLO OF NORTH CAROLINA RECOMMENDED HER TO US AS A RISING STAR IN HIS BIOTECH CORRIDOR.

DOCTOR BANNER, MEET--

BRUCE. SO GREAT TO SEE YOU AGAIN.

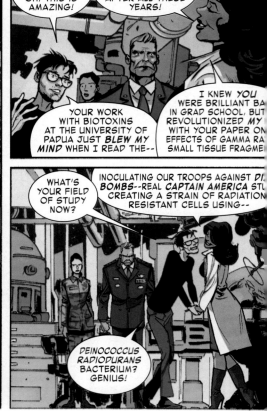

MONICA *RAPPACCINI!?!* OH, THIS IS AMAZING!

I KNOW--*FINALLY* WORKING TOGETHER AFTER ALL THESE YEARS!

YOUR WORK WITH BIOTOXINS AT THE UNIVERSITY OF PADUA JUST *BLEW MY MIND* WHEN I READ THE--

I KNEW *YOU* WERE BRILLIANT BA[CK] IN GRAD SCHOOL, BUT REVOLUTIONIZED *MY* WITH YOUR PAPER ON EFFECTS OF GAMMA RA[YS] SMALL TISSUE FRAGME[NTS]

WHAT'S YOUR FIELD OF STUDY NOW?

INOCULATING OUR TROOPS AGAINST *DI[RTY] BOMBS*--REAL *CAPTAIN AMERICA* STU[FF] CREATING A STRAIN OF RADIATION[-]RESISTANT CELLS USING--

DEINOCOCCUS RADIODURANS BACTERIUM? GENIUS!

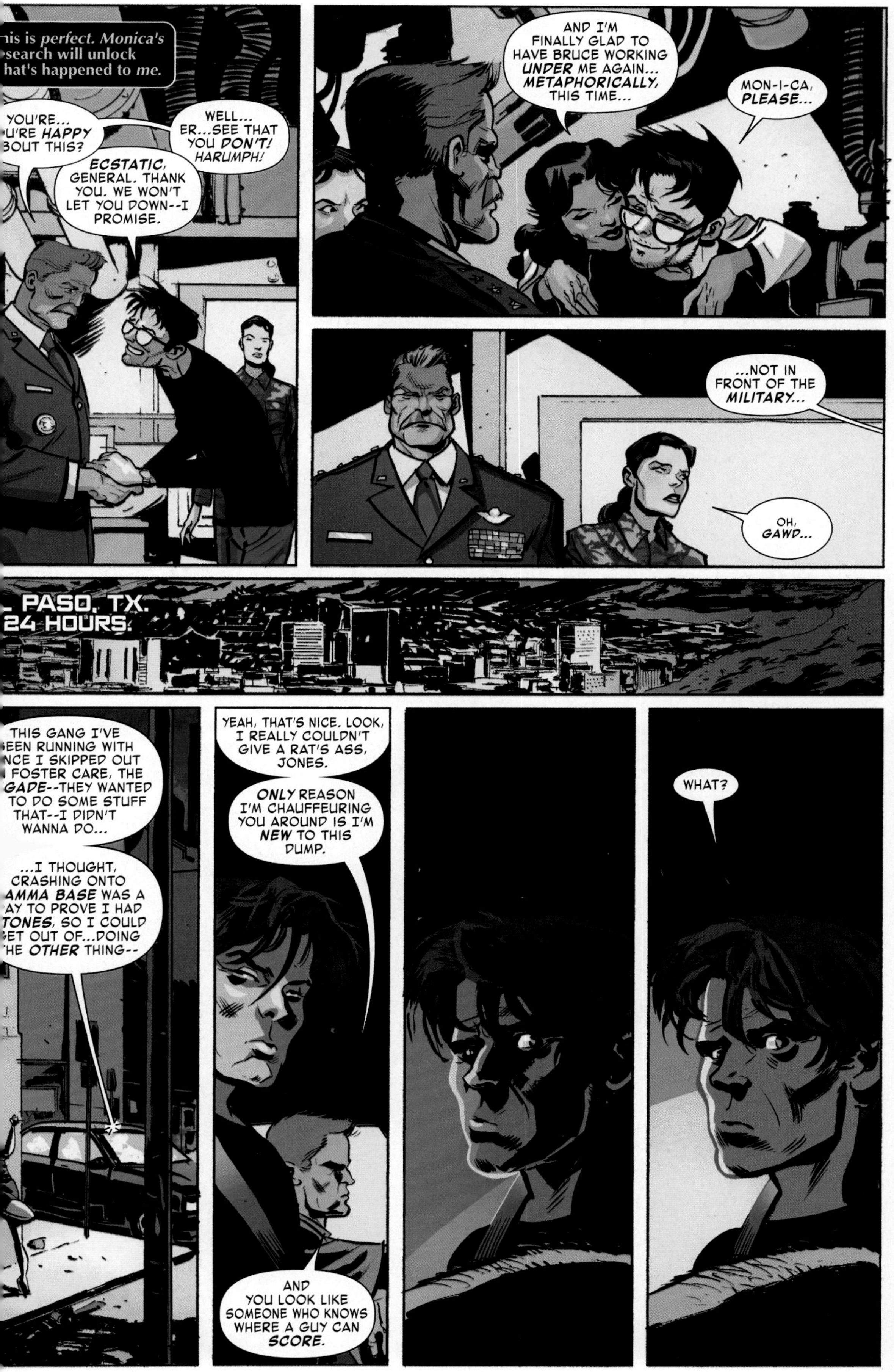

is is perfect. Monica's
search will unlock
hat's happened to me.
YOU'RE... U'RE HAPPY BOUT THIS?
ECSTATIC, GENERAL. THANK YOU. WE WON'T LET YOU DOWN--I PROMISE.
WELL... ER...SEE THAT YOU DON'T! HARUMPH!
AND I'M FINALLY GLAD TO HAVE BRUCE WORKING UNDER ME AGAIN... METAPHORICALLY, THIS TIME...
MON-I-CA, PLEASE...
...NOT IN FRONT OF THE MILITARY...
OH, GAWD...
L PASO, TX.
24 HOURS.
THIS GANG I'VE EEN RUNNING WITH NCE I SKIPPED OUT FOSTER CARE, THE GADE--THEY WANTED TO DO SOME STUFF THAT--I DIDN'T WANNA DO...
...I THOUGHT, CRASHING ONTO AMMA BASE WAS A AY TO PROVE I HAD TONES, SO I COULD ET OUT OF...DOING HE OTHER THING--
YEAH, THAT'S NICE. LOOK, I REALLY COULDN'T GIVE A RAT'S ASS, JONES.
ONLY REASON I'M CHAUFFEURING YOU AROUND IS I'M NEW TO THIS DUMP.
AND YOU LOOK LIKE SOMEONE WHO KNOWS WHERE A GUY CAN SCORE.
WHAT?

HAH! *JONES. TOLD* YOU HE'D BE BACK, *ESE.*

YOU OWE ME *TWENTY,* STEVE-O.

DANG.

HEY, RICARDO, HEARD ABOUT YOU BUSTING ONTO THE MILITARY BASE ON THE NEWS, THAT WAS *BADASS.*

AIN'T NO *THING,* SCUMMY, JUST HOW I ROLL, YOUKNOWWHATI'MSAYIN'?

THOUGHT FOR SURE THEY WERE GONNA SEND YOUR A DOWN TO *GUANTANA* SPEND THE REST OF YO LIFE WITH A *BAG* OV YOUR HEAD--

NAW, I JUST PLAYED IT COOL, MAN, THEY POPPED ME RIGHT OUT--

YEAH, MAYBE *TOO* COOL. YOU AIN'T GONE *SNITCH* ON US, HAVE YOU, RICARDO?

YOU NOT MAN ENOUGH TO GRAB A *SCALP*--CHECK THIS SCHOOLGIRL FOR A *WIRE.*

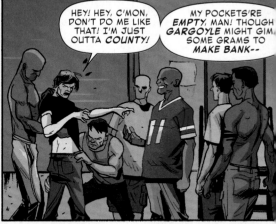

HEY! HEY, C'MON, DON'T DO ME LIKE THAT! I'M JUST OUTTA *COUNTY!*

MY POCKETS'RE *EMPTY,* MAN! THOUGH *GARGOYLE* MIGHT GIM SOME GRAMS TO *MAKE BANK*--

YOU THINK *WRONG,* JONES.

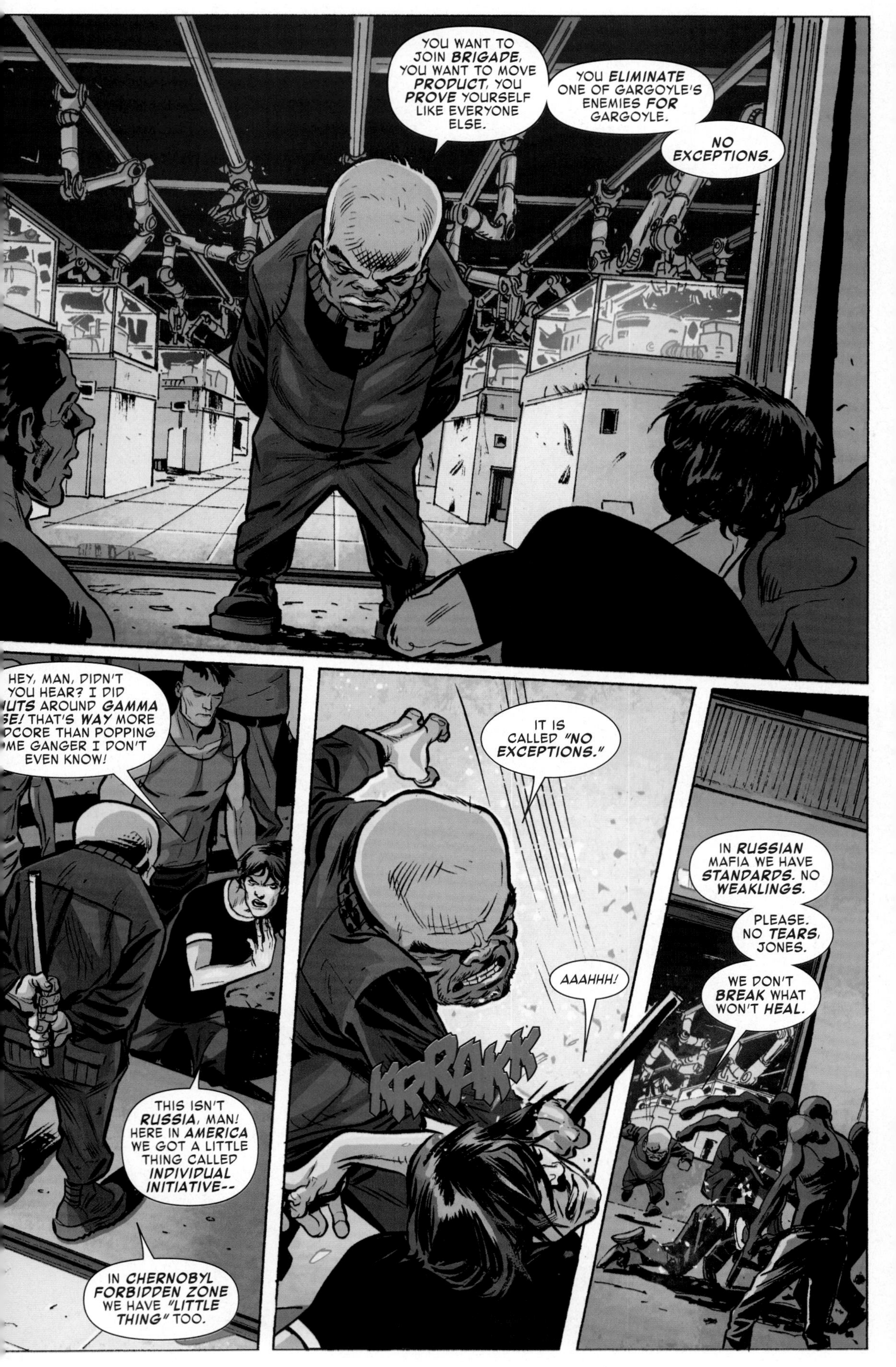
YOU WANT TO JOIN BRIGADE, YOU WANT TO MOVE PRODUCT, YOU PROVE YOURSELF LIKE EVERYONE ELSE.
YOU ELIMINATE ONE OF GARGOYLE'S ENEMIES FOR GARGOYLE.
NO EXCEPTIONS.
HEY, MAN, DIDN'T YOU HEAR? I DID
UTS AROUND GAMMA
SE! THAT'S WAY MORE
DCORE THAN POPPING
ME GANGER I DON'T EVEN KNOW!
THIS ISN'T RUSSIA, MAN! HERE IN AMERICA WE GOT A LITTLE THING CALLED INDIVIDUAL INITIATIVE--
IN CHERNOBYL FORBIDDEN ZONE WE HAVE "LITTLE THING" TOO.
IT IS CALLED "NO EXCEPTIONS."
AAAHHH!
KRRAKK
IN RUSSIAN MAFIA WE HAVE STANDARDS. NO WEAKLINGS.
PLEASE. NO TEARS, JONES.
WE DON'T BREAK WHAT WON'T HEAL.

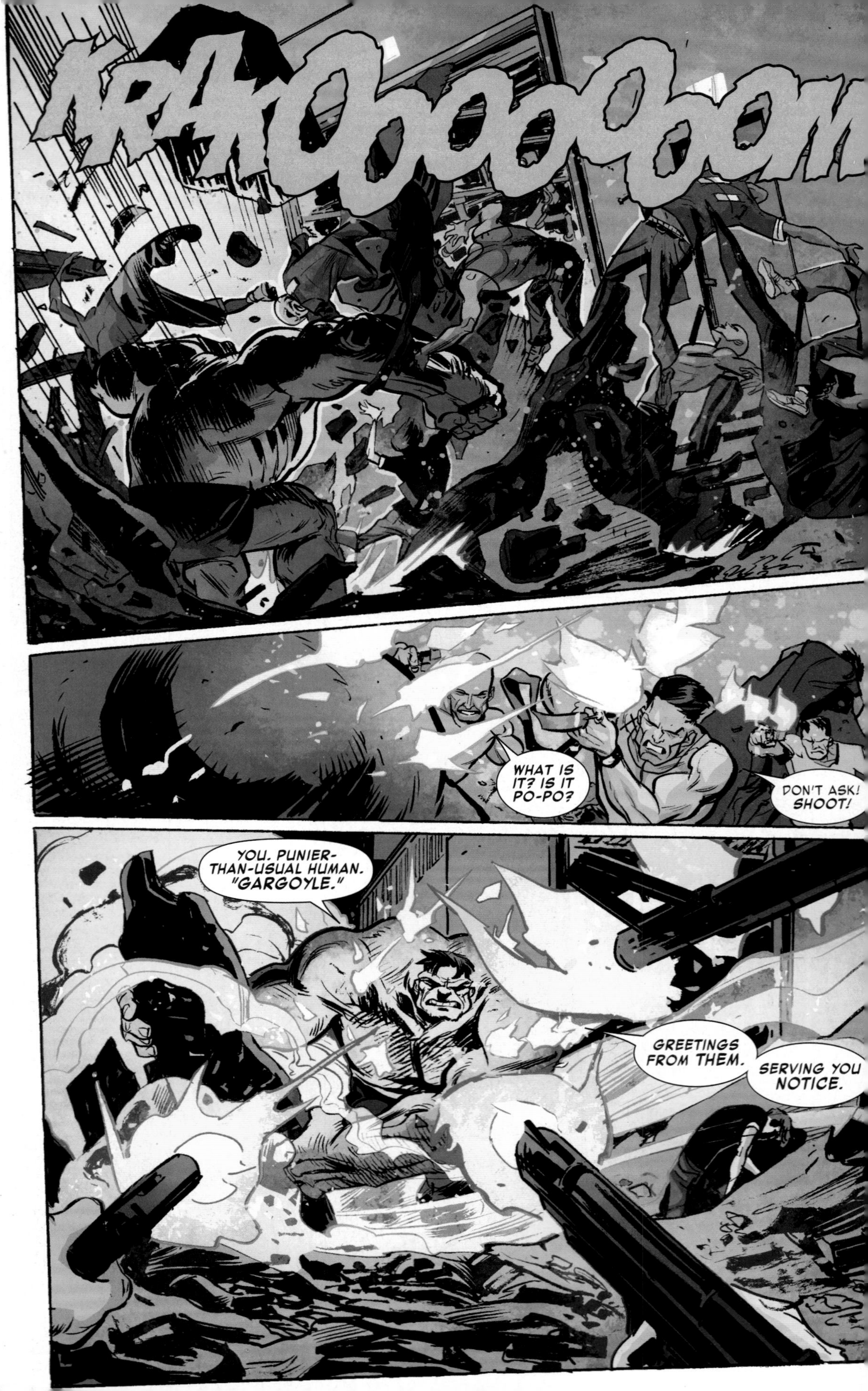
KRAKOOOOOOOM
WHAT IS IT? IS IT PO-PO?
DON'T ASK! SHOOT!
YOU. PUNIER-THAN-USUAL HUMAN. "GARGOYLE."
GREETINGS FROM THEM.
SERVING YOU NOTICE.

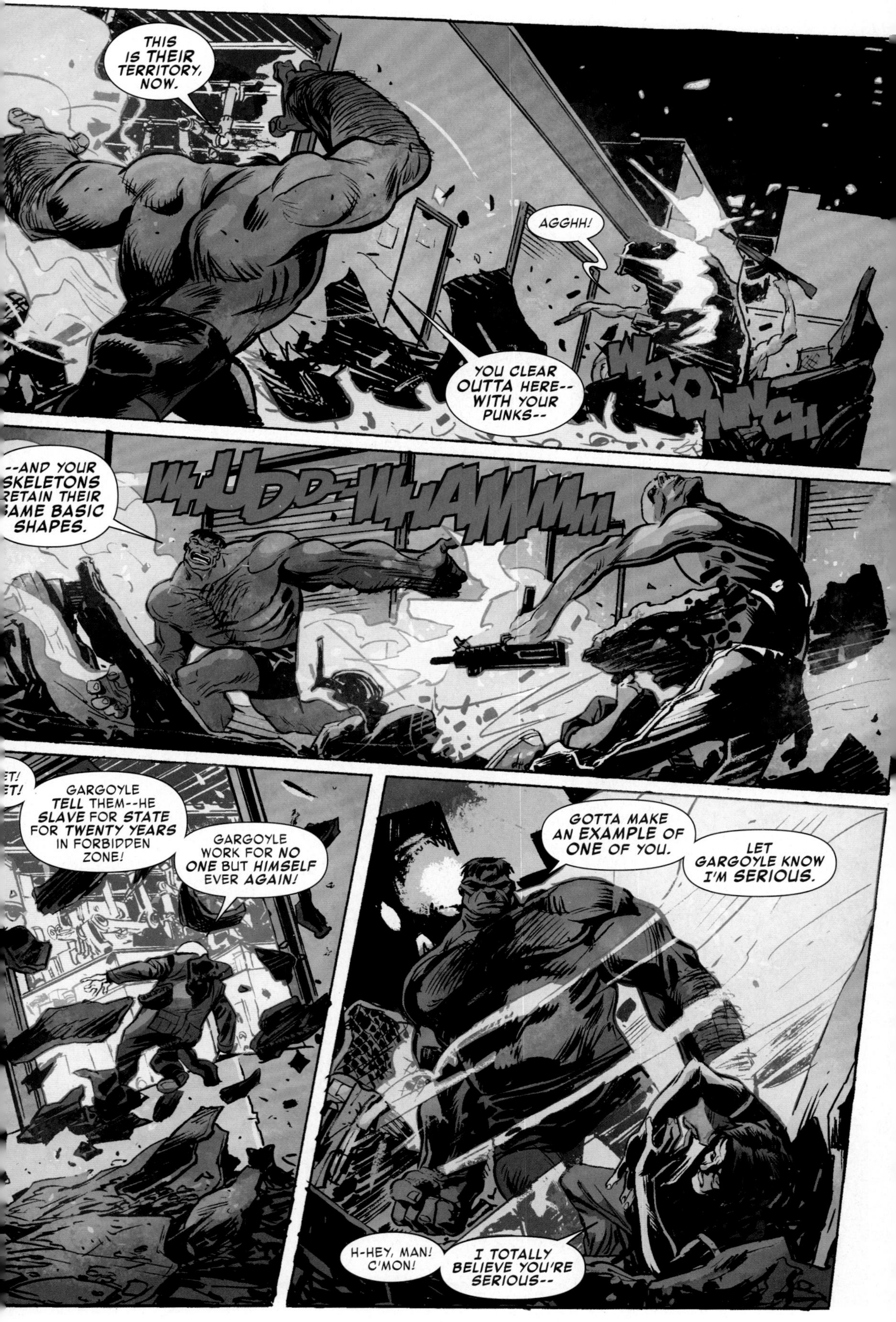
THIS IS THEIR TERRITORY, NOW.
AGGHH!
YOU CLEAR OUTTA HERE-- WITH YOUR PUNKS--
WRONNCH
--AND YOUR SKELETONS RETAIN THEIR SAME BASIC SHAPES.
WHUDD-WHAMMM
GARGOYLE TELL THEM--HE SLAVE FOR STATE FOR TWENTY YEARS IN FORBIDDEN ZONE!
GARGOYLE WORK FOR NO ONE BUT HIMSELF EVER AGAIN!
GOTTA MAKE AN EXAMPLE OF ONE OF YOU.
LET GARGOYLE KNOW I'M SERIOUS.
H-HEY, MAN! C'MON!
I TOTALLY BELIEVE YOU'RE SERIOUS--

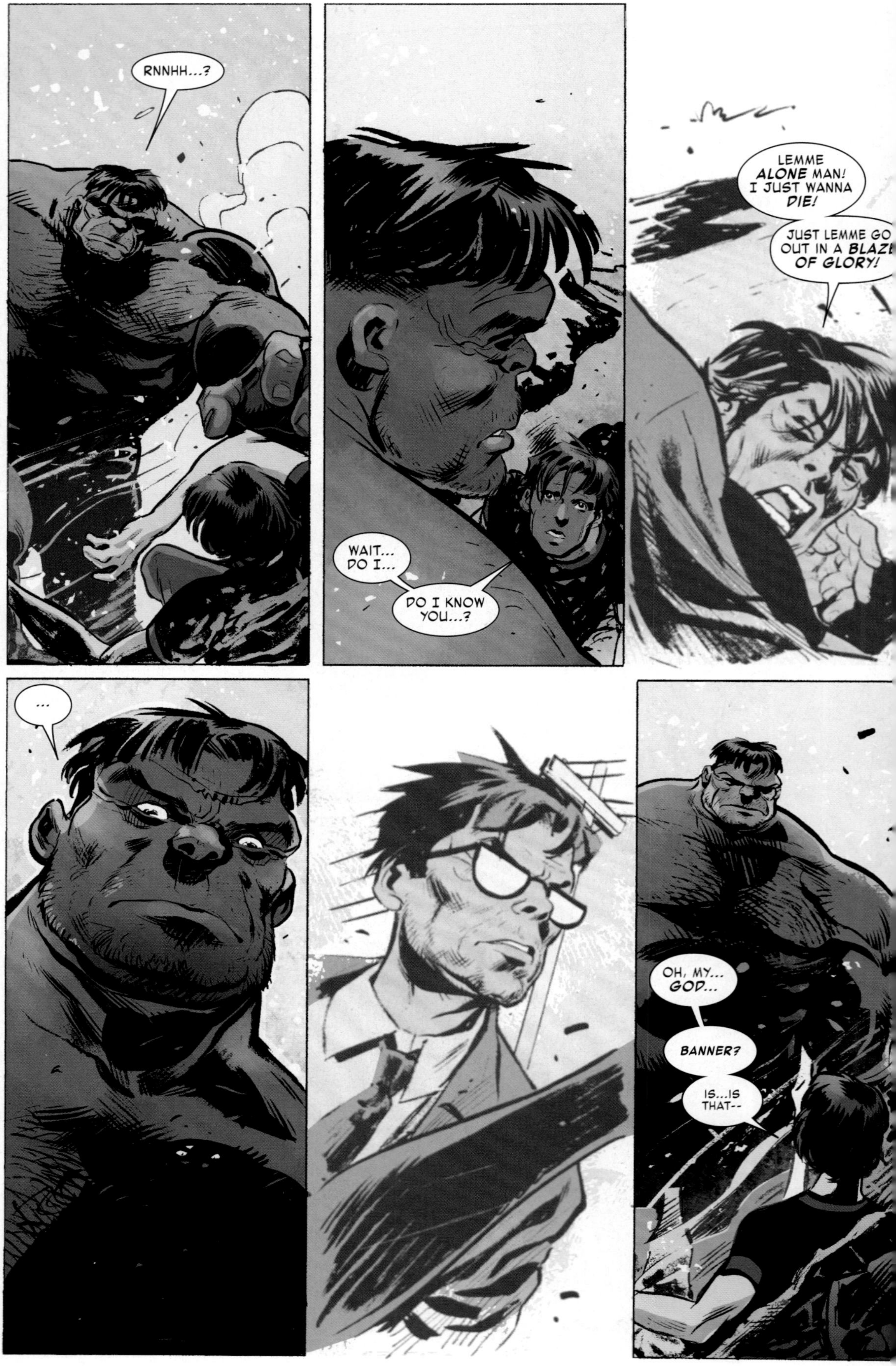
RNNHH...?
WAIT... DO I...
DO I KNOW YOU...?
LEMME ALONE MAN! I JUST WANNA DIE!
JUST LEMME GO OUT IN A BLAZE OF GLORY!
...
OH, MY... GOD...
BANNER?
IS...IS THAT--

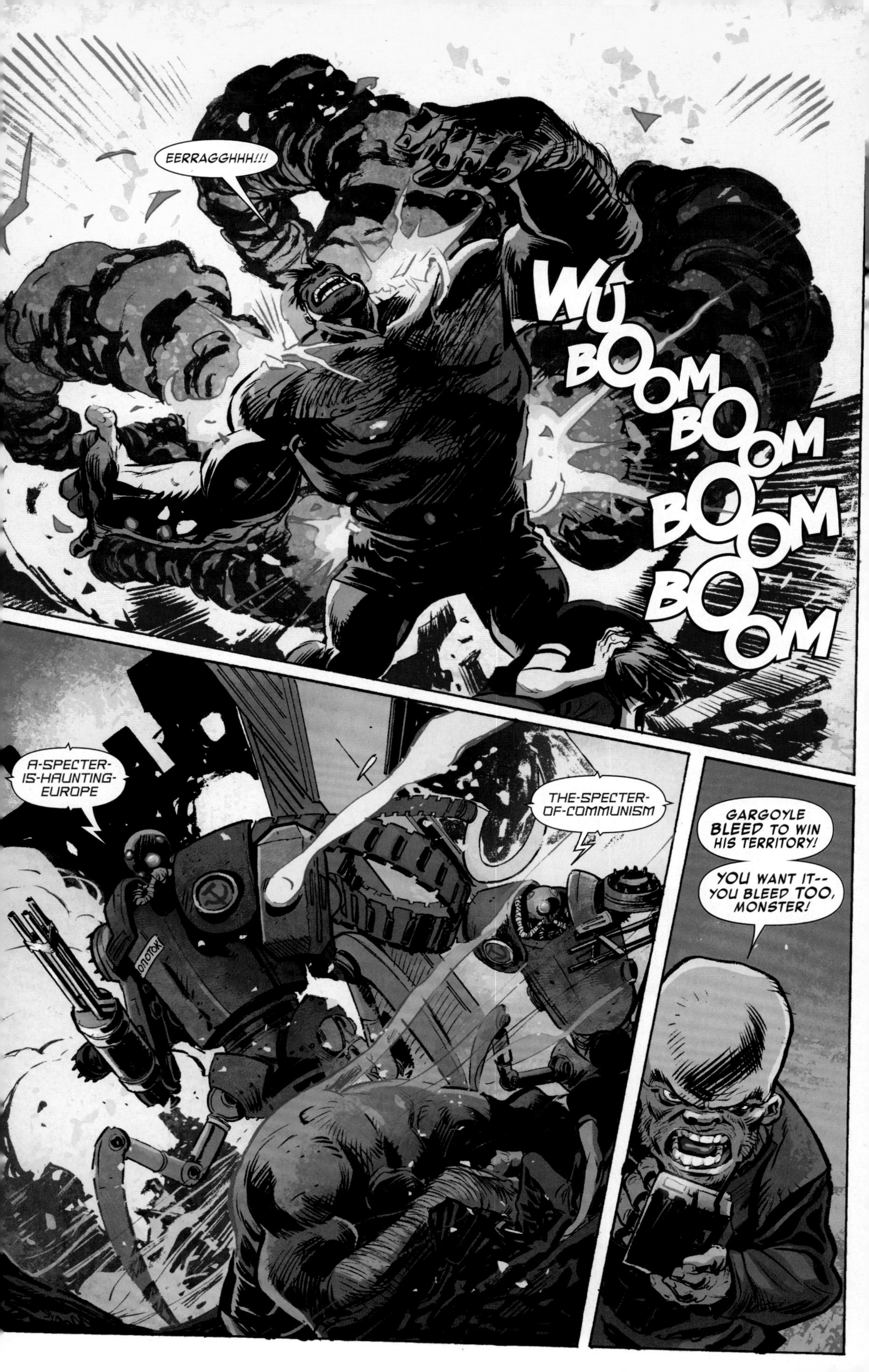
EERRAGGHHH!!!
WUBOOMBOOMBOOMBOOM
A-SPECTER-IS-HAUNTING-EUROPE
THE-SPECTER-OF-COMMUNISM
GARGOYLE BLEED TO WIN HIS TERRITORY!
YOU WANT IT-- YOU BLEED TOO, MONSTER!

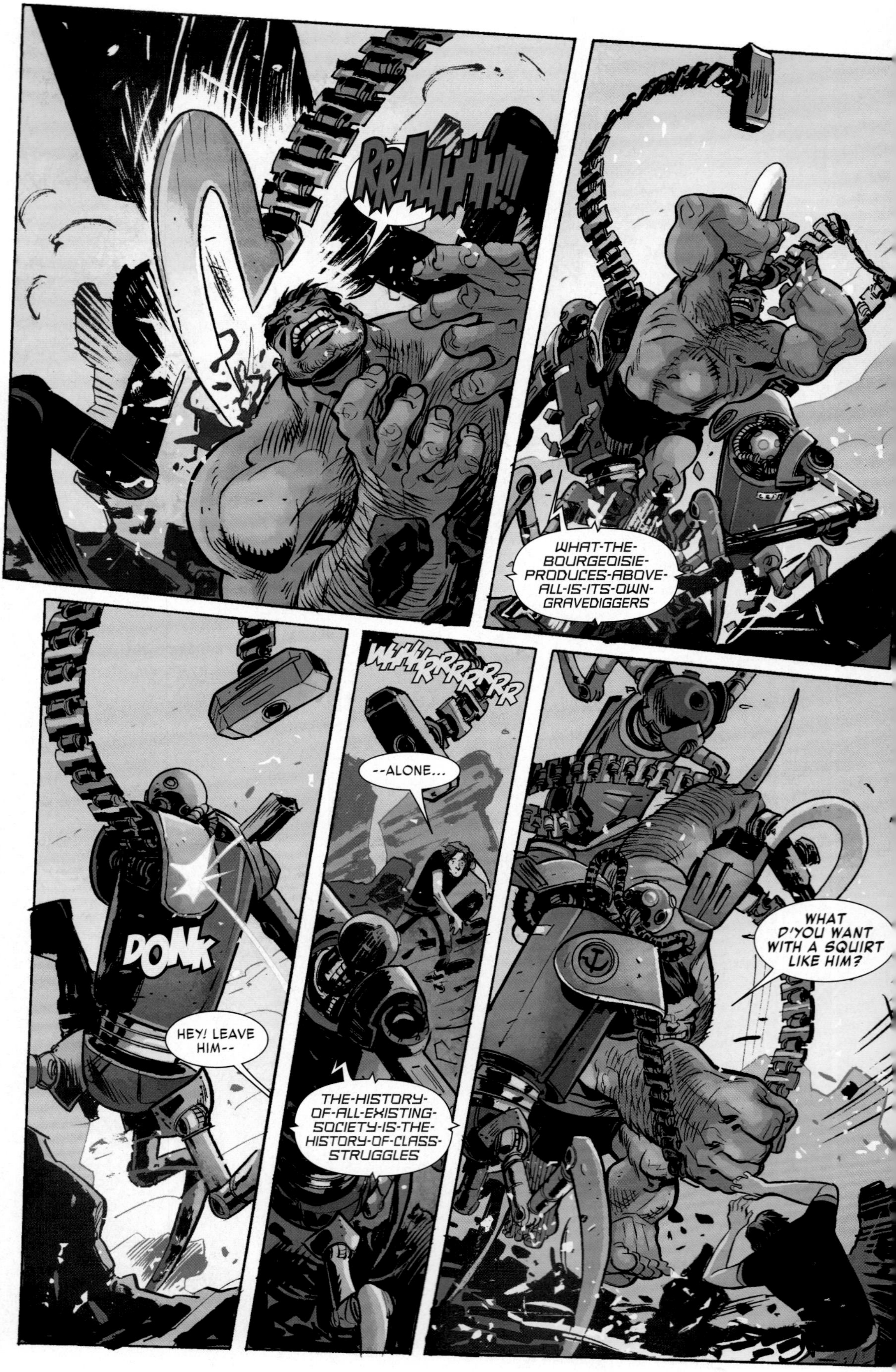
RRAAHHH!!!
WHAT-THE-BOURGEOISIE-PRODUCES-ABOVE-ALL-IS-ITS-OWN-GRAVEDIGGERS
DONK
HEY! LEAVE HIM--
WHHRRRRRRR
--ALONE...
THE-HISTORY-OF-ALL-EXISTING-SOCIETY-IS-THE-HISTORY-OF-CLASS-STRUGGLES
WHAT D'YOU WANT WITH A SQUIRT LIKE HIM?

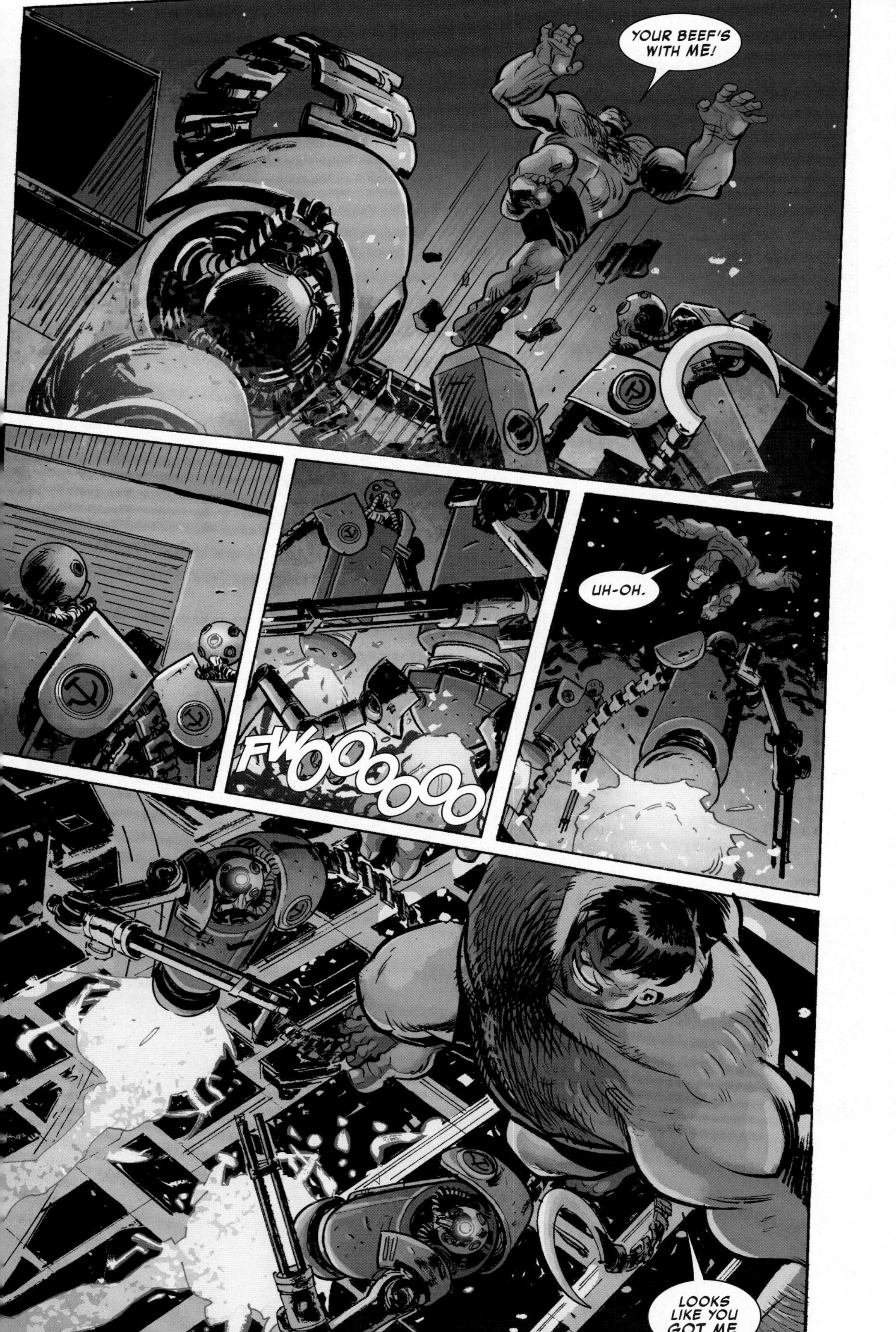
YOUR BEEF'S WITH ME!
FWOOOOOOO
UH-OH.
LOOKS LIKE YOU GOT ME.

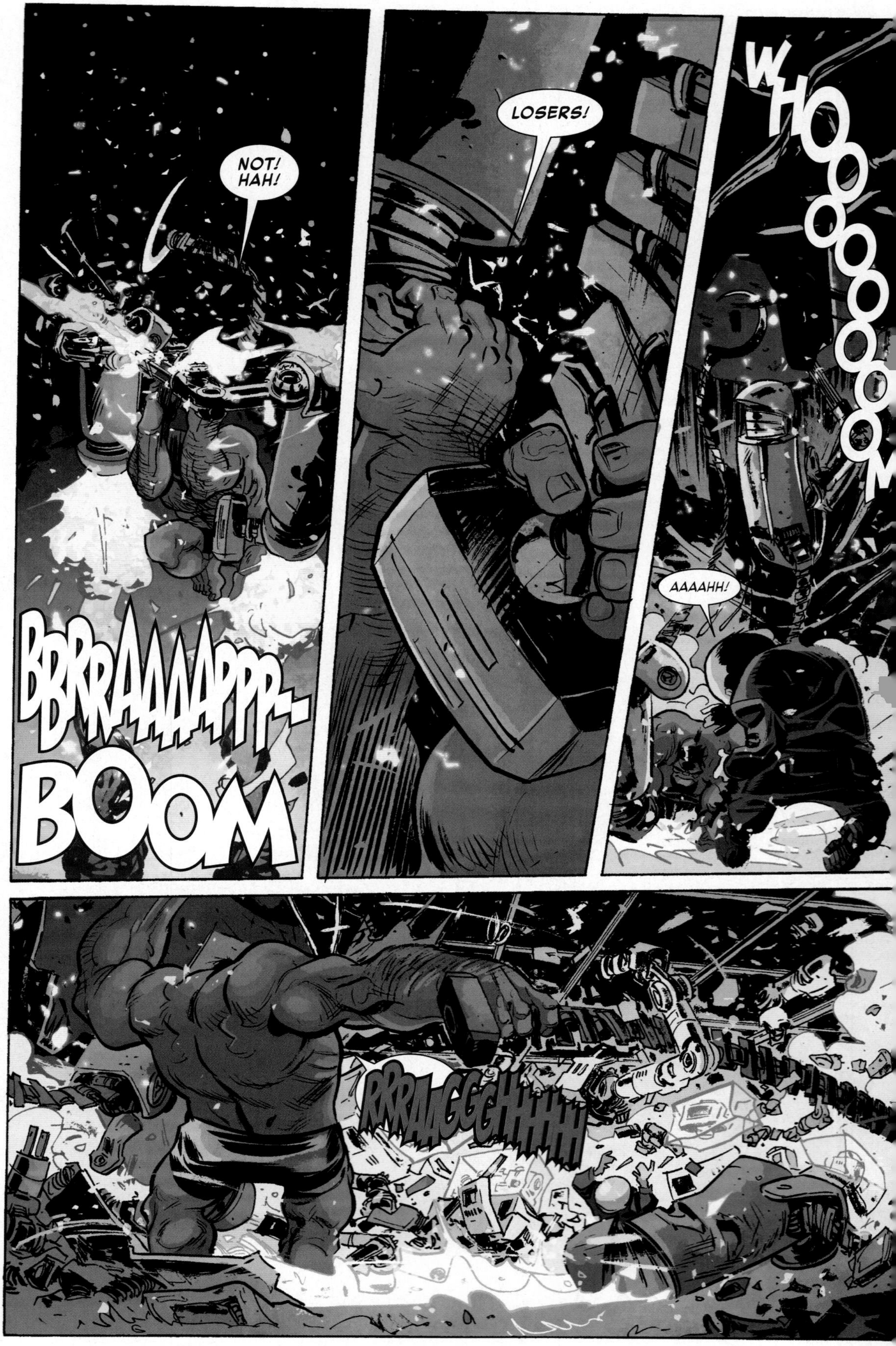
NOT! HAH!
BBRRAAAAPPP--
BOOM
LOSERS!
WHOOOOOOOOOM
AAAAHH!
RRRAAGGGHHHHH

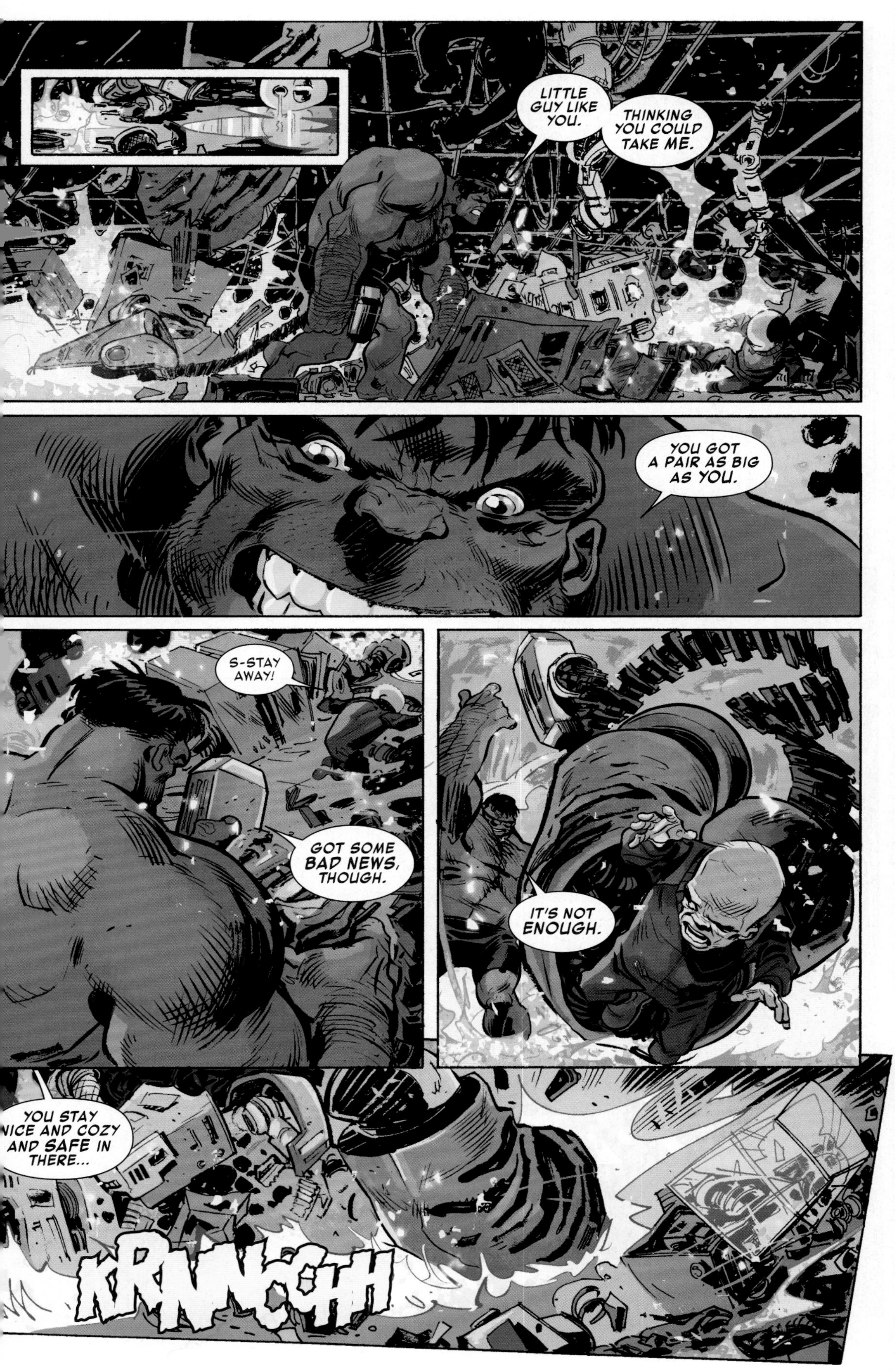

LITTLE GUY LIKE YOU.
THINKING YOU COULD TAKE ME.
YOU GOT A PAIR AS BIG AS YOU.
S-STAY AWAY!
GOT SOME BAD NEWS, THOUGH.
IT'S NOT ENOUGH.
YOU STAY NICE AND COZY AND SAFE IN THERE...
KRNNCHH

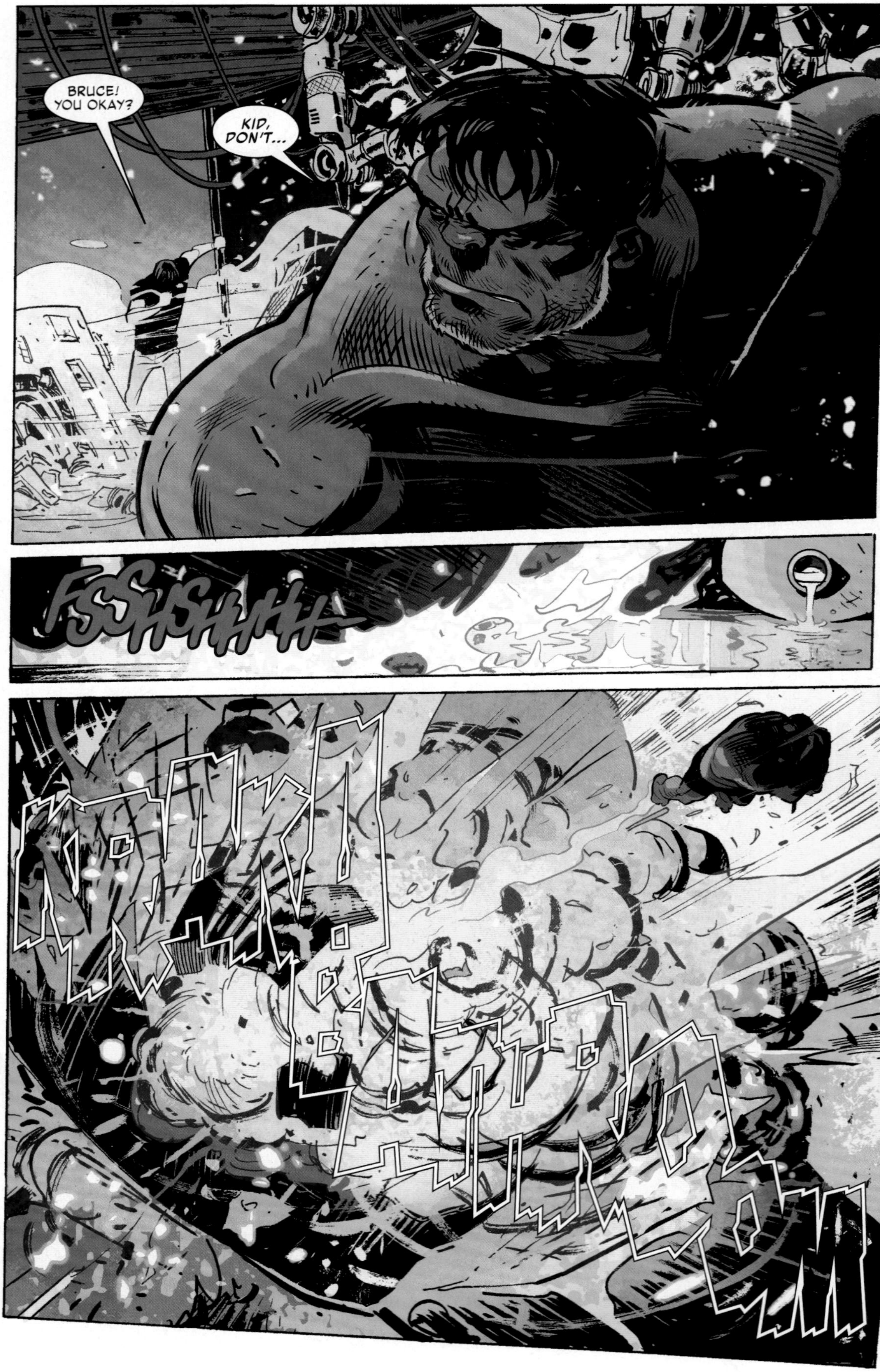
BRUCE! YOU OKAY?
KID, DON'T...
FSSHSHHHH

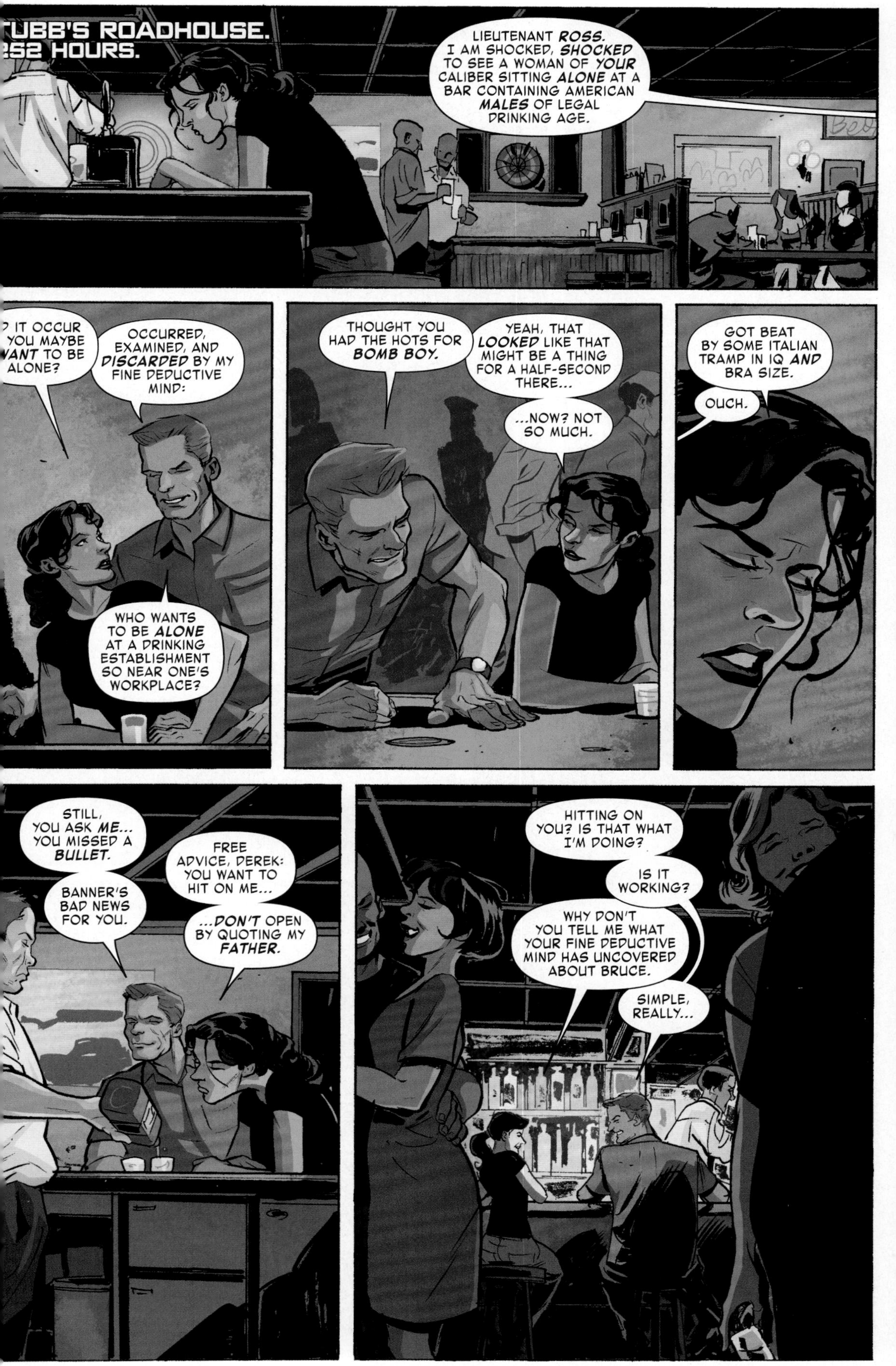

TUBB'S ROADHOUSE.
252 HOURS.
LIEUTENANT ROSS. I AM SHOCKED, SHOCKED TO SEE A WOMAN OF YOUR CALIBER SITTING ALONE AT A BAR CONTAINING AMERICAN MALES OF LEGAL DRINKING AGE.
IT OCCUR YOU MAYBE WANT TO BE ALONE?
OCCURRED, EXAMINED, AND DISCARDED BY MY FINE DEDUCTIVE MIND:
WHO WANTS TO BE ALONE AT A DRINKING ESTABLISHMENT SO NEAR ONE'S WORKPLACE?
THOUGHT YOU HAD THE HOTS FOR BOMB BOY.
YEAH, THAT LOOKED LIKE THAT MIGHT BE A THING FOR A HALF-SECOND THERE...
...NOW? NOT SO MUCH.
GOT BEAT BY SOME ITALIAN TRAMP IN IQ AND BRA SIZE.
OUCH.
STILL, YOU ASK ME... YOU MISSED A BULLET.
BANNER'S BAD NEWS FOR YOU.
FREE ADVICE, DEREK: YOU WANT TO HIT ON ME...
...DON'T OPEN BY QUOTING MY FATHER.
HITTING ON YOU? IS THAT WHAT I'M DOING?
IS IT WORKING?
WHY DON'T YOU TELL ME WHAT YOUR FINE DEDUCTIVE MIND HAS UNCOVERED ABOUT BRUCE.
SIMPLE, REALLY...

"...BANNER IS *HIDING* SOMETHING.

"IT'S ONLY A MATTER OF *TIME* BEFORE I FIGURE OUT WHAT IT IS.

"THEN EVERYTHING THAT WENT WRONG WITH LITTLE GREEN MAN WILL BE REVEALED.

"AND I'M GONNA NAIL HIM TO THE WALL.

"HOW CAN I BE SO SURE, YOU ASK?

"EASY.

"*TAKES* ONE TO *KNOW* ONE."

REALLY? DO I GET TO SEE YOUR HIDDEN SIDE?

DUNNO. THAT REQUIRES A LOT OF TRUST.

LET'S SEE HOW TONIGHT GOES FIRST, SHALL WE?

ALL RIGHT.

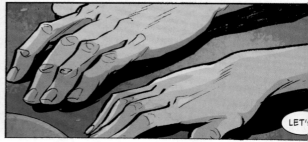

LET'S

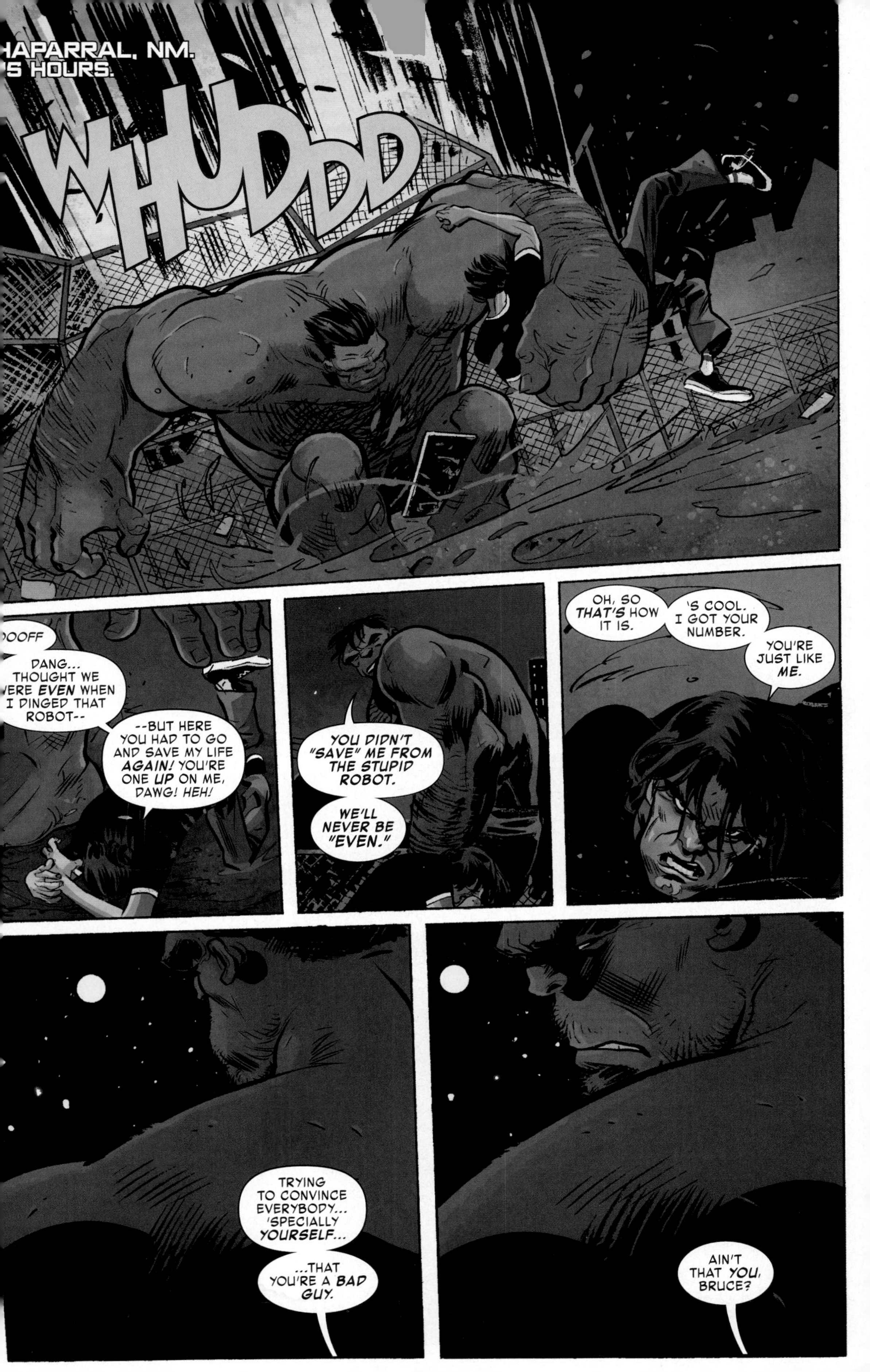

HAPARRAL, NM.
'S HOURS.
WHUDDD
OOFF
DANG... THOUGHT WE WERE EVEN WHEN I DINGED THAT ROBOT--
--BUT HERE YOU HAD TO GO AND SAVE MY LIFE AGAIN! YOU'RE ONE UP ON ME, DAWG! HEH!
YOU DIDN'T "SAVE" ME FROM THE STUPID ROBOT.
WE'LL NEVER BE "EVEN."
OH, SO THAT'S HOW IT IS.
'S COOL. I GOT YOUR NUMBER.
YOU'RE JUST LIKE ME.
TRYING TO CONVINCE EVERYBODY... 'SPECIALLY YOURSELF...
...THAT YOU'RE A BAD GUY.
AIN'T THAT YOU, BRUCE?

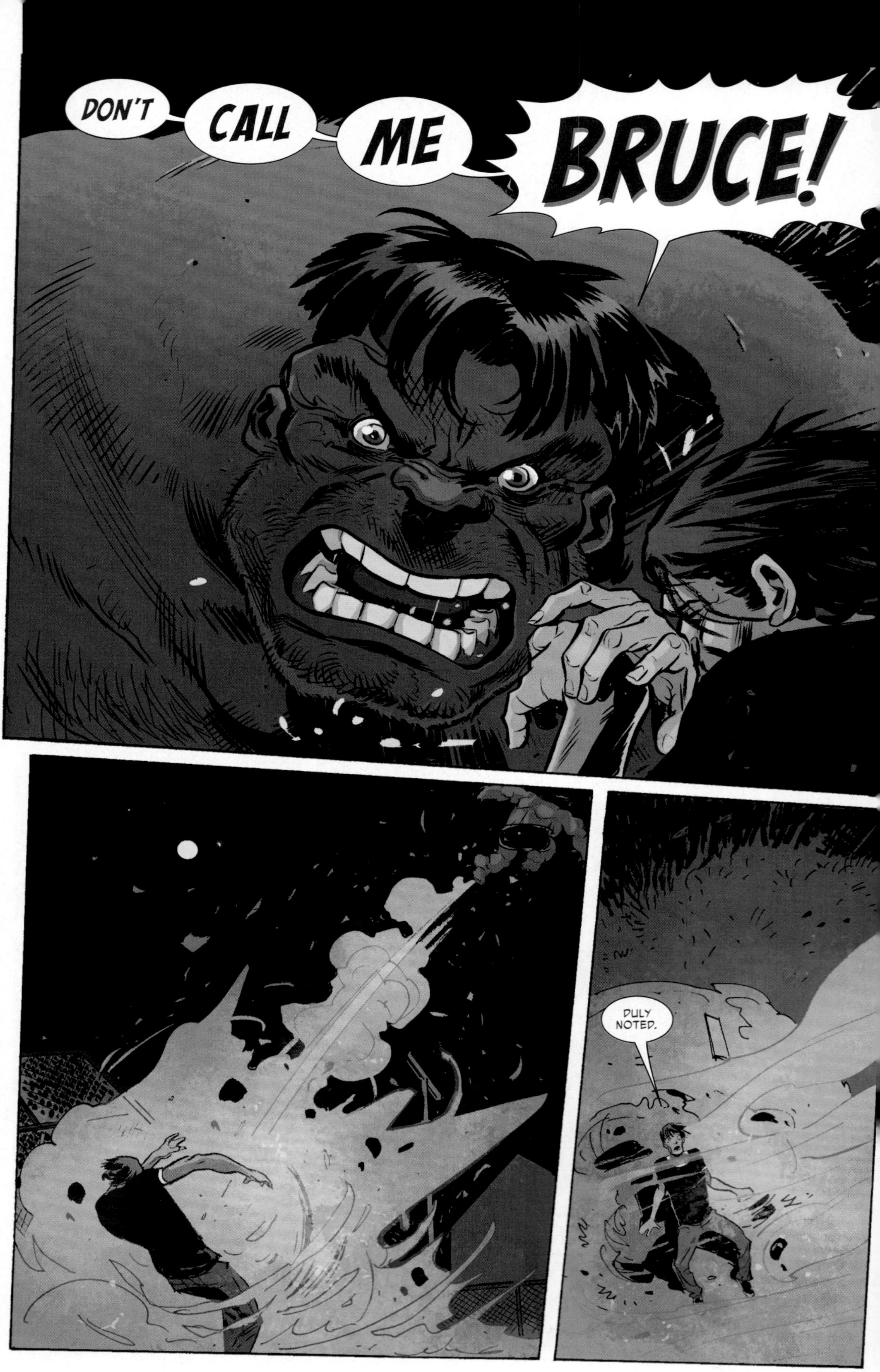
DON'T
CALL
ME
BRUCE!
DULY NOTED.

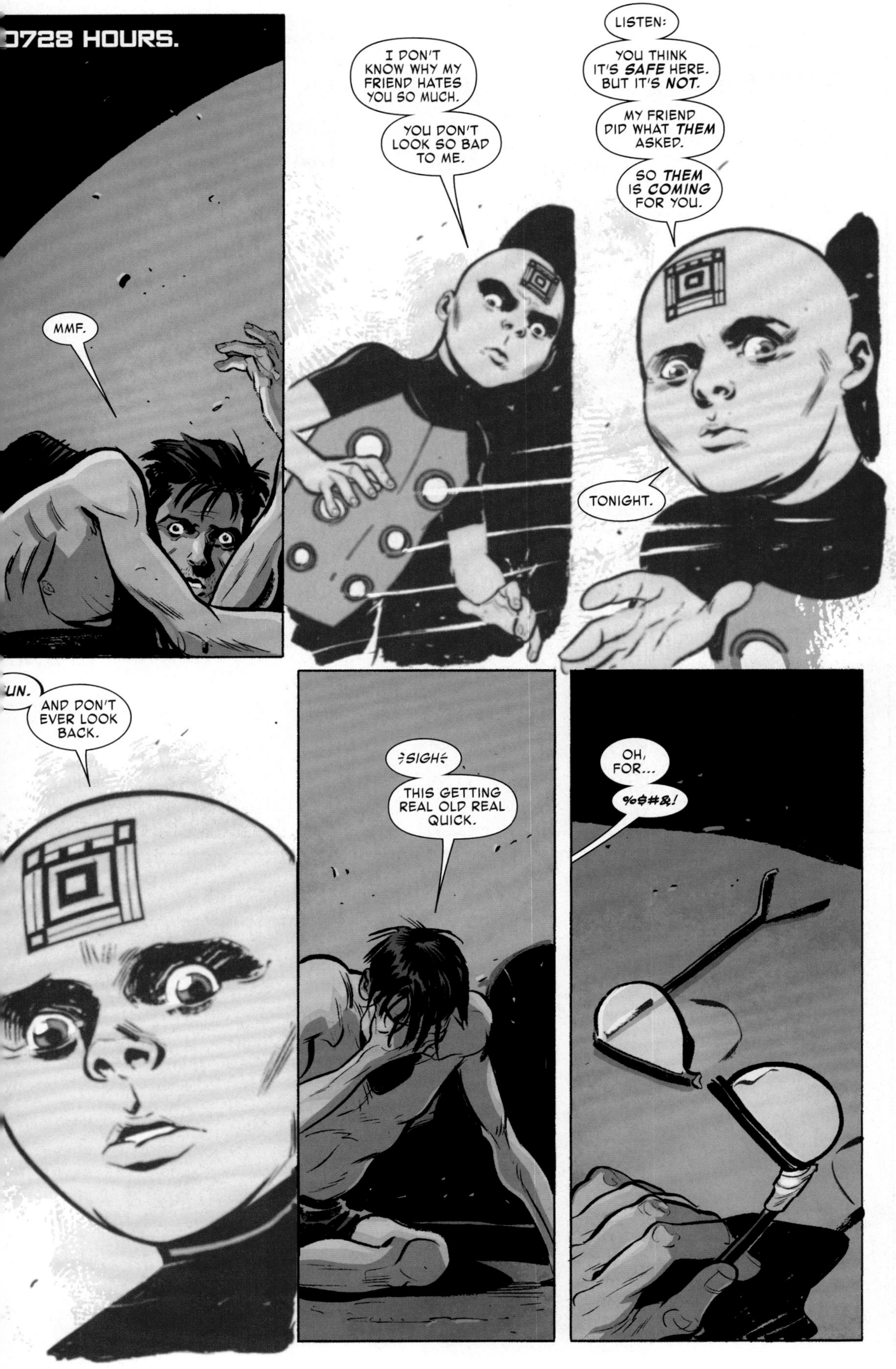
0728 HOURS.
MMF.
I DON'T KNOW WHY MY FRIEND HATES YOU SO MUCH.
YOU DON'T LOOK SO BAD TO ME.
LISTEN:
YOU THINK IT'S SAFE HERE. BUT IT'S NOT.
MY FRIEND DID WHAT THEM ASKED.
SO THEM IS COMING FOR YOU.
TONIGHT.
UN.
AND DON'T EVER LOOK BACK.
SIGH
THIS GETTING REAL OLD REAL QUICK.
OH, FOR...
%$#&!

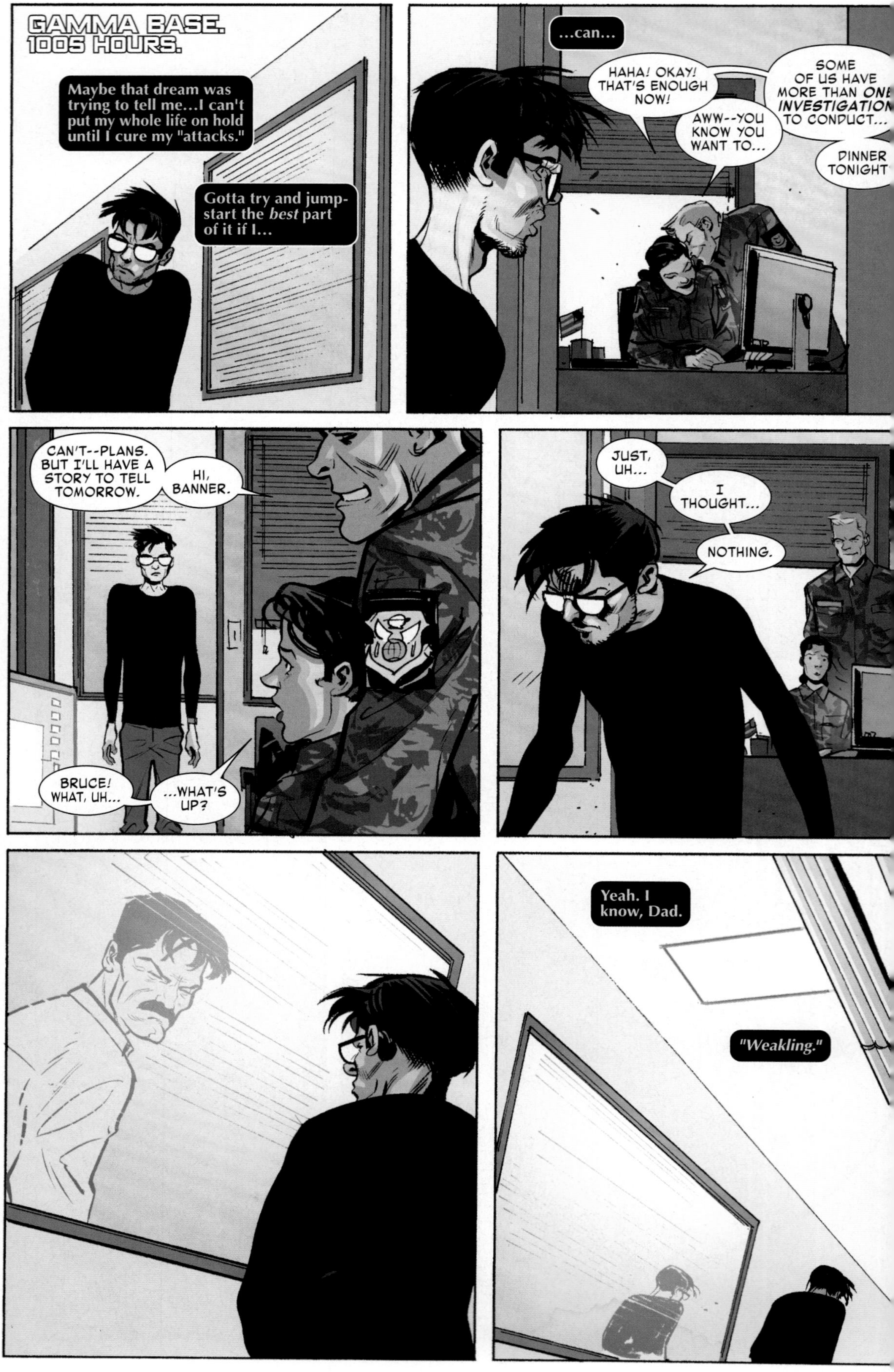
GAMMA BASE. 1005 HOURS.
Maybe that dream was trying to tell me...I can't put my whole life on hold until I cure my "attacks."
Gotta try and jump-start the *best* part of it if I...
...can...
HAHA! OKAY! THAT'S ENOUGH NOW!
AWW--YOU KNOW YOU WANT TO...
SOME OF US HAVE MORE THAN ONE INVESTIGATION TO CONDUCT...
DINNER TONIGHT
CAN'T--PLANS. BUT I'LL HAVE A STORY TO TELL TOMORROW.
HI, BANNER.
BRUCE! WHAT, UH...
...WHAT'S UP?
JUST, UH...
I THOUGHT...
NOTHING.
Yeah. I know, Dad.
"Weakling."

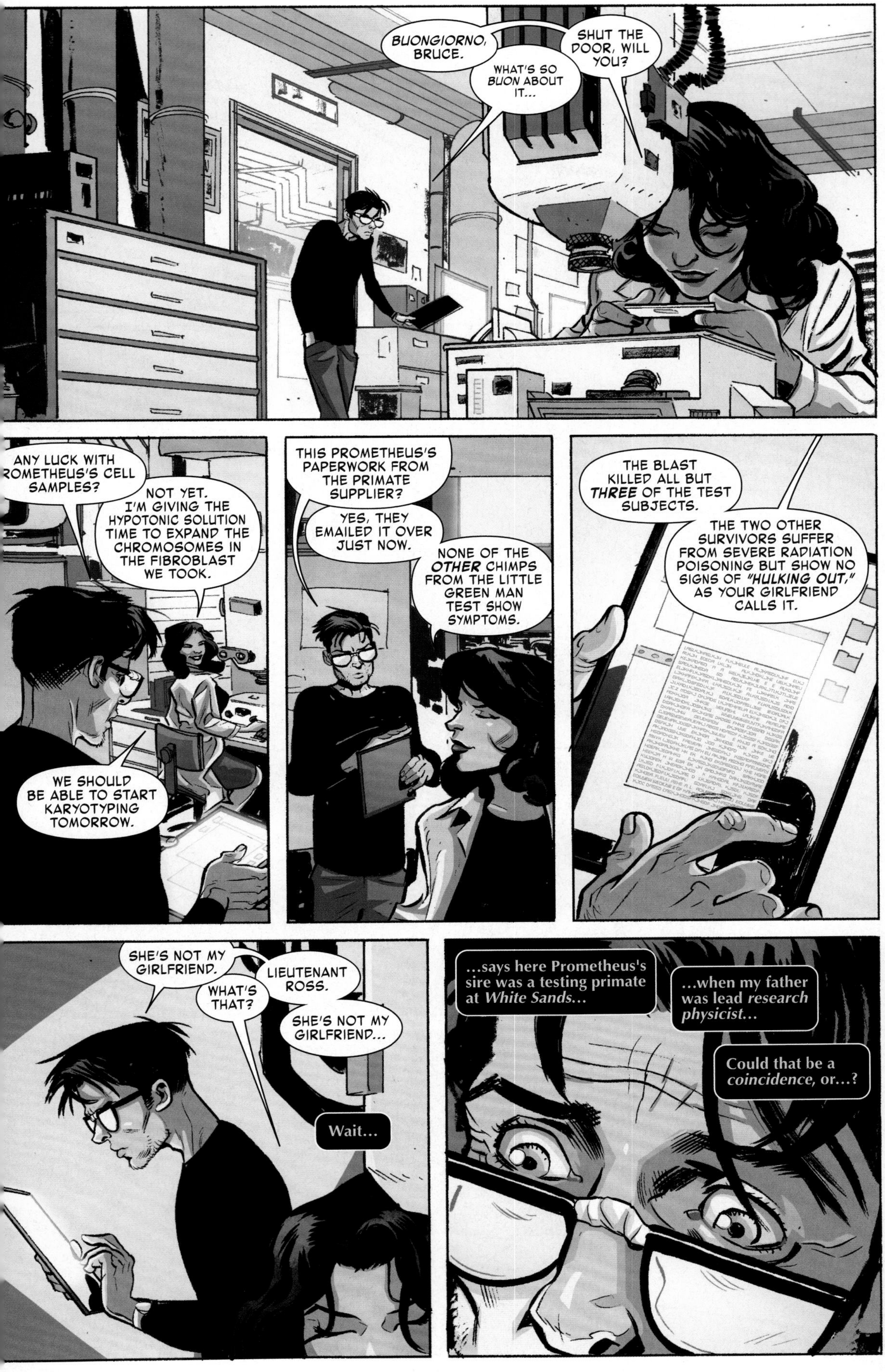
BUONGIORNO, BRUCE.
WHAT'S SO BUON ABOUT IT...
SHUT THE DOOR, WILL YOU?
ANY LUCK WITH PROMETHEUS'S CELL SAMPLES?
NOT YET. I'M GIVING THE HYPOTONIC SOLUTION TIME TO EXPAND THE CHROMOSOMES IN THE FIBROBLAST WE TOOK.
WE SHOULD BE ABLE TO START KARYOTYPING TOMORROW.
THIS PROMETHEUS'S PAPERWORK FROM THE PRIMATE SUPPLIER?
YES, THEY EMAILED IT OVER JUST NOW.
NONE OF THE OTHER CHIMPS FROM THE LITTLE GREEN MAN TEST SHOW SYMPTOMS.
THE BLAST KILLED ALL BUT THREE OF THE TEST SUBJECTS.
THE TWO OTHER SURVIVORS SUFFER FROM SEVERE RADIATION POISONING BUT SHOW NO SIGNS OF "HULKING OUT," AS YOUR GIRLFRIEND CALLS IT.
SHE'S NOT MY GIRLFRIEND.
WHAT'S THAT?
LIEUTENANT ROSS.
SHE'S NOT MY GIRLFRIEND...
Wait...
...says here Prometheus's sire was a testing primate at White Sands...
...when my father was lead research physicist...
Could that be a coincidence, or...?

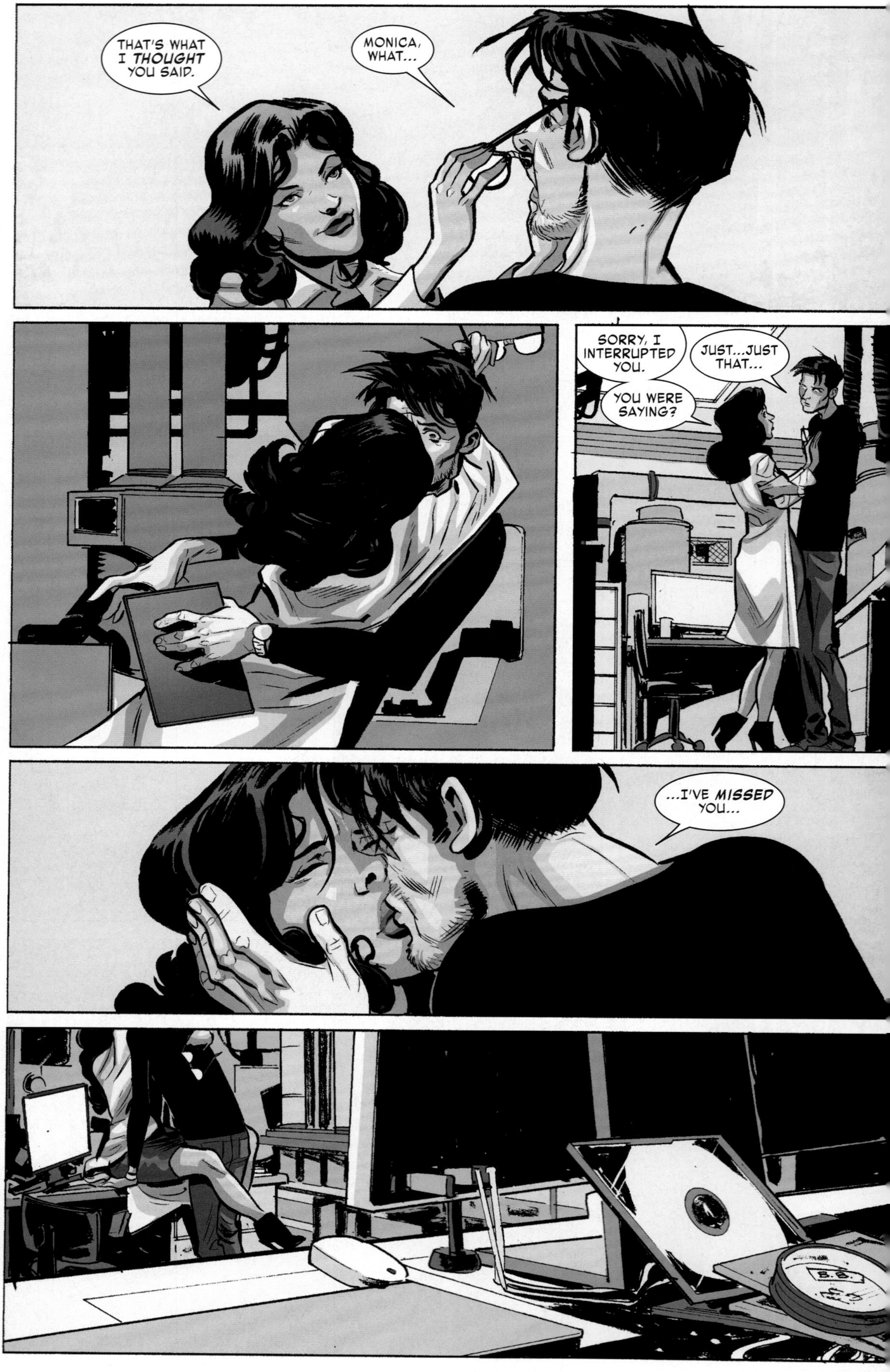
THAT'S WHAT I *THOUGHT* YOU SAID.
MONICA, WHAT...
SORRY, I INTERRUPTED YOU.
YOU WERE SAYING?
JUST...JUST THAT...
...I'VE *MISSED* YOU...
B.B.

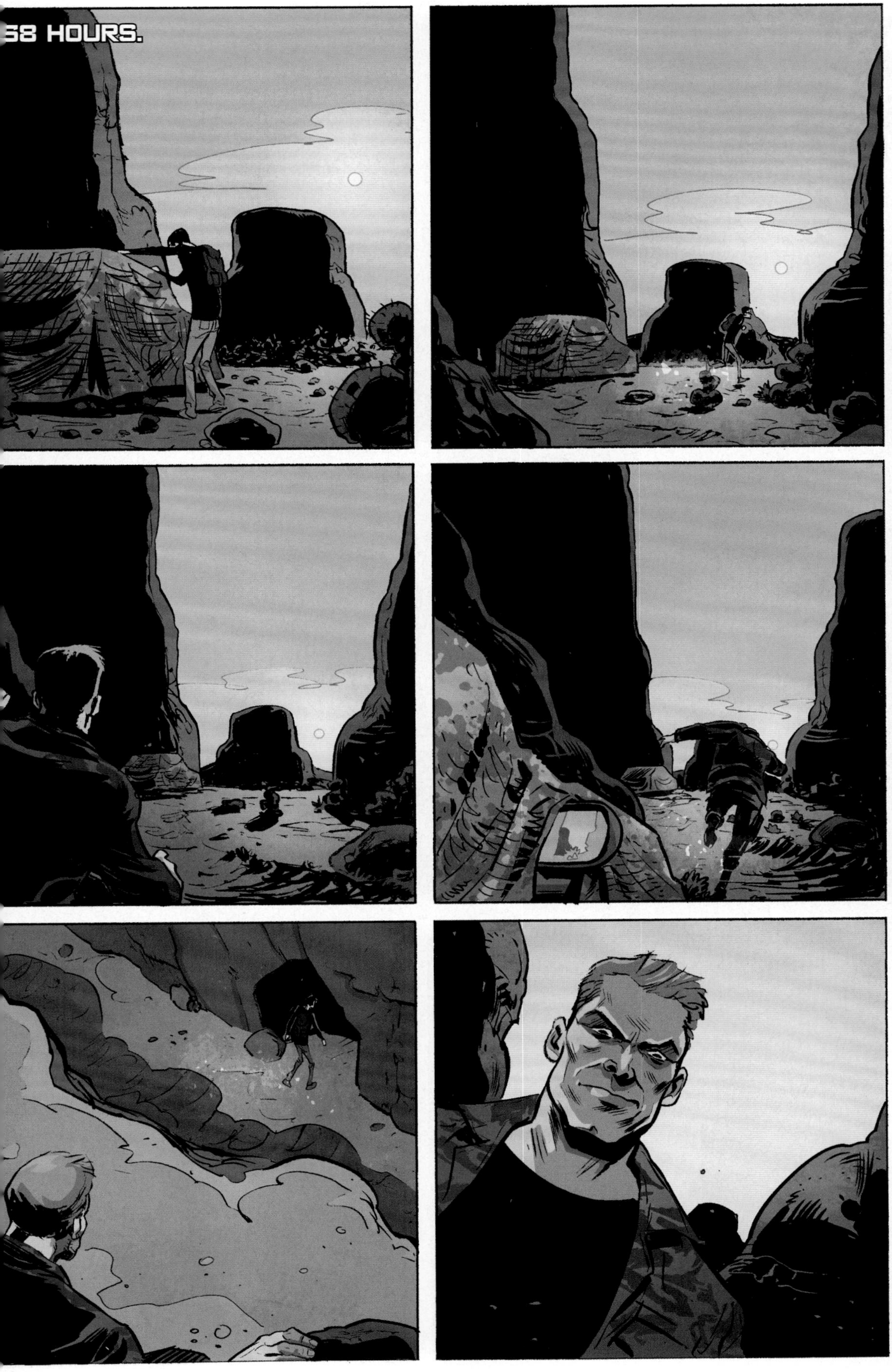

68 HOURS.

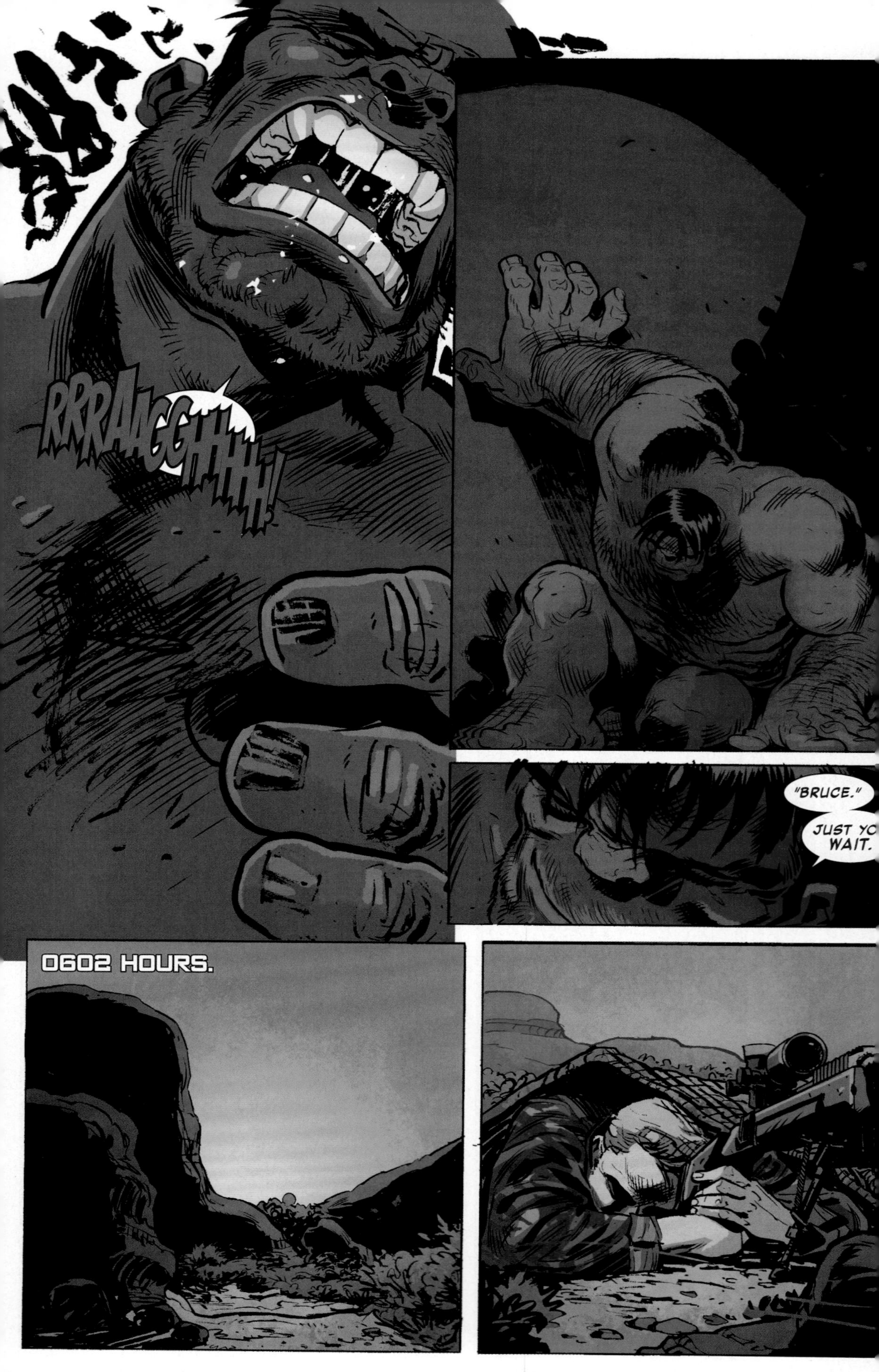

RRRAAGGHHHH!
"BRUCE."
JUST YO
WAIT.
0602 HOURS.

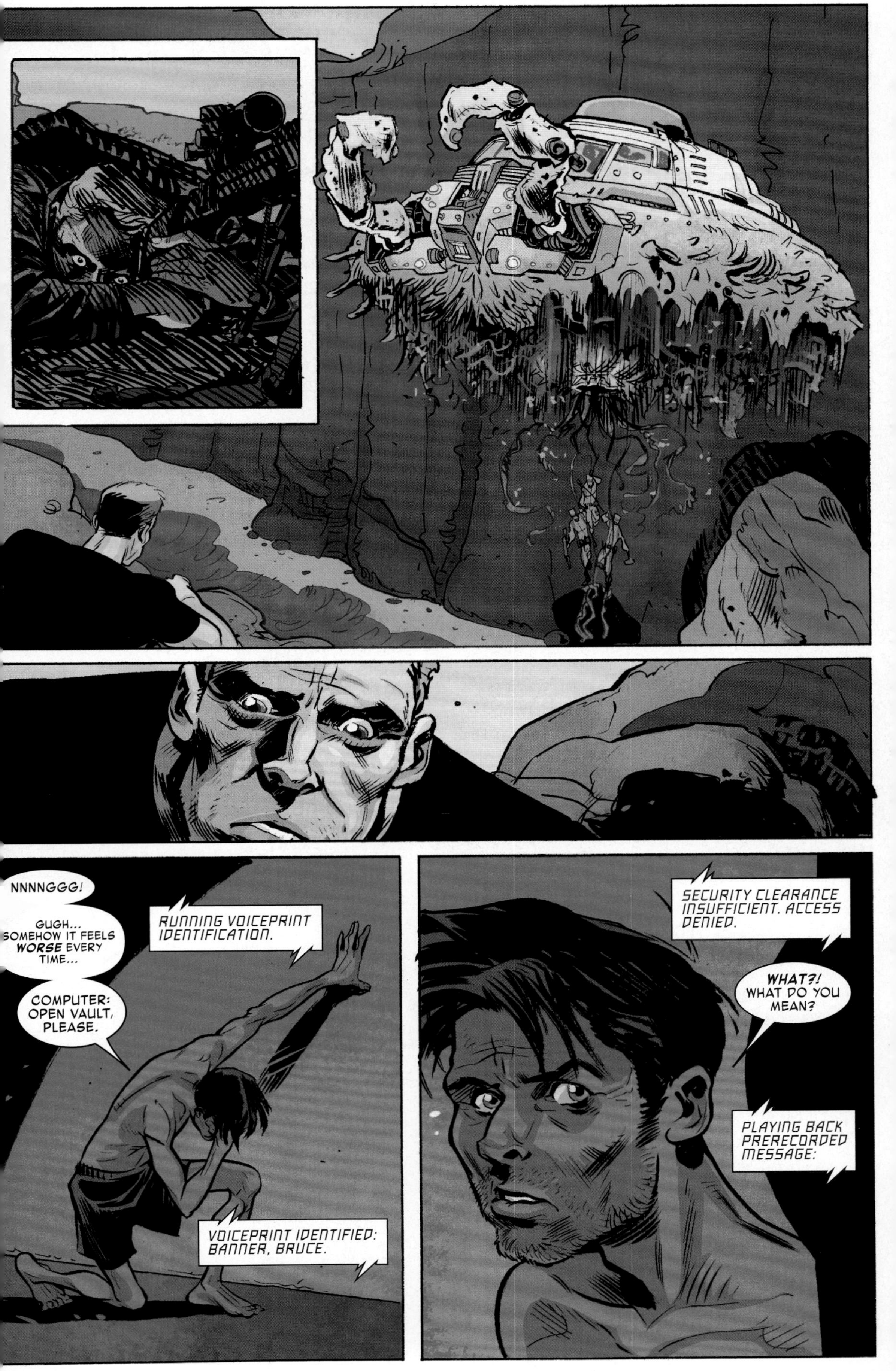

NNNNGGG!
GUGH... SOMEHOW IT FEELS WORSE EVERY TIME...
COMPUTER: OPEN VAULT, PLEASE.
RUNNING VOICEPRINT IDENTIFICATION.
VOICEPRINT IDENTIFIED: BANNER, BRUCE.
SECURITY CLEARANCE INSUFFICIENT. ACCESS DENIED.
WHAT?! WHAT DO YOU MEAN?
PLAYING BACK PRERECORDED MESSAGE:

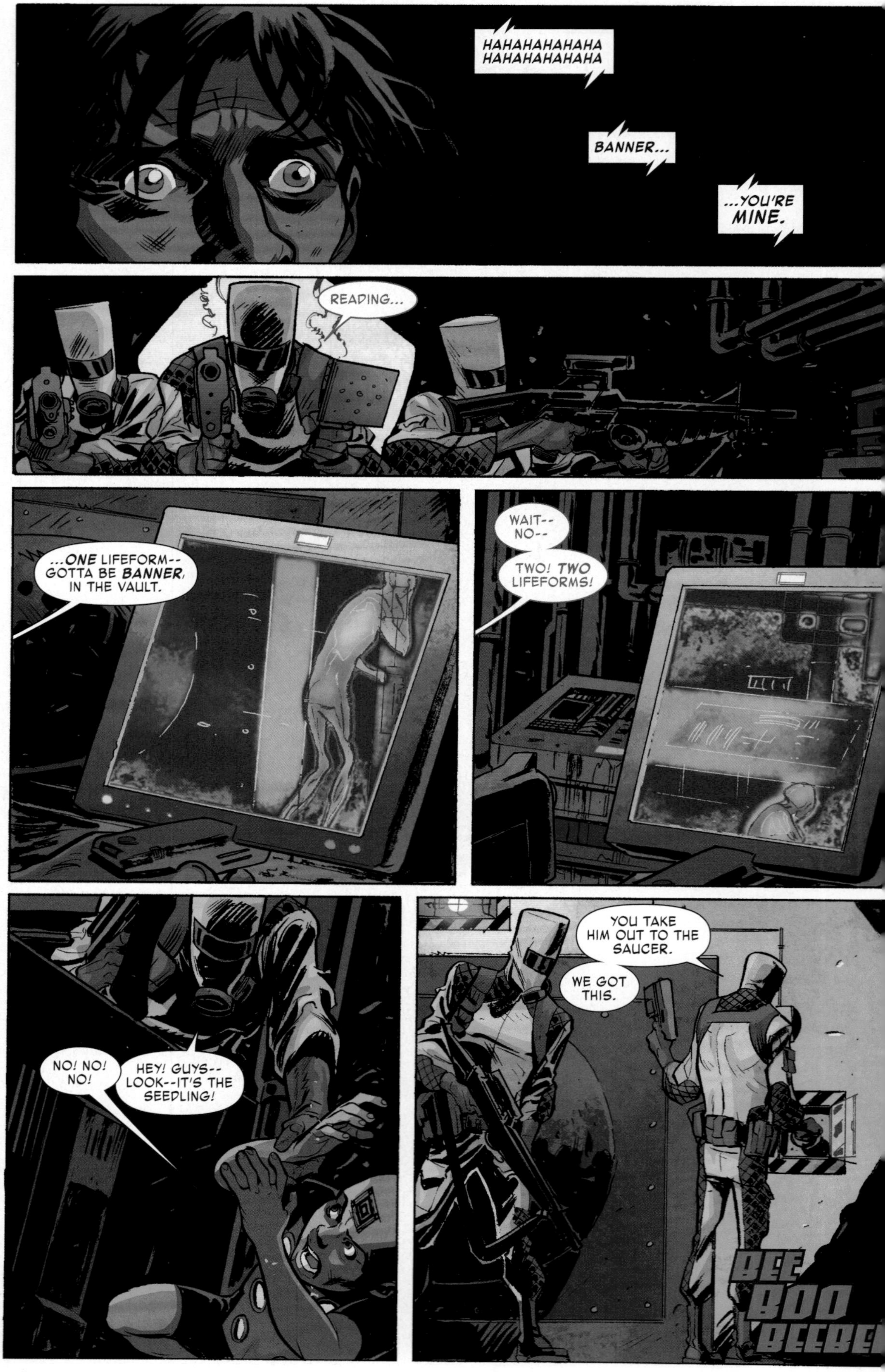
HAHAHAHAHAHA
HAHAHAHAHAHA
BANNER...
...YOU'RE MINE.
READING...
...ONE LIFEFORM-- GOTTA BE BANNER, IN THE VAULT.
WAIT-- NO--
TWO! TWO LIFEFORMS!
NO! NO! NO!
HEY! GUYS-- LOOK--IT'S THE SEEDLING!
YOU TAKE HIM OUT TO THE SAUCER.
WE GOT THIS.
BEE BOO BEEBE

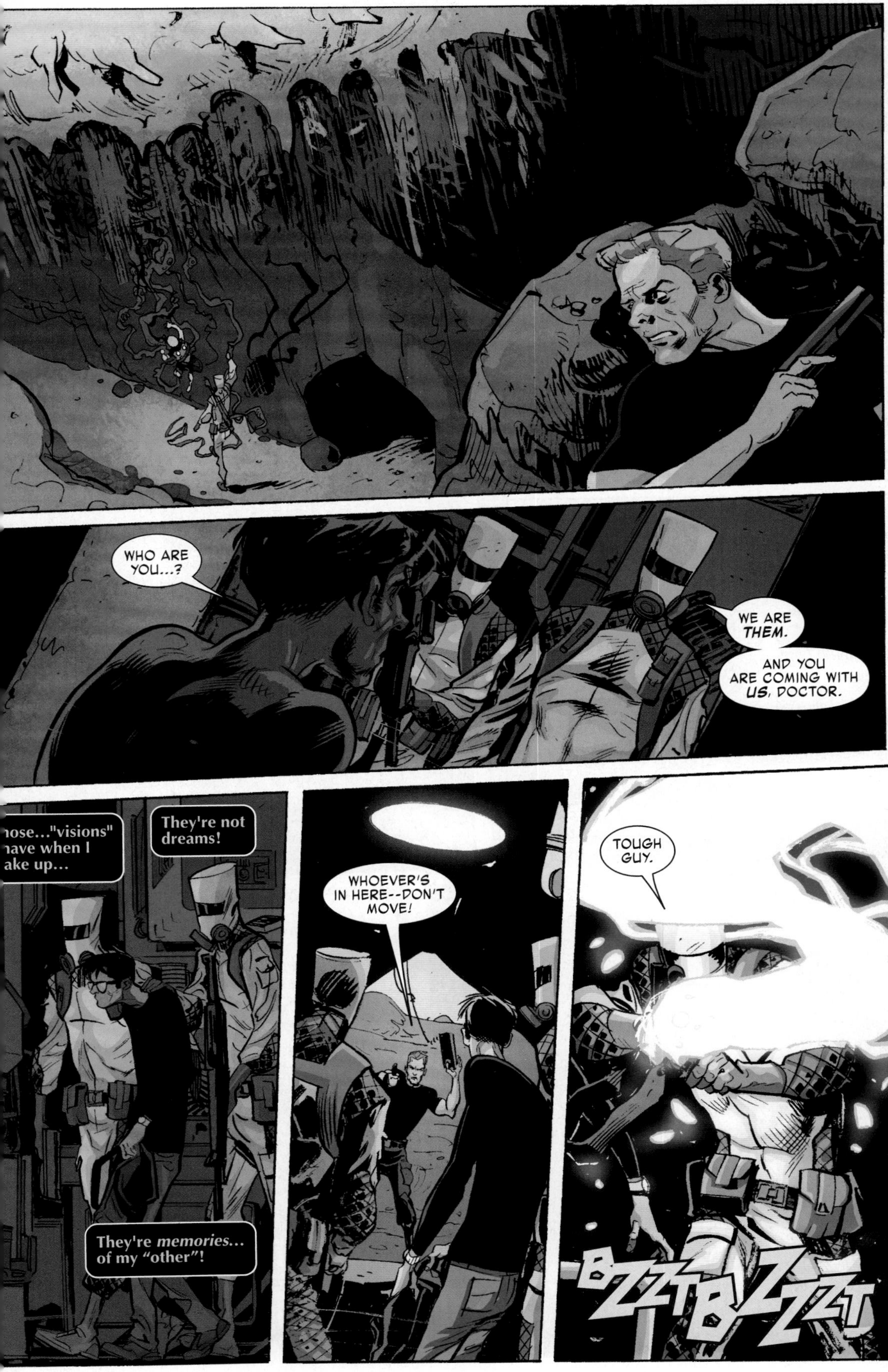
WHO ARE YOU...?
WE ARE *THEM.*
AND YOU ARE COMING WITH *US*, DOCTOR.
hose..."visions" ıave when I ake up...
They're not dreams!
They're *memories*... of my "other"!
WHOEVER'S IN HERE--DON'T MOVE!
TOUGH GUY.
BZZZT BZZZZT

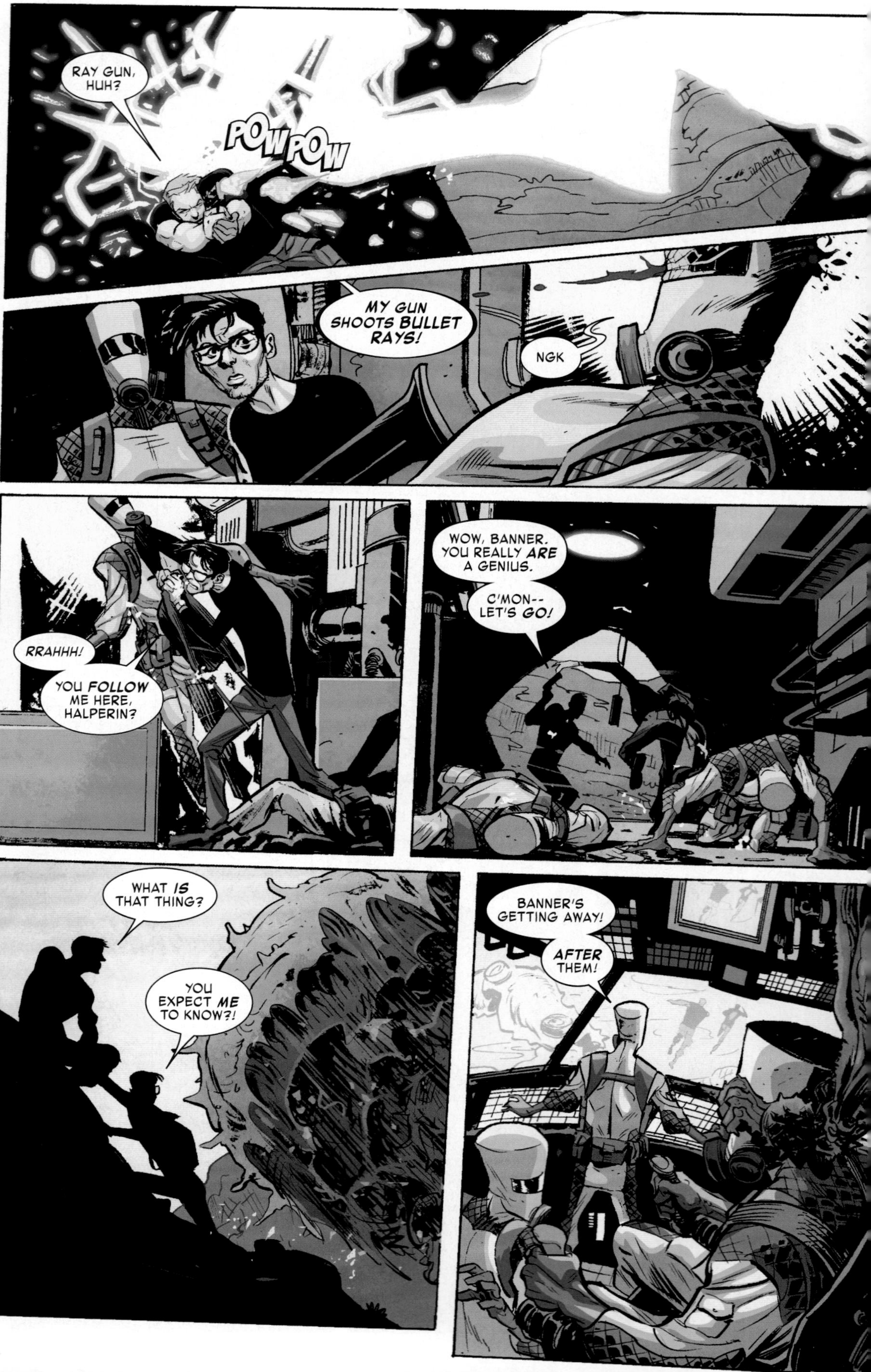
RAY GUN, HUH?
POWPOW
MY GUN SHOOTS BULLET RAYS!
NGK
RRAHHH!
YOU FOLLOW ME HERE, HALPERIN?
WOW, BANNER. YOU REALLY ARE A GENIUS.
C'MON-- LET'S GO!
WHAT IS THAT THING?
YOU EXPECT ME TO KNOW?!
BANNER'S GETTING AWAY!
AFTER THEM!

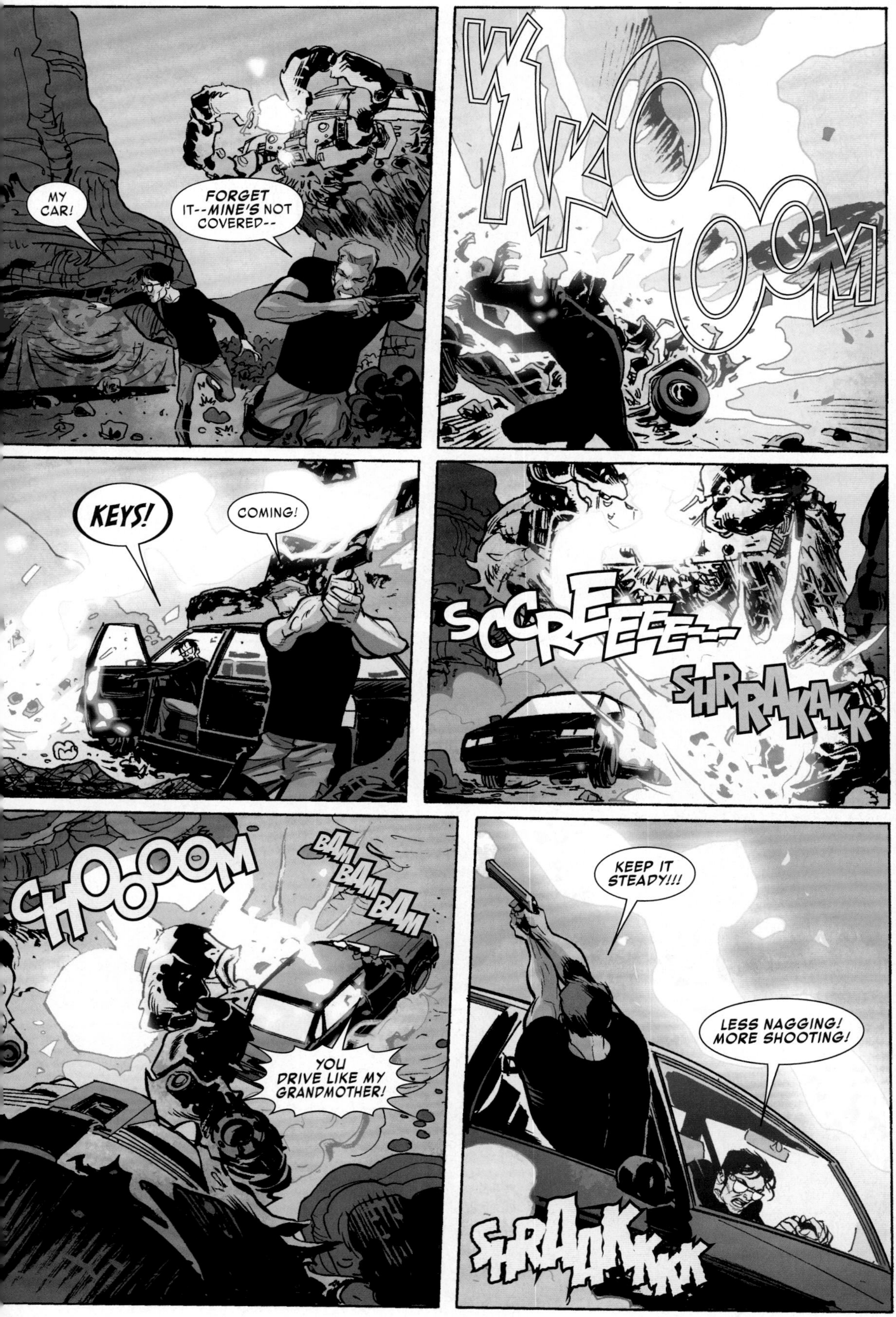
MY CAR!
FORGET IT--MINE'S NOT COVERED--
KAKOOOOM
KEYS!
COMING!
SCCREEEEE---
SHRRAKAKKK
CHOOOOM
BAM BAM BAM
YOU DRIVE LIKE MY GRANDMOTHER!
KEEP IT STEADY!!!
LESS NAGGING! MORE SHOOTING!
SHRAAKKKK

HURRY UP AND **BLAST** 'EM! THIS KID **BITES!**

MMMMMMMM!!

CAN'T QUITE GET A BEAD. JUST A...

AW, DAMN IT.

"HE MUST'VE CALLED FOR **BACKUP.**"

"THE IMPERATOR WON'T WANT US TO BE IDENTIFIED."

WE'RE OUTTA HERE.

AT LEAST WE GOT THE SEEDLING.

SH RA KKKK

LOOK OU--

SKREEE--

RMMMBBB

BBBLLLLLL

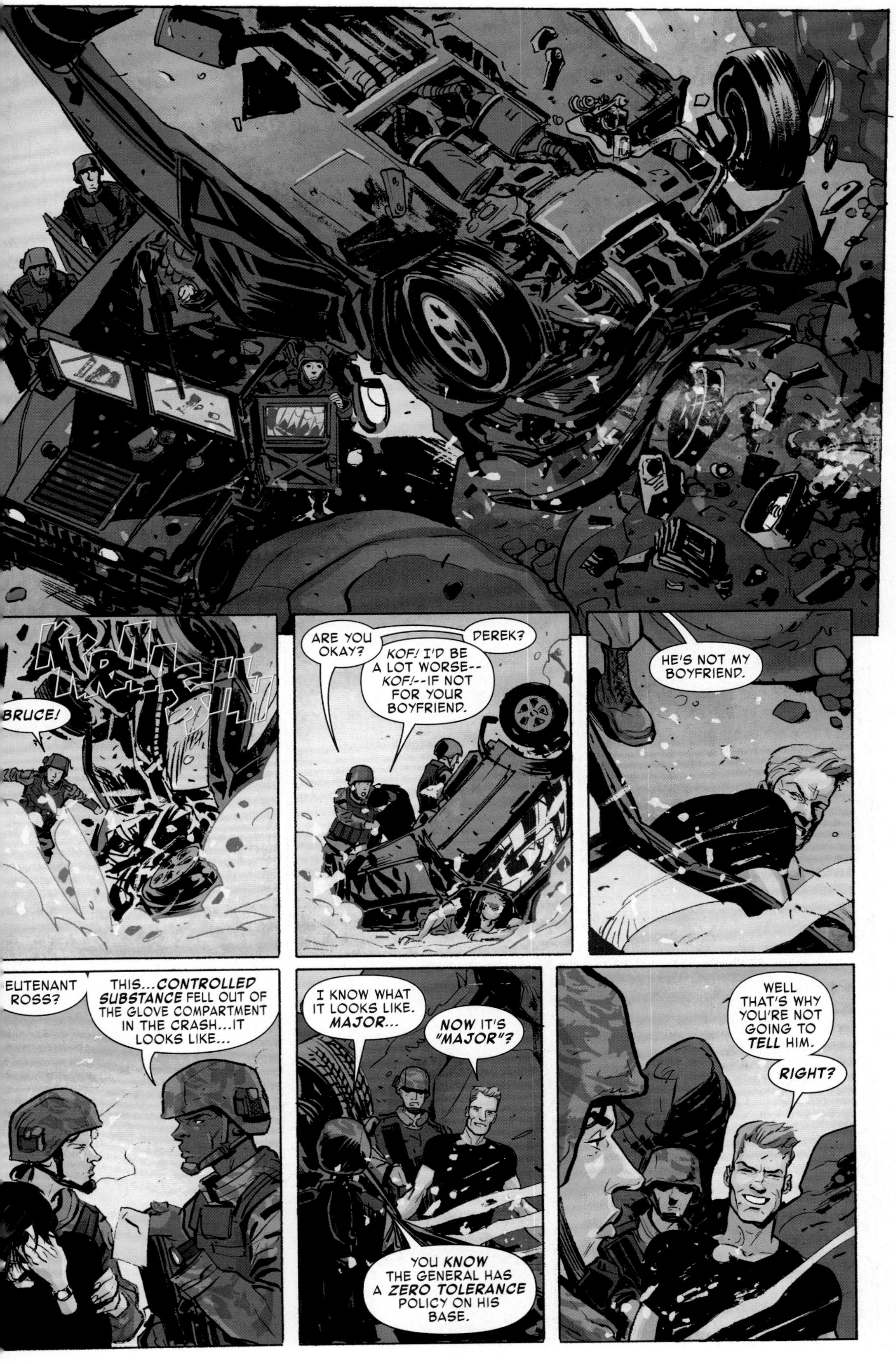
BRUCE!
ARE YOU OKAY?
DEREK?
KOF! I'D BE A LOT WORSE--KOF!--IF NOT FOR YOUR BOYFRIEND.
HE'S NOT MY BOYFRIEND.
EUTENANT ROSS?
THIS...CONTROLLED SUBSTANCE FELL OUT OF THE GLOVE COMPARTMENT IN THE CRASH...IT LOOKS LIKE...
I KNOW WHAT IT LOOKS LIKE. MAJOR...
NOW IT'S "MAJOR"?
YOU KNOW THE GENERAL HAS A ZERO TOLERANCE POLICY ON HIS BASE.
WELL THAT'S WHY YOU'RE NOT GOING TO TELL HIM.
RIGHT?

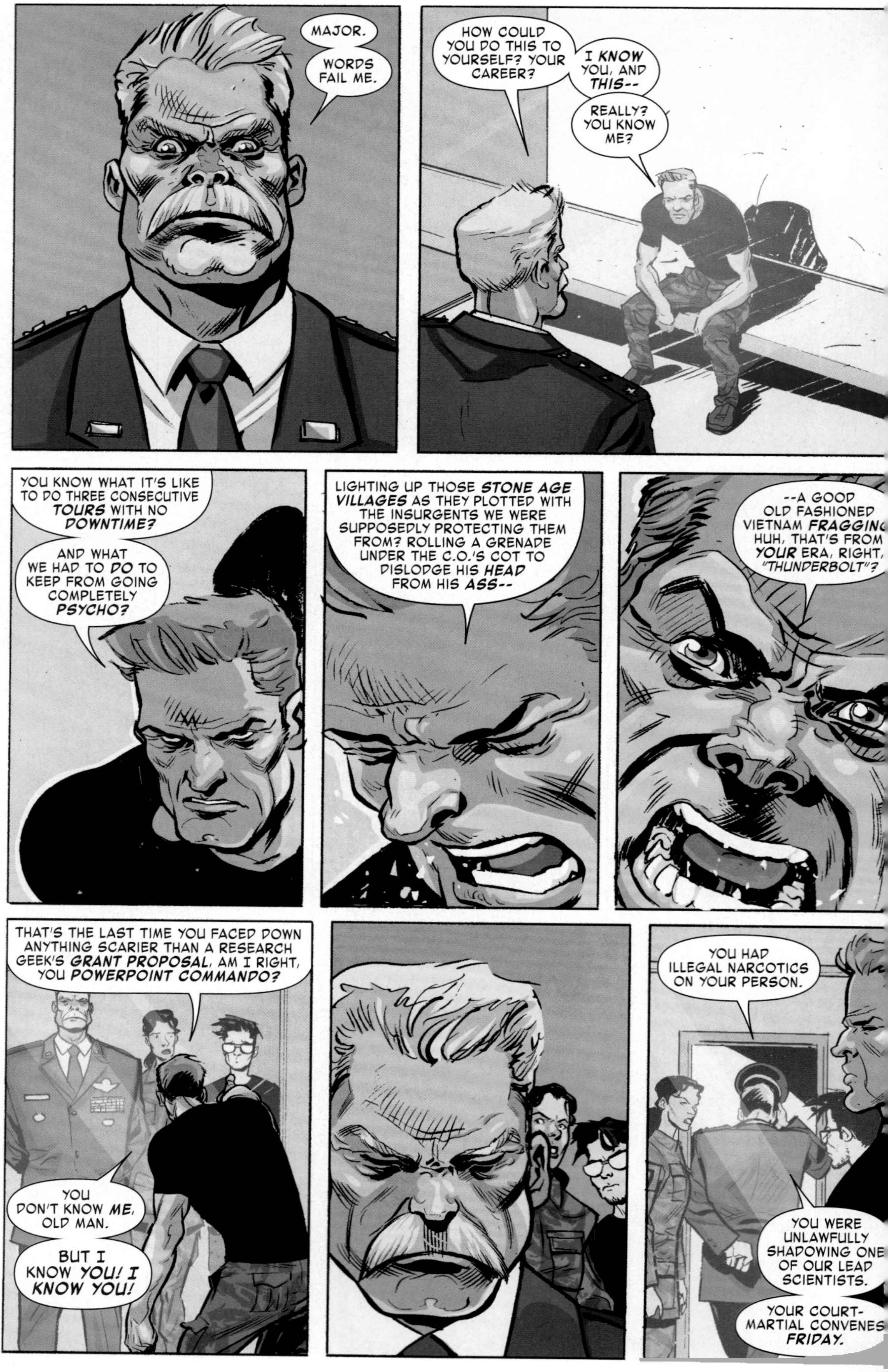
MAJOR.
WORDS FAIL ME.
HOW COULD YOU DO THIS TO YOURSELF? YOUR CAREER?
I KNOW YOU, AND THIS--
REALLY? YOU KNOW ME?
YOU KNOW WHAT IT'S LIKE TO DO THREE CONSECUTIVE TOURS WITH NO DOWNTIME?
AND WHAT WE HAD TO DO TO KEEP FROM GOING COMPLETELY PSYCHO?
LIGHTING UP THOSE STONE AGE VILLAGES AS THEY PLOTTED WITH THE INSURGENTS WE WERE SUPPOSEDLY PROTECTING THEM FROM? ROLLING A GRENADE UNDER THE C.O.'S COT TO DISLODGE HIS HEAD FROM HIS ASS--
--A GOOD OLD FASHIONED VIETNAM FRAGGING HUH, THAT'S FROM YOUR ERA, RIGHT, "THUNDERBOLT"?
THAT'S THE LAST TIME YOU FACED DOWN ANYTHING SCARIER THAN A RESEARCH GEEK'S GRANT PROPOSAL, AM I RIGHT, YOU POWERPOINT COMMANDO?
YOU DON'T KNOW ME, OLD MAN.
BUT I KNOW YOU! I KNOW YOU!
YOU HAD ILLEGAL NARCOTICS ON YOUR PERSON.
YOU WERE UNLAWFULLY SHADOWING ONE OF OUR LEAD SCIENTISTS.
YOUR COURT-MARTIAL CONVENES FRIDAY.

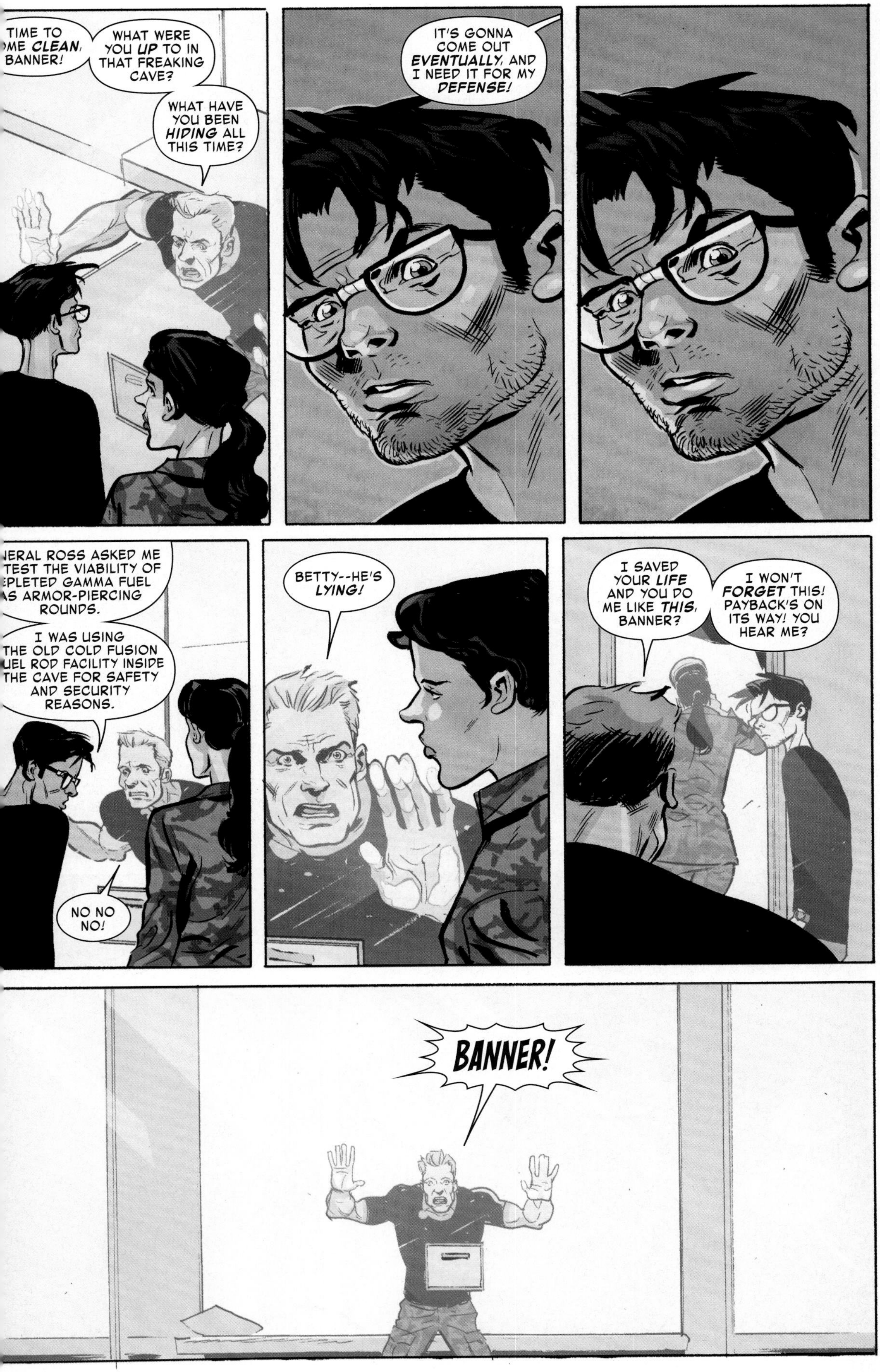

TIME TO OME CLEAN, BANNER!
WHAT WERE YOU UP TO IN THAT FREAKING CAVE?
WHAT HAVE YOU BEEN HIDING ALL THIS TIME?
IT'S GONNA COME OUT EVENTUALLY, AND I NEED IT FOR MY DEFENSE!
NERAL ROSS ASKED ME TEST THE VIABILITY OF EPLETED GAMMA FUEL AS ARMOR-PIERCING ROUNDS.
I WAS USING THE OLD COLD FUSION UEL ROD FACILITY INSIDE THE CAVE FOR SAFETY AND SECURITY REASONS.
NO NO NO!
BETTY--HE'S LYING!
I SAVED YOUR LIFE AND YOU DO ME LIKE THIS, BANNER?
I WON'T FORGET THIS! PAYBACK'S ON ITS WAY! YOU HEAR ME?
BANNER!

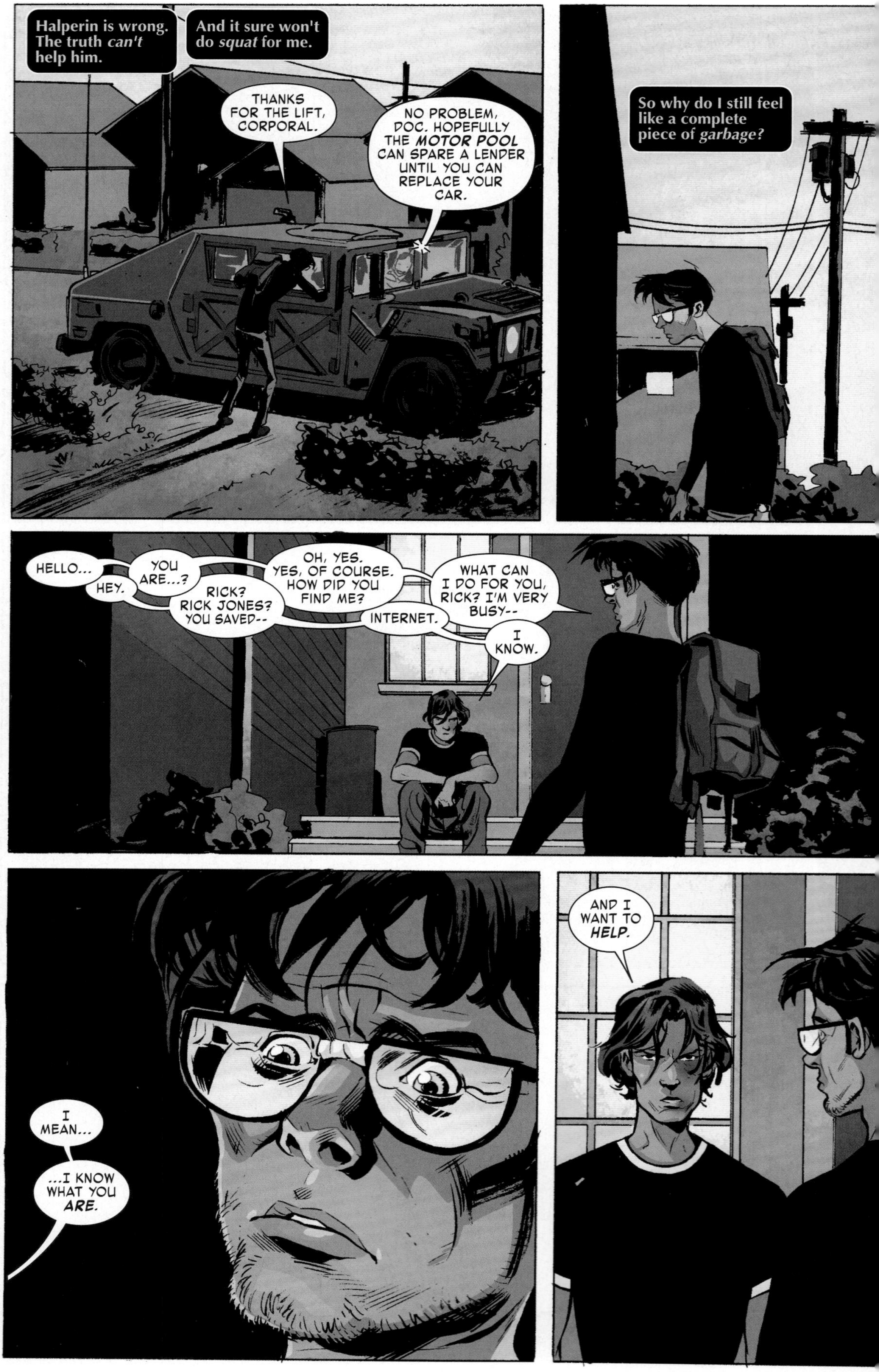

Halperin is wrong. The truth *can't* help him.
And it sure won't do *squat* for me.
THANKS FOR THE LIFT, CORPORAL.
NO PROBLEM, DOC. HOPEFULLY THE ***MOTOR POOL*** CAN SPARE A LENDER UNTIL YOU CAN REPLACE YOUR CAR.
So why do I still feel like a complete piece of *garbage?*
HELLO...
HEY.
YOU ARE...?
RICK? RICK JONES? YOU SAVED--
OH, YES. YES, OF COURSE. HOW DID YOU FIND ME?
INTERNET.
WHAT CAN I DO FOR YOU, RICK? I'M VERY BUSY--
I KNOW.
I MEAN...
...I KNOW WHAT YOU ***ARE.***
AND I WANT TO ***HELP.***

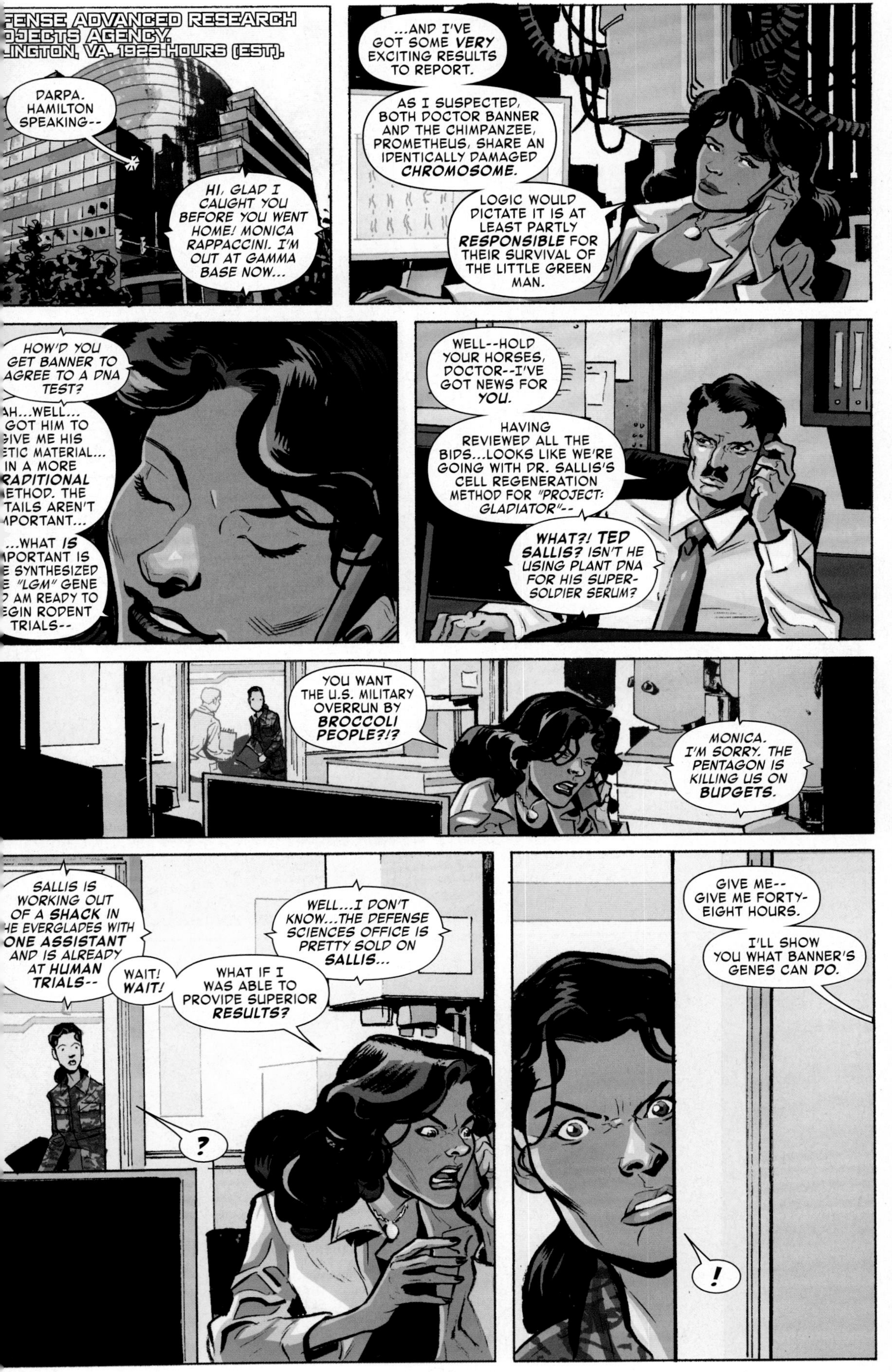

FENSE ADVANCED RESEARCH
OJECTS AGENCY.
LINGTON, VA. 1925 HOURS (EST).
DARPA. HAMILTON SPEAKING--
HI, GLAD I CAUGHT YOU BEFORE YOU WENT HOME! MONICA RAPPACCINI. I'M OUT AT GAMMA BASE NOW...
...AND I'VE GOT SOME VERY EXCITING RESULTS TO REPORT.
AS I SUSPECTED, BOTH DOCTOR BANNER AND THE CHIMPANZEE, PROMETHEUS, SHARE AN IDENTICALLY DAMAGED CHROMOSOME.
LOGIC WOULD DICTATE IT IS AT LEAST PARTLY RESPONSIBLE FOR THEIR SURVIVAL OF THE LITTLE GREEN MAN.
HOW'D YOU GET BANNER TO AGREE TO A DNA TEST?
AH...WELL... GOT HIM TO GIVE ME HIS ETIC MATERIAL... IN A MORE RADITIONAL METHOD. THE TAILS AREN'T MPORTANT...
...WHAT IS MPORTANT IS E SYNTHESIZED E "LGM" GENE D AM READY TO EGIN RODENT TRIALS--
WELL--HOLD YOUR HORSES, DOCTOR--I'VE GOT NEWS FOR YOU.
HAVING REVIEWED ALL THE BIDS...LOOKS LIKE WE'RE GOING WITH DR. SALLIS'S CELL REGENERATION METHOD FOR "PROJECT: GLADIATOR"--
WHAT?! TED SALLIS? ISN'T HE USING PLANT DNA FOR HIS SUPER-SOLDIER SERUM?
YOU WANT THE U.S. MILITARY OVERRUN BY BROCCOLI PEOPLE?!?
MONICA. I'M SORRY. THE PENTAGON IS KILLING US ON BUDGETS.
SALLIS IS WORKING OUT OF A SHACK IN HE EVERGLADES WITH ONE ASSISTANT AND IS ALREADY AT HUMAN TRIALS--
WELL...I DON'T KNOW...THE DEFENSE SCIENCES OFFICE IS PRETTY SOLD ON SALLIS...
WAIT! WAIT!
WHAT IF I WAS ABLE TO PROVIDE SUPERIOR RESULTS?
?
GIVE ME-- GIVE ME FORTY-EIGHT HOURS.
I'LL SHOW YOU WHAT BANNER'S GENES CAN DO.
!

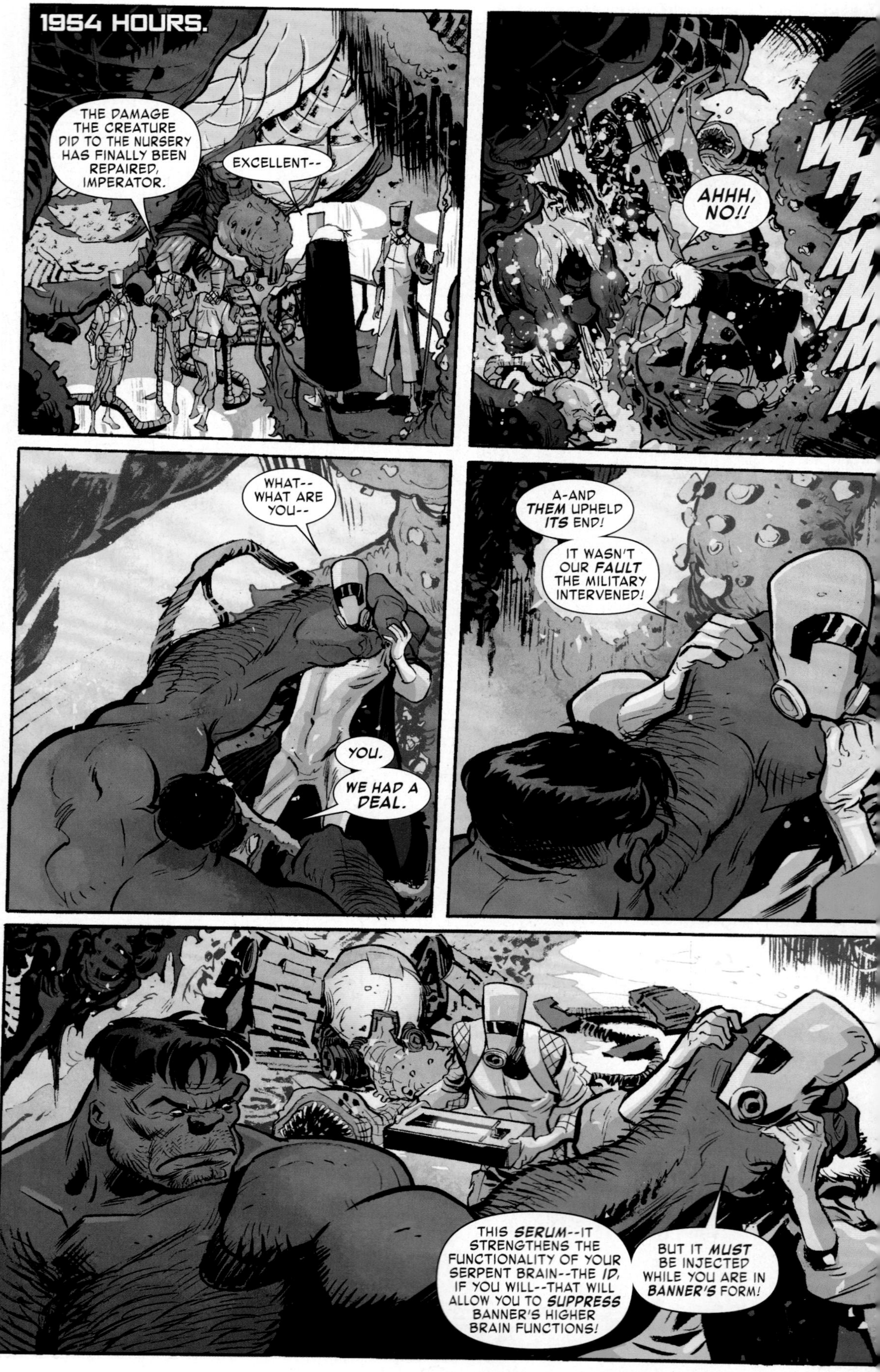
1954 HOURS.
THE DAMAGE THE CREATURE DID TO THE NURSERY HAS FINALLY BEEN REPAIRED, IMPERATOR.
EXCELLENT--
AHHH, NO!!
WHAT-- WHAT ARE YOU--
YOU.
WE HAD A DEAL.
A-AND THEM UPHELD ITS END!
IT WASN'T OUR FAULT THE MILITARY INTERVENED!
THIS SERUM--IT STRENGTHENS THE FUNCTIONALITY OF YOUR SERPENT BRAIN--THE ID, IF YOU WILL--THAT WILL ALLOW YOU TO SUPPRESS BANNER'S HIGHER BRAIN FUNCTIONS!
BUT IT MUST BE INJECTED WHILE YOU ARE IN BANNER'S FORM!

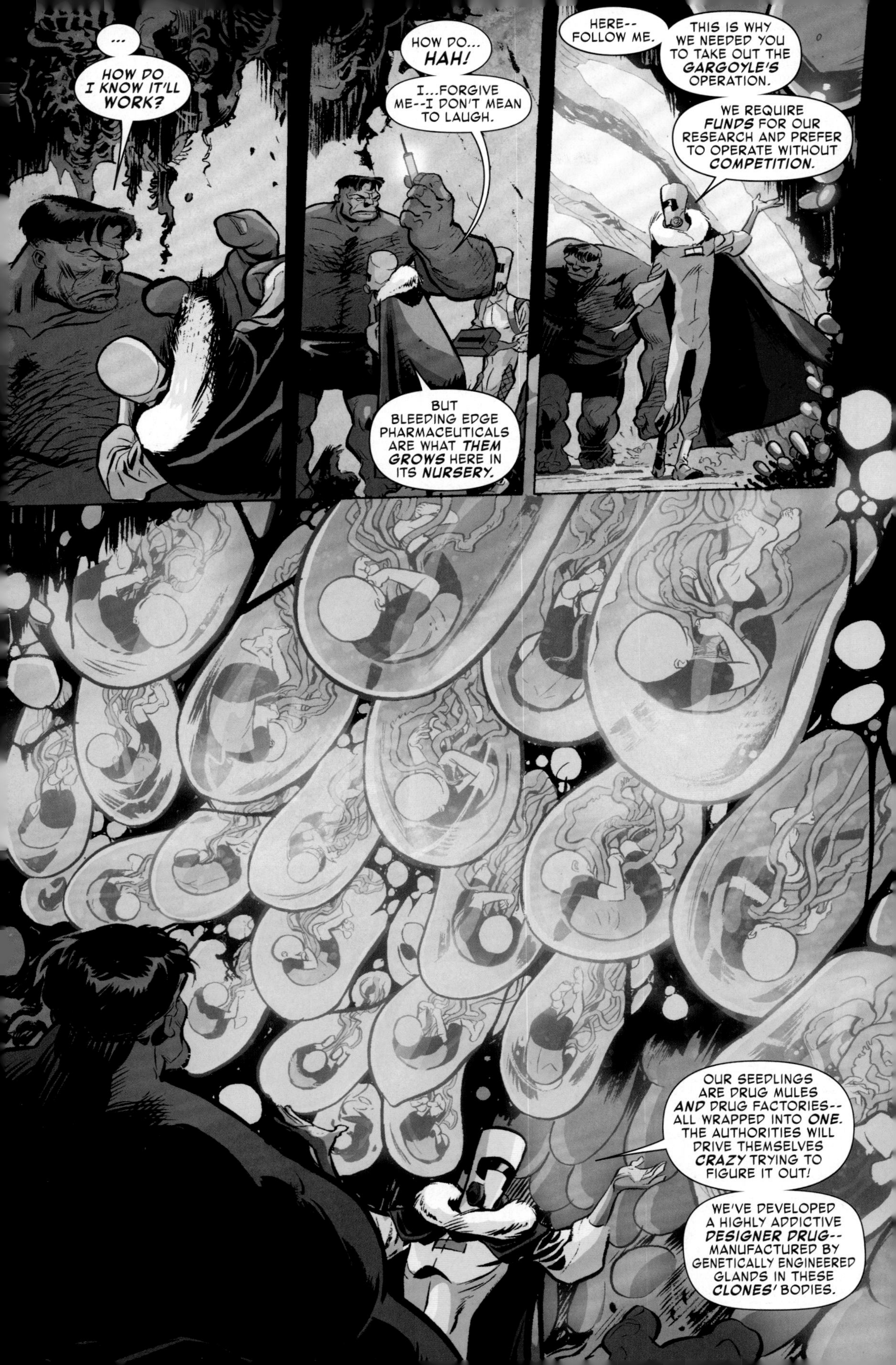
...
HOW DO I KNOW IT'LL WORK?
HOW DO... HAH!
I...FORGIVE ME--I DON'T MEAN TO LAUGH.
BUT BLEEDING EDGE PHARMACEUTICALS ARE WHAT THEM GROWS HERE IN ITS NURSERY.
HERE-- FOLLOW ME.
THIS IS WHY WE NEEDED YOU TO TAKE OUT THE GARGOYLE'S OPERATION.
WE REQUIRE FUNDS FOR OUR RESEARCH AND PREFER TO OPERATE WITHOUT COMPETITION.
OUR SEEDLINGS ARE DRUG MULES AND DRUG FACTORIES-- ALL WRAPPED INTO ONE. THE AUTHORITIES WILL DRIVE THEMSELVES CRAZY TRYING TO FIGURE IT OUT!
WE'VE DEVELOPED A HIGHLY ADDICTIVE DESIGNER DRUG-- MANUFACTURED BY GENETICALLY ENGINEERED GLANDS IN THESE CLONES' BODIES.

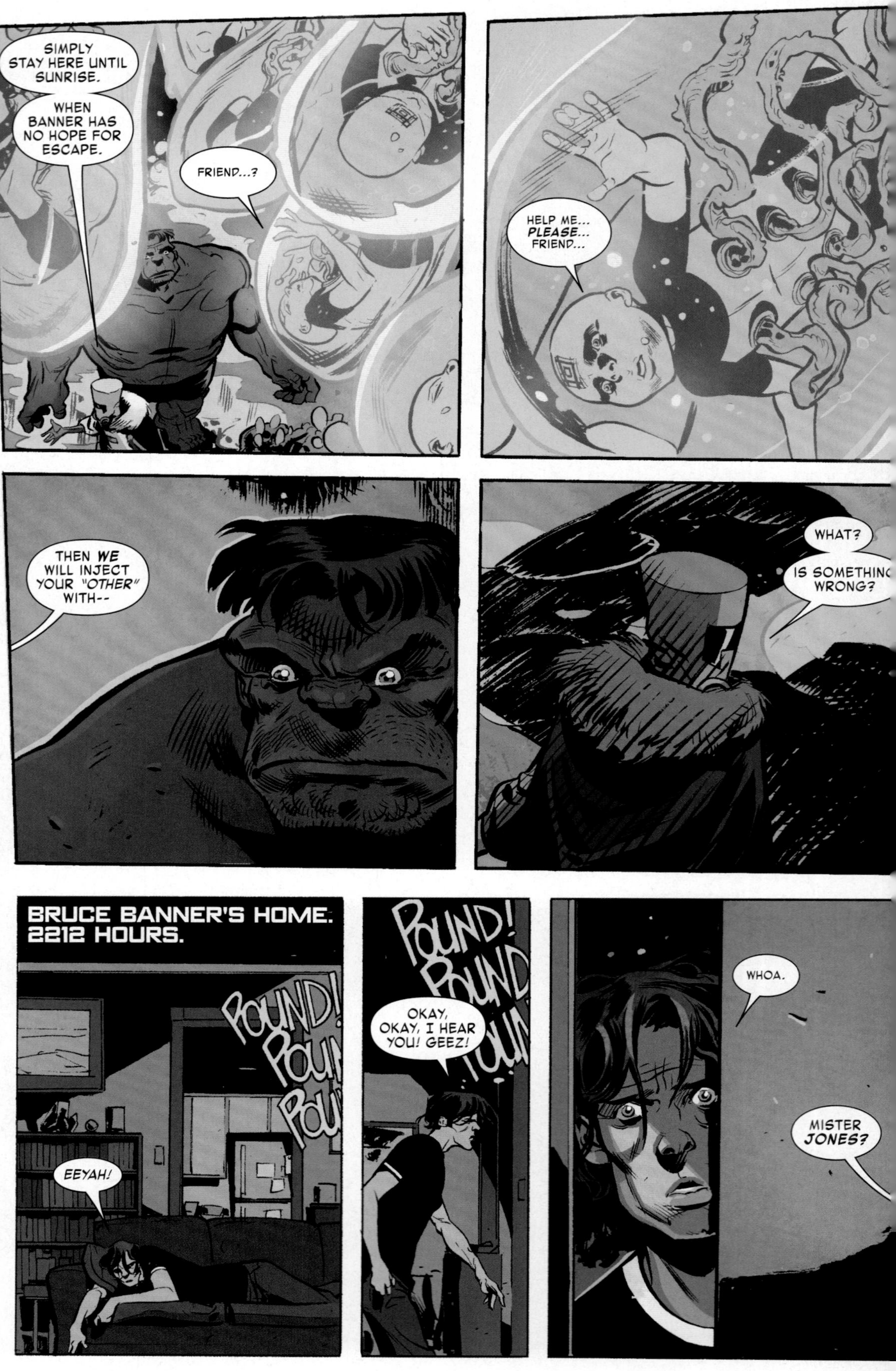
SIMPLY STAY HERE UNTIL SUNRISE.
WHEN BANNER HAS NO HOPE FOR ESCAPE.
FRIEND...?
HELP ME... PLEASE... FRIEND...
THEN WE WILL INJECT YOUR "OTHER" WITH--
WHAT?
IS SOMETHING WRONG?
BRUCE BANNER'S HOME. 2212 HOURS.
POUND! POUND! POUND!
EEYAH!
POUND! POUND! POUND!
OKAY, OKAY, I HEAR YOU! GEEZ!
WHOA.
MISTER JONES?

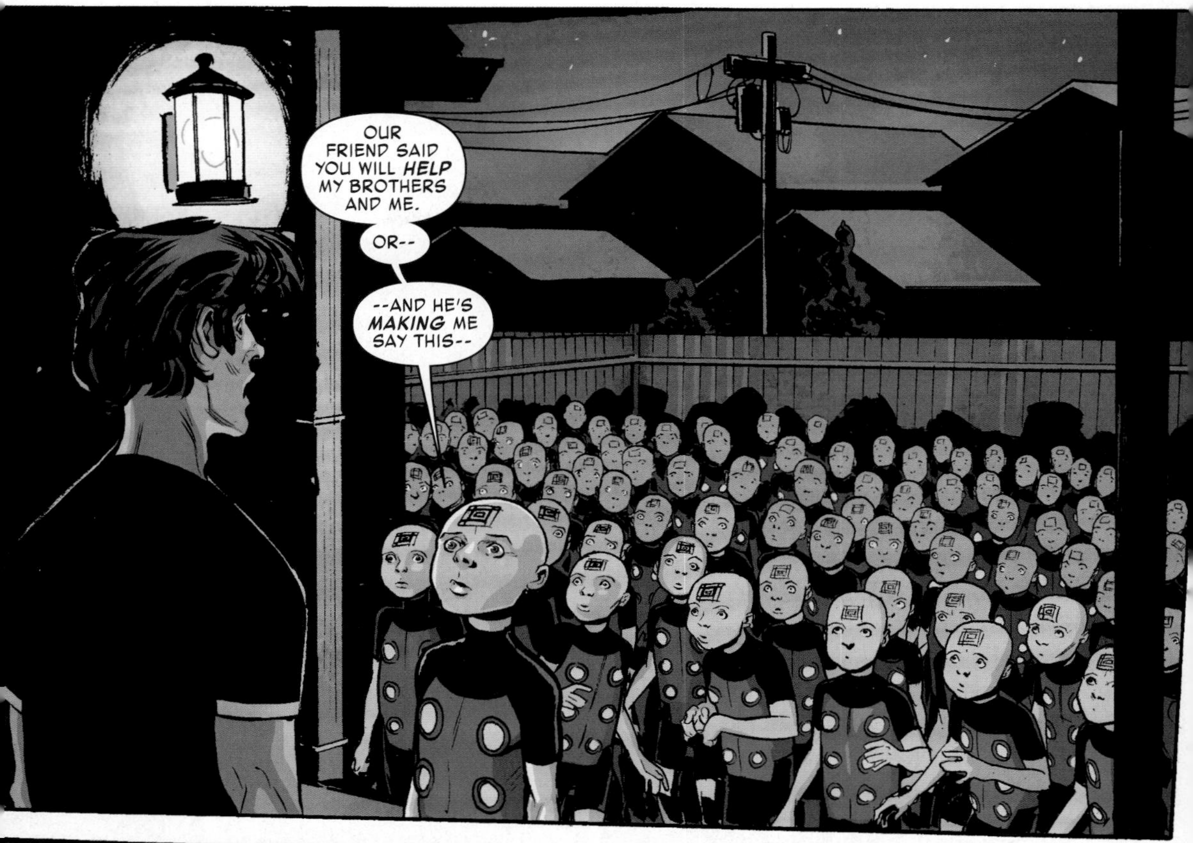
OUR FRIEND SAID YOU WILL HELP MY BROTHERS AND ME.
OR--
--AND HE'S MAKING ME SAY THIS--

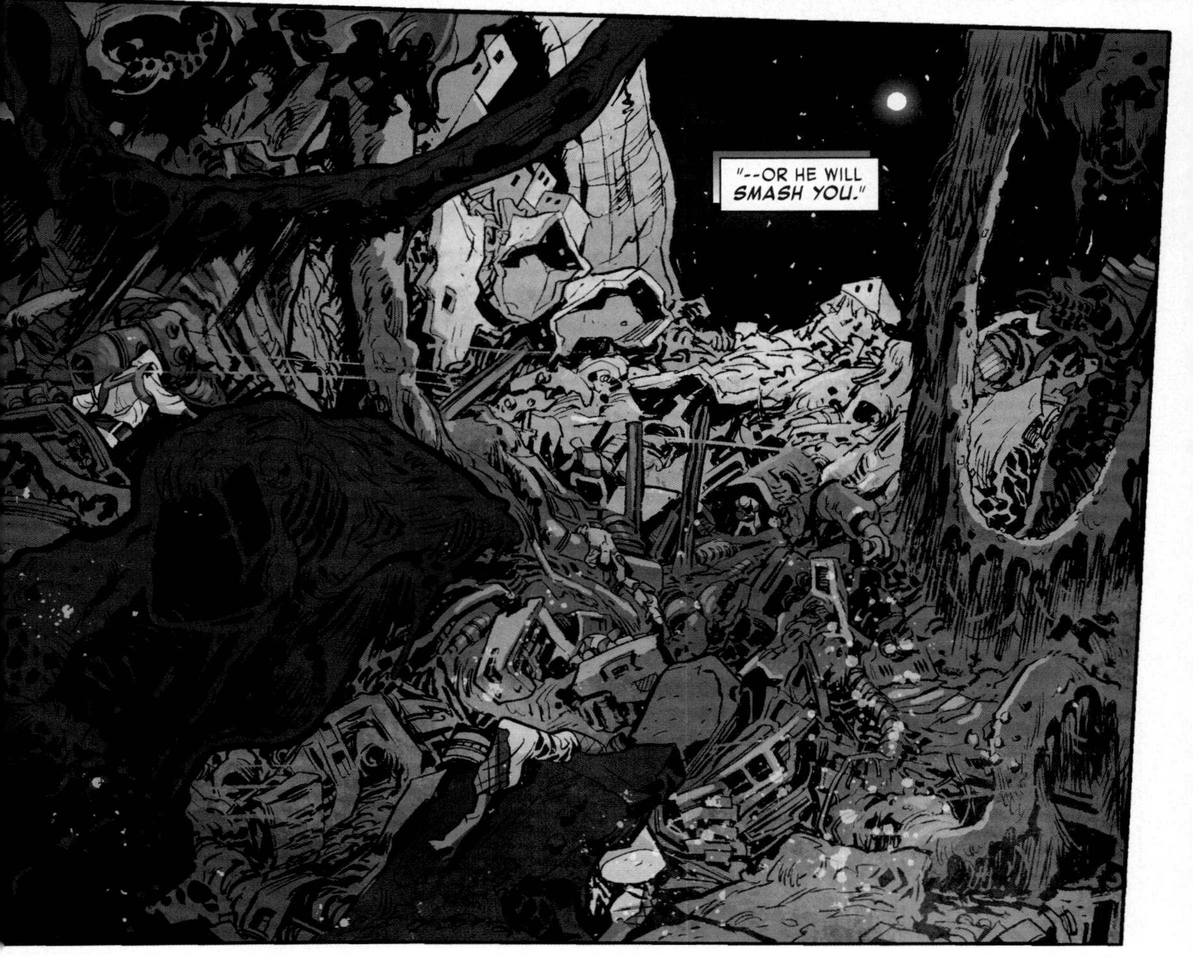
"--OR HE WILL SMASH YOU."

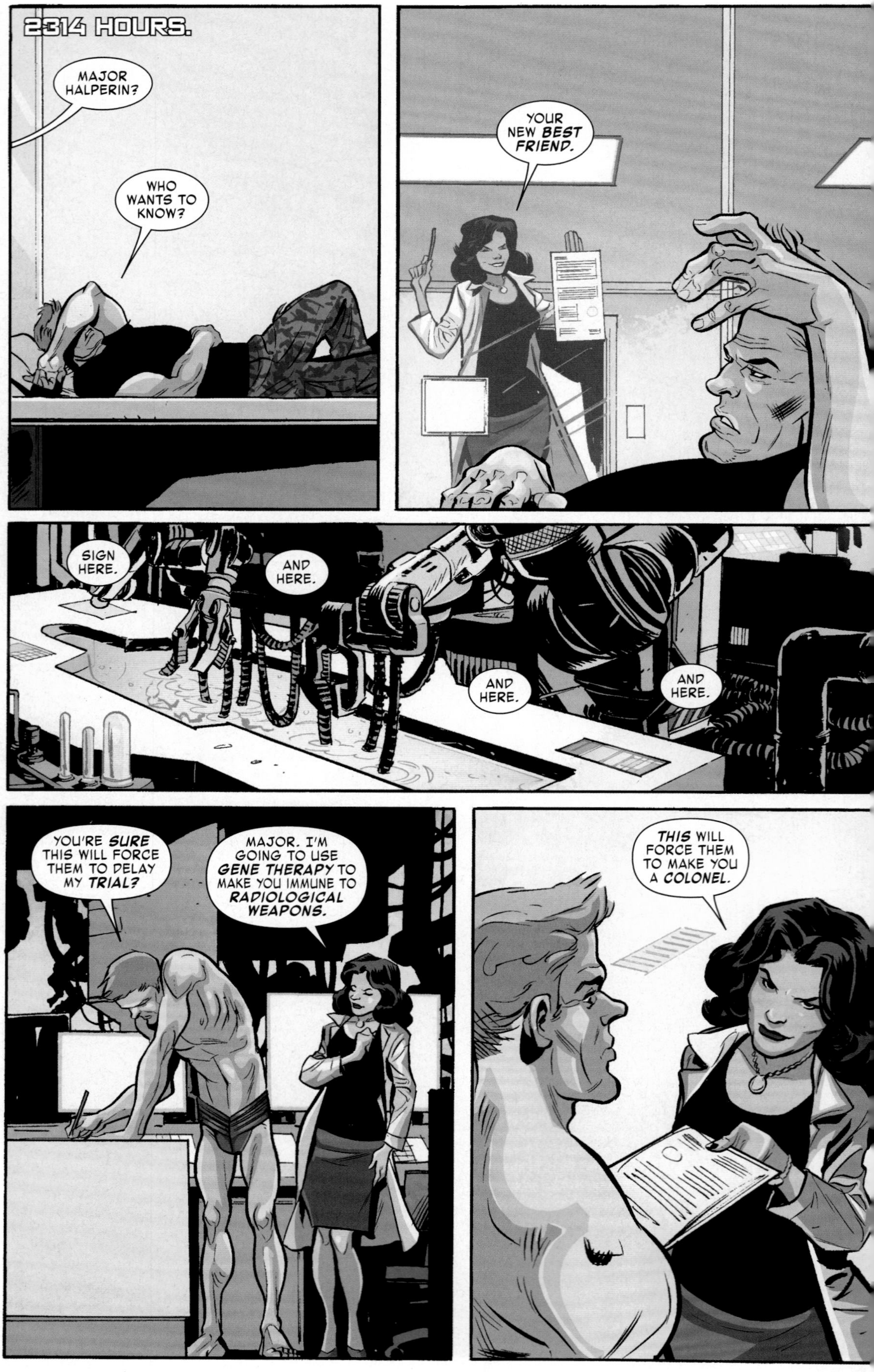
2314 HOURS.
MAJOR HALPERIN?
WHO WANTS TO KNOW?
YOUR NEW BEST FRIEND.
SIGN HERE.
AND HERE.
AND HERE.
AND HERE.
YOU'RE SURE THIS WILL FORCE THEM TO DELAY MY TRIAL?
MAJOR. I'M GOING TO USE GENE THERAPY TO MAKE YOU IMMUNE TO RADIOLOGICAL WEAPONS.
THIS WILL FORCE THEM TO MAKE YOU A COLONEL.

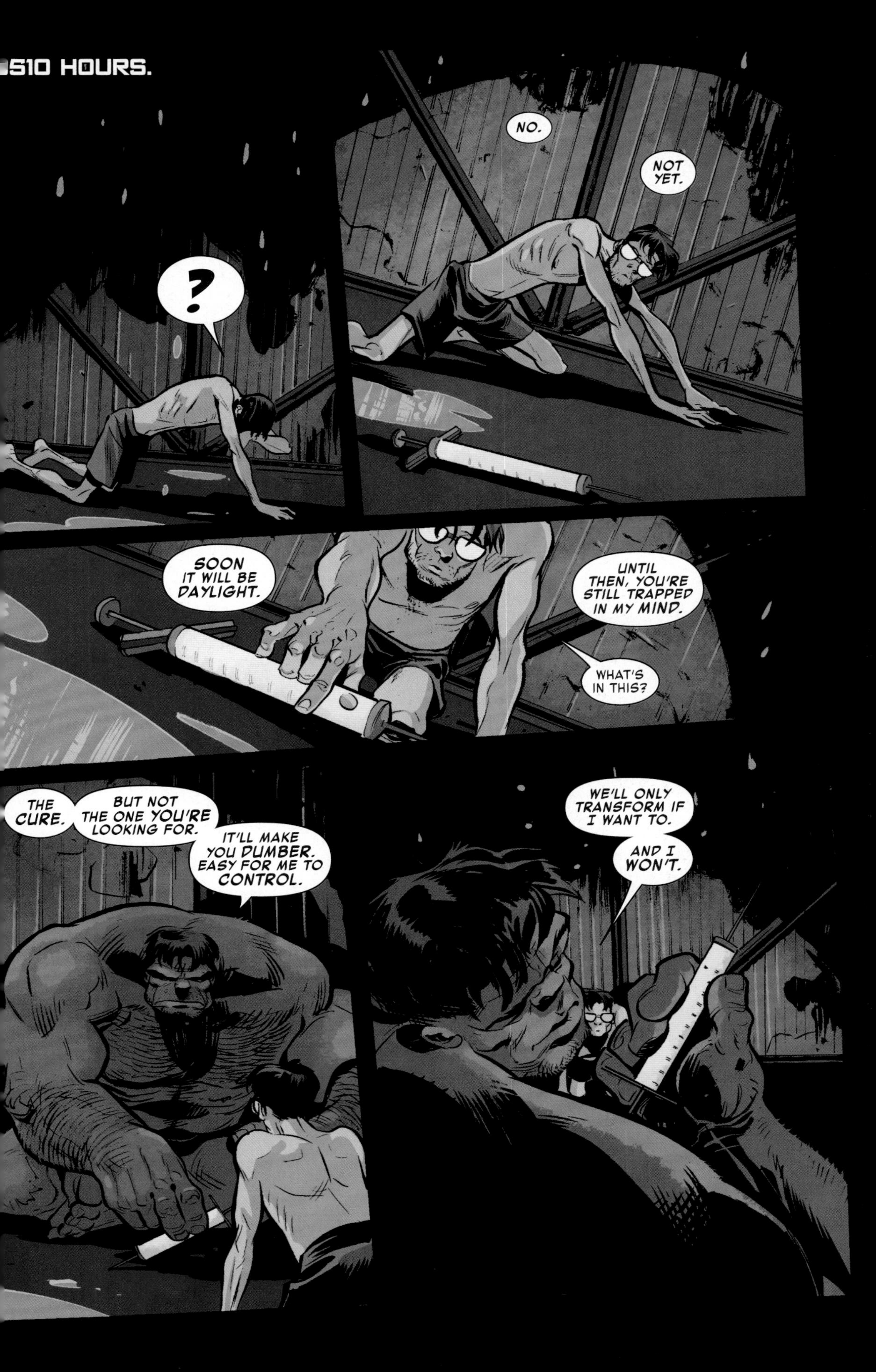

510 HOURS.
?
NO.
NOT YET.
SOON IT WILL BE DAYLIGHT.
UNTIL THEN, YOU'RE STILL TRAPPED IN MY MIND.
WHAT'S IN THIS?
THE CURE.
BUT NOT THE ONE YOU'RE LOOKING FOR.
IT'LL MAKE YOU DUMBER. EASY FOR ME TO CONTROL.
WE'LL ONLY TRANSFORM IF I WANT TO.
AND I WON'T.

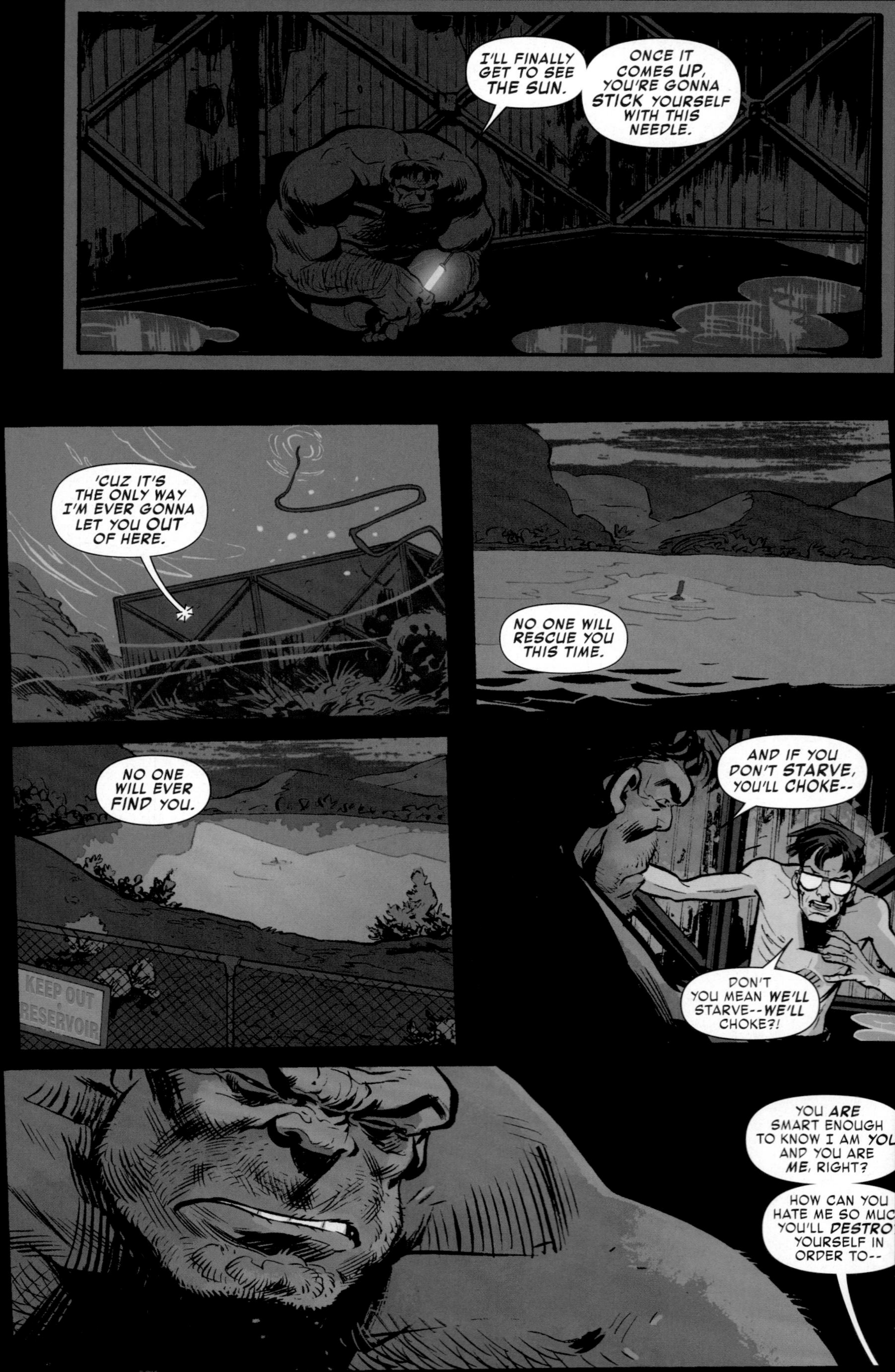
I'LL FINALLY GET TO SEE THE SUN.
ONCE IT COMES UP, YOU'RE GONNA STICK YOURSELF WITH THIS NEEDLE.
'CUZ IT'S THE ONLY WAY I'M EVER GONNA LET YOU OUT OF HERE.
NO ONE WILL RESCUE YOU THIS TIME.
NO ONE WILL EVER FIND YOU.
KEEP OUT
RESERVOIR
AND IF YOU DON'T STARVE, YOU'LL CHOKE--
DON'T YOU MEAN WE'LL STARVE--WE'LL CHOKE?!
YOU ARE SMART ENOUGH TO KNOW I AM YOU AND YOU ARE ME, RIGHT?
HOW CAN YOU HATE ME SO MUC YOU'LL DESTRO YOURSELF IN ORDER TO--

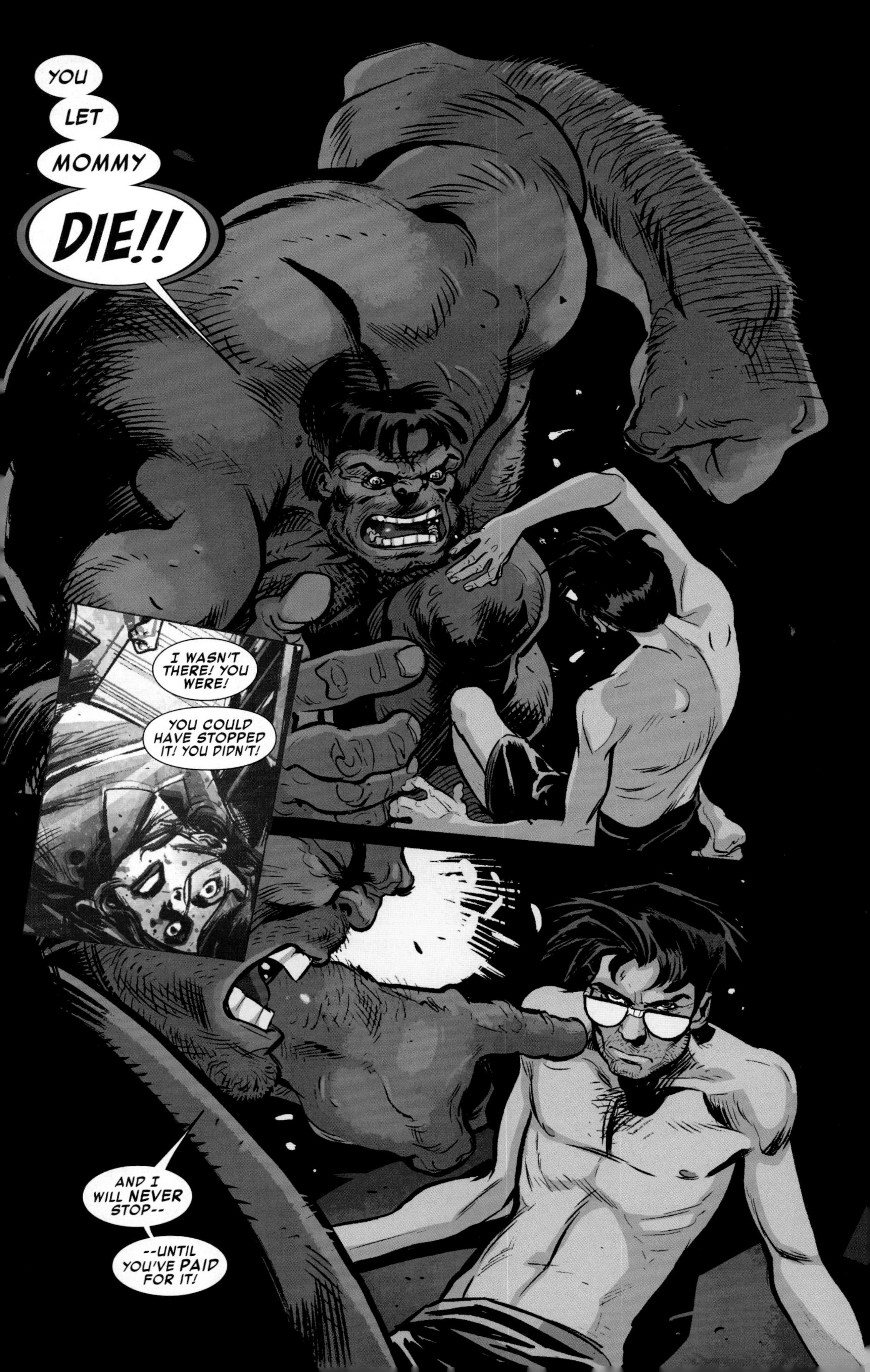
YOU
LET
MOMMY
DIE!!
I WASN'T THERE! YOU WERE!
YOU COULD HAVE STOPPED IT! YOU DIDN'T!
AND I WILL NEVER STOP--
--UNTIL YOU'VE PAID FOR IT!

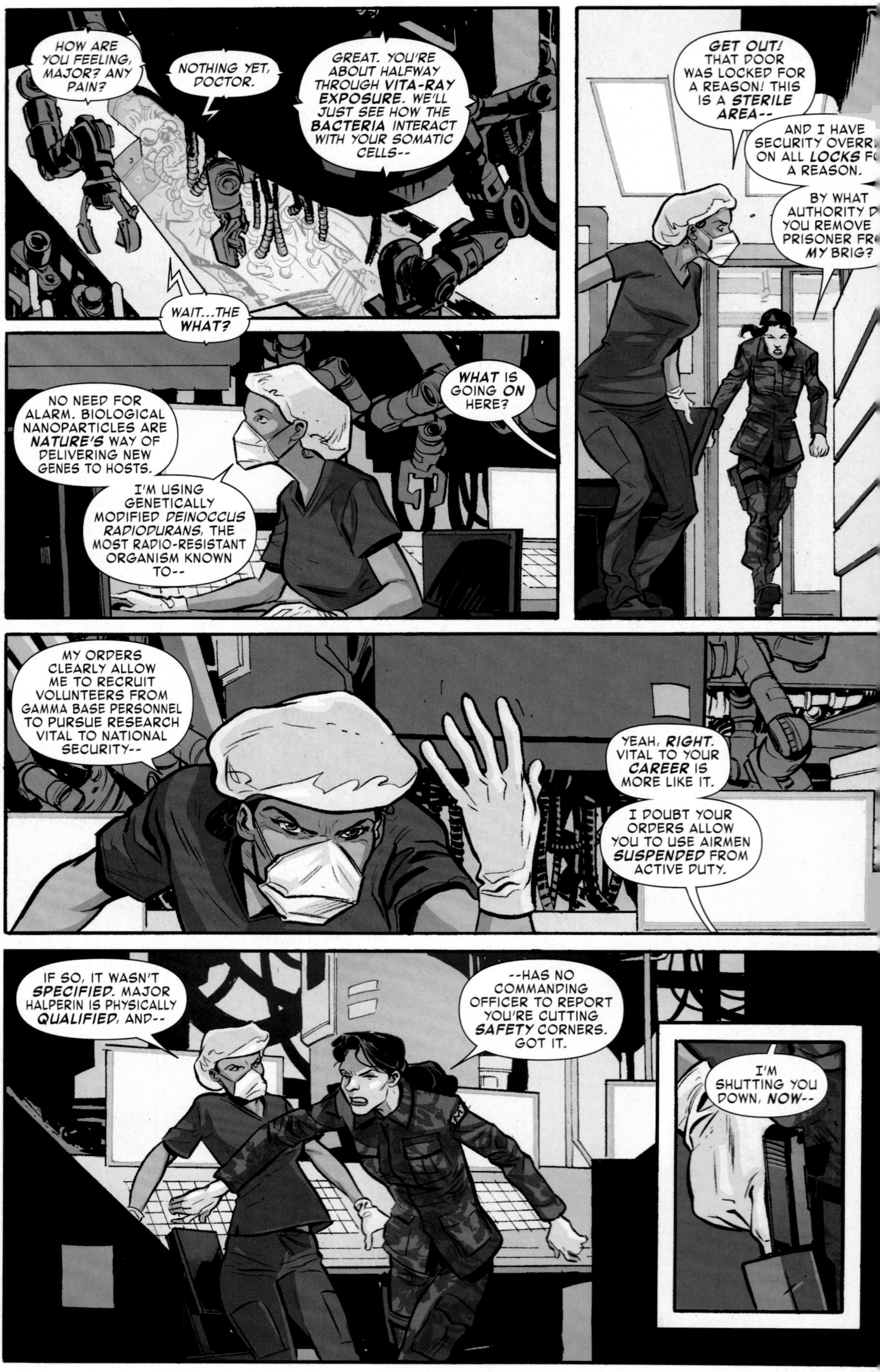
HOW ARE YOU FEELING, MAJOR? ANY PAIN?
NOTHING YET, DOCTOR.
GREAT. YOU'RE ABOUT HALFWAY THROUGH VITA-RAY EXPOSURE. WE'LL JUST SEE HOW THE BACTERIA INTERACT WITH YOUR SOMATIC CELLS--
WAIT...THE WHAT?
NO NEED FOR ALARM. BIOLOGICAL NANOPARTICLES ARE NATURE'S WAY OF DELIVERING NEW GENES TO HOSTS.
I'M USING GENETICALLY MODIFIED DEINOCCUS RADIODURANS, THE MOST RADIO-RESISTANT ORGANISM KNOWN TO--
WHAT IS GOING ON HERE?
GET OUT! THAT DOOR WAS LOCKED FOR A REASON! THIS IS A STERILE AREA--
AND I HAVE SECURITY OVERR ON ALL LOCKS F A REASON.
BY WHAT AUTHORITY D YOU REMOVE PRISONER FR MY BRIG?
MY ORDERS CLEARLY ALLOW ME TO RECRUIT VOLUNTEERS FROM GAMMA BASE PERSONNEL TO PURSUE RESEARCH VITAL TO NATIONAL SECURITY--
YEAH, RIGHT. VITAL TO YOUR CAREER IS MORE LIKE IT.
I DOUBT YOUR ORDERS ALLOW YOU TO USE AIRMEN SUSPENDED FROM ACTIVE DUTY.
IF SO, IT WASN'T SPECIFIED. MAJOR HALPERIN IS PHYSICALLY QUALIFIED, AND--
--HAS NO COMMANDING OFFICER TO REPORT YOU'RE CUTTING SAFETY CORNERS. GOT IT.
I'M SHUTTING YOU DOWN, NOW--

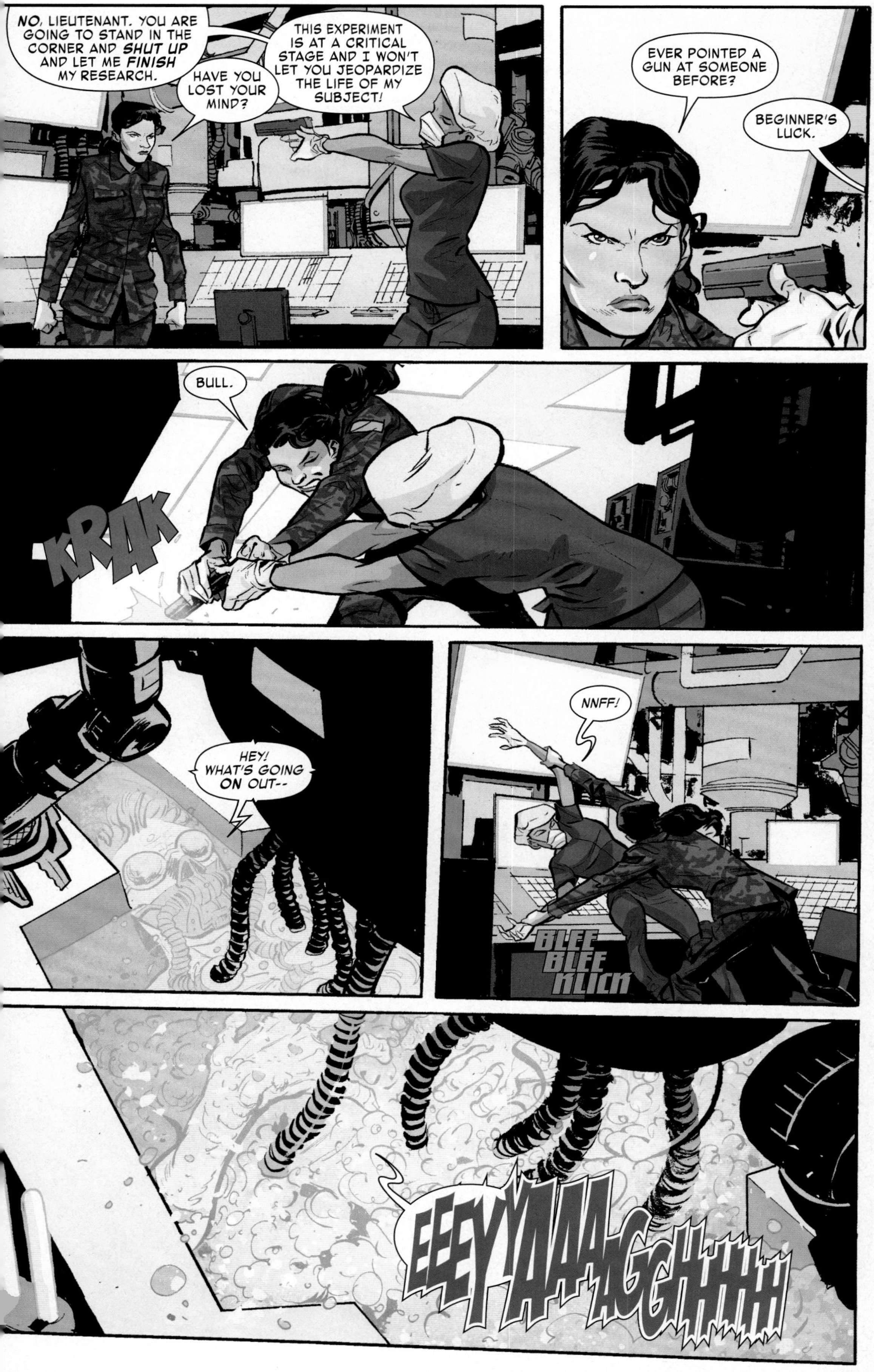
NO, LIEUTENANT. YOU ARE GOING TO STAND IN THE CORNER AND SHUT UP AND LET ME FINISH MY RESEARCH.
HAVE YOU LOST YOUR MIND?
THIS EXPERIMENT IS AT A CRITICAL STAGE AND I WON'T LET YOU JEOPARDIZE THE LIFE OF MY SUBJECT!
EVER POINTED A GUN AT SOMEONE BEFORE?
BEGINNER'S LUCK.
BULL.
KRAK
HEY! WHAT'S GOING ON OUT--
NNFF!
BLEE
BLEE
KLICK
EEEYAAAAGHHHH

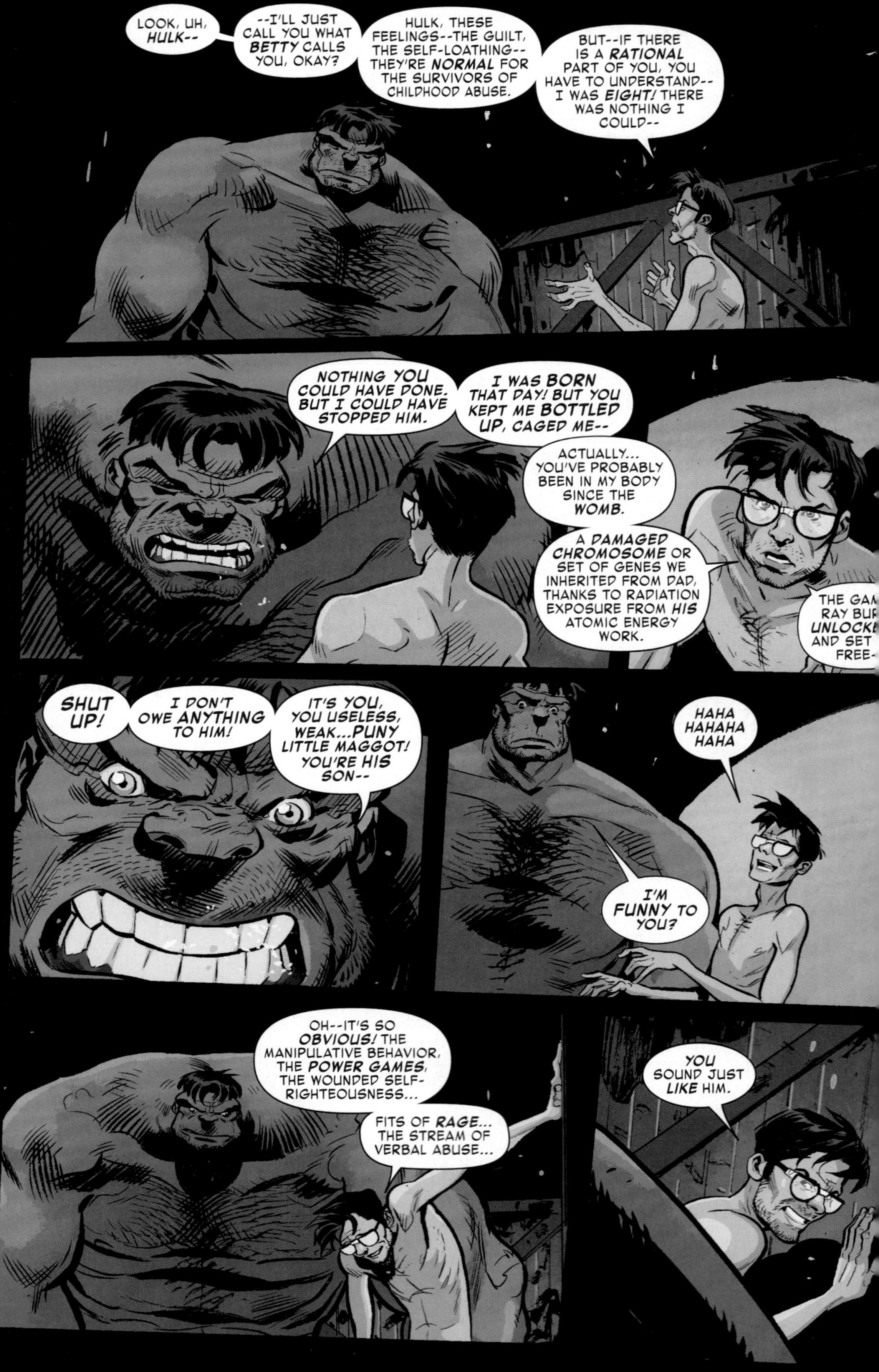

LOOK, UH, HULK--
--I'LL JUST CALL YOU WHAT BETTY CALLS YOU, OKAY?
HULK, THESE FEELINGS--THE GUILT, THE SELF-LOATHING--THEY'RE NORMAL FOR THE SURVIVORS OF CHILDHOOD ABUSE.
BUT--IF THERE IS A RATIONAL PART OF YOU, YOU HAVE TO UNDERSTAND--I WAS EIGHT! THERE WAS NOTHING I COULD--
NOTHING YOU COULD HAVE DONE. BUT I COULD HAVE STOPPED HIM.
I WAS BORN THAT DAY! BUT YOU KEPT ME BOTTLED UP, CAGED ME--
ACTUALLY... YOU'VE PROBABLY BEEN IN MY BODY SINCE THE WOMB.
A DAMAGED CHROMOSOME OR SET OF GENES WE INHERITED FROM DAD, THANKS TO RADIATION EXPOSURE FROM HIS ATOMIC ENERGY WORK.
SHUT UP!
I DON'T OWE ANYTHING TO HIM!
IT'S YOU, YOU USELESS, WEAK...PUNY LITTLE MAGGOT! YOU'RE HIS SON--
HAHA HAHAHA HAHA
I'M FUNNY TO YOU?
OH--IT'S SO OBVIOUS! THE MANIPULATIVE BEHAVIOR, THE POWER GAMES, THE WOUNDED SELF-RIGHTEOUSNESS...
FITS OF RAGE... THE STREAM OF VERBAL ABUSE...
YOU SOUND JUST LIKE HIM.

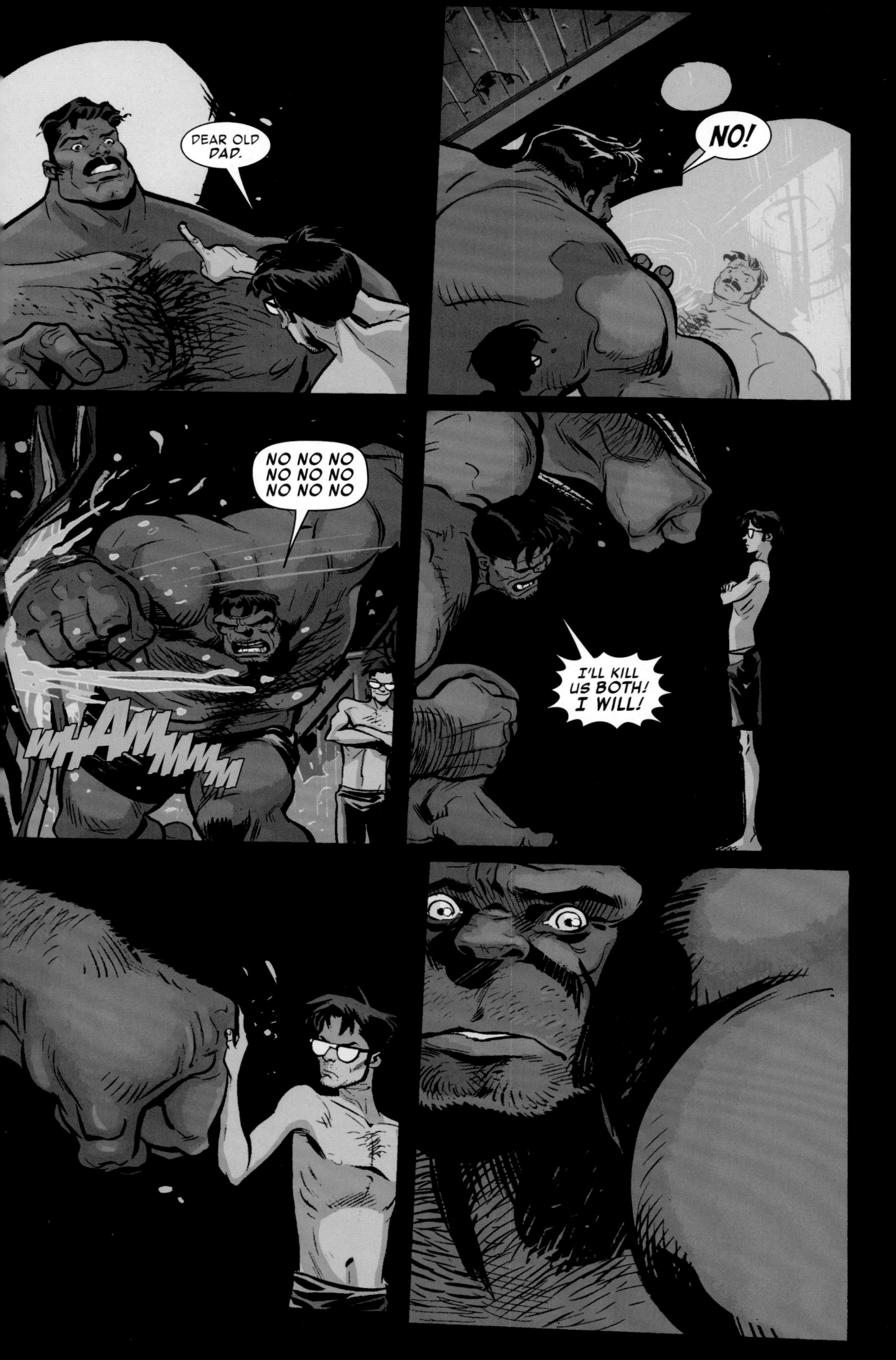
DEAR OLD DAD.
NO!
NO NO NO NO NO NO NO NO NO
WHAMMMM
I'LL KILL US BOTH! I WILL!

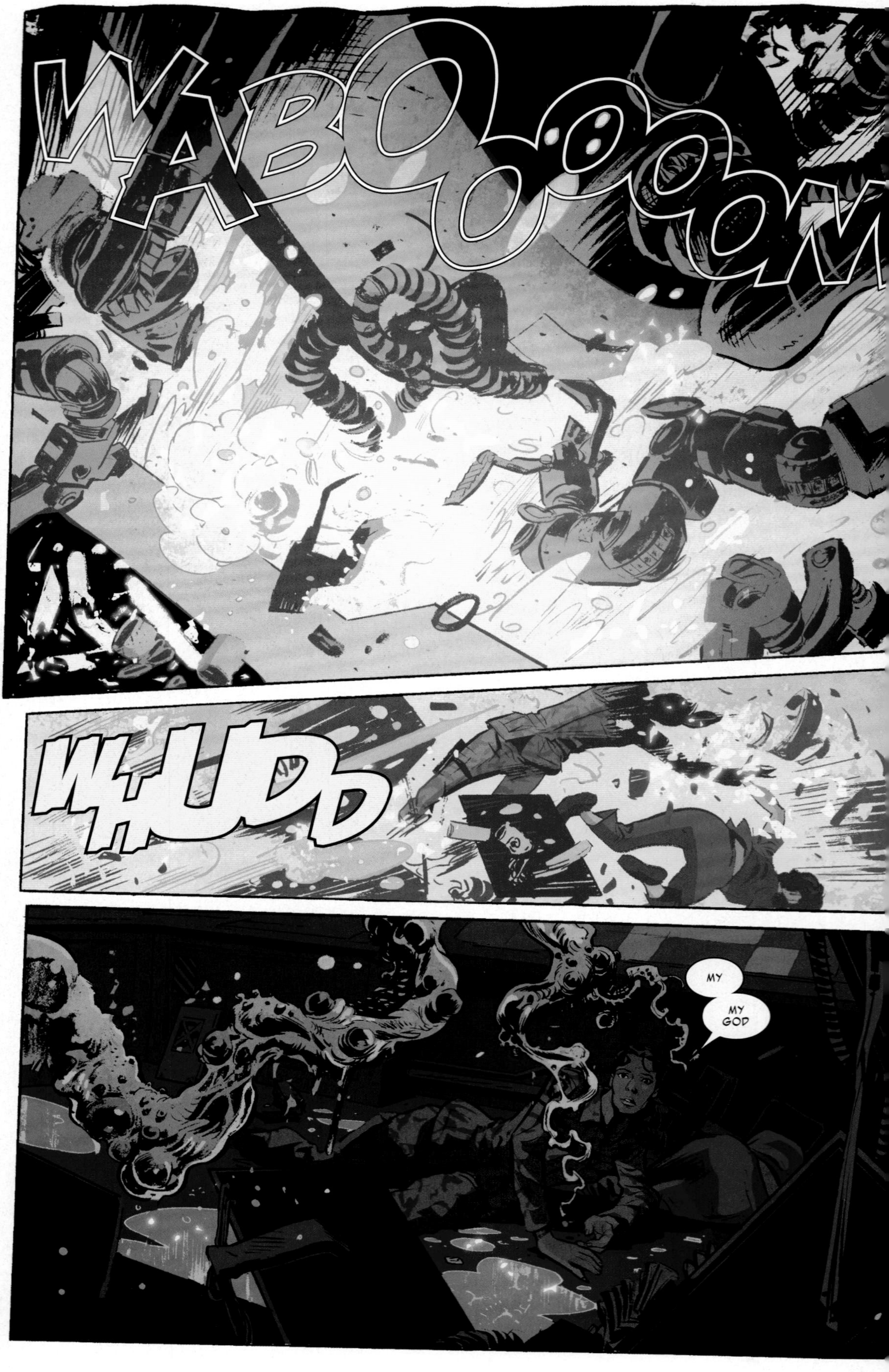
WABOOOOOOM
WHUDD
MY
MY GOD

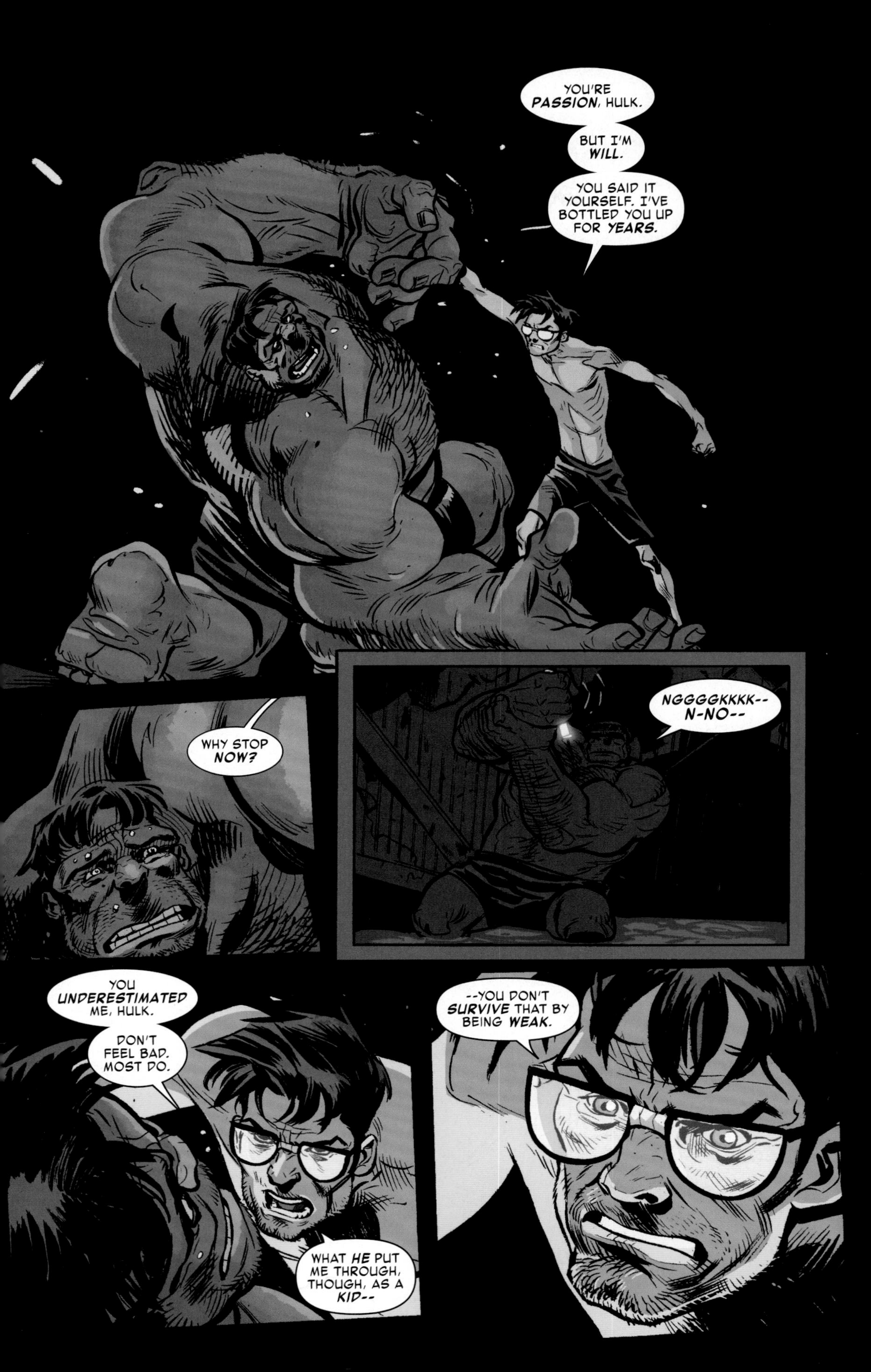
YOU'RE PASSION, HULK.
BUT I'M WILL.
YOU SAID IT YOURSELF. I'VE BOTTLED YOU UP FOR YEARS.
WHY STOP NOW?
NGGGGKKKK-- N-NO--
YOU UNDERESTIMATED ME, HULK.
DON'T FEEL BAD. MOST DO.
WHAT HE PUT ME THROUGH, THOUGH, AS A KID--
--YOU DON'T SURVIVE THAT BY BEING WEAK.

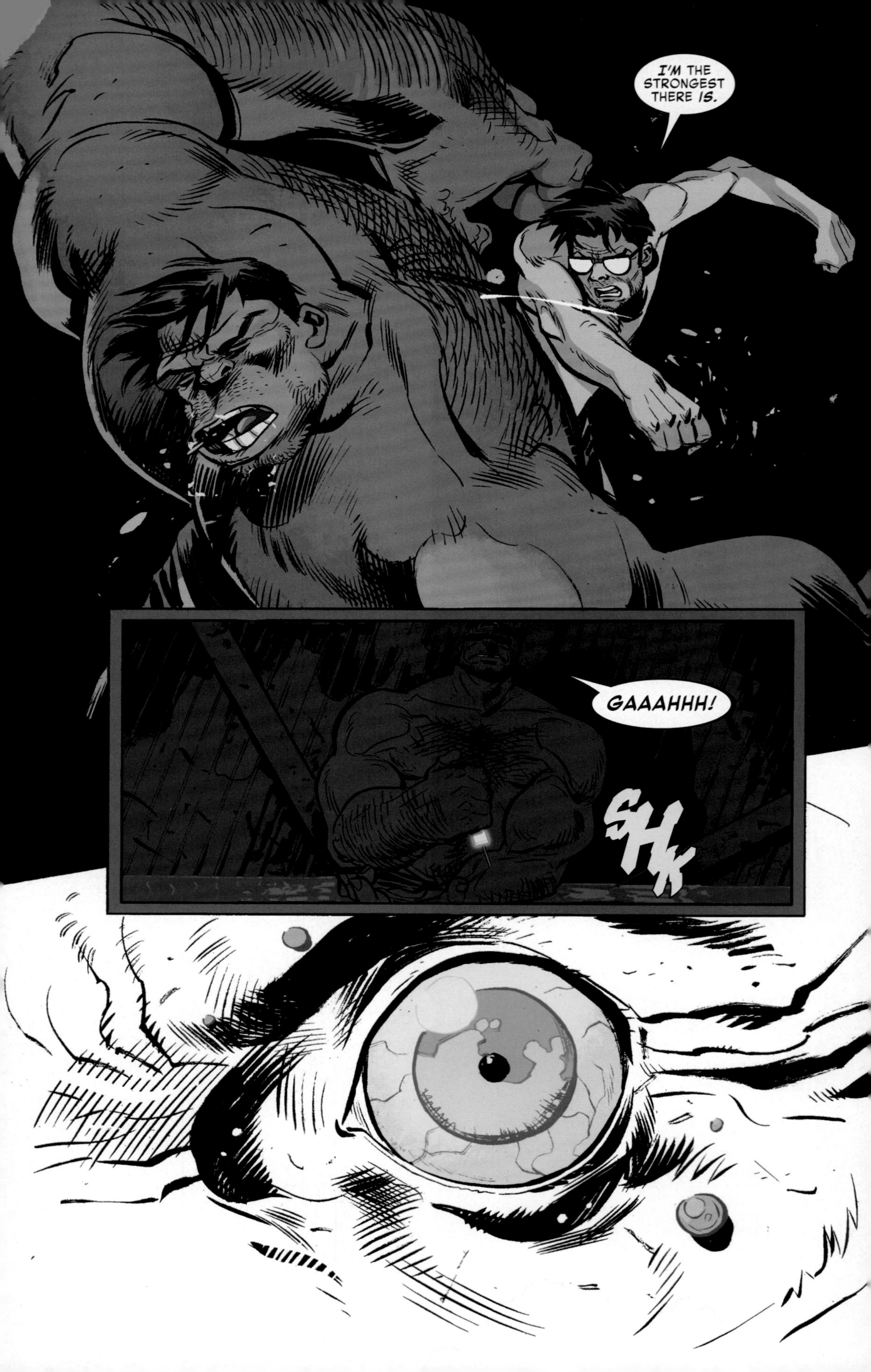
I'M THE STRONGEST THERE IS.
GAAAHHH!
SHK

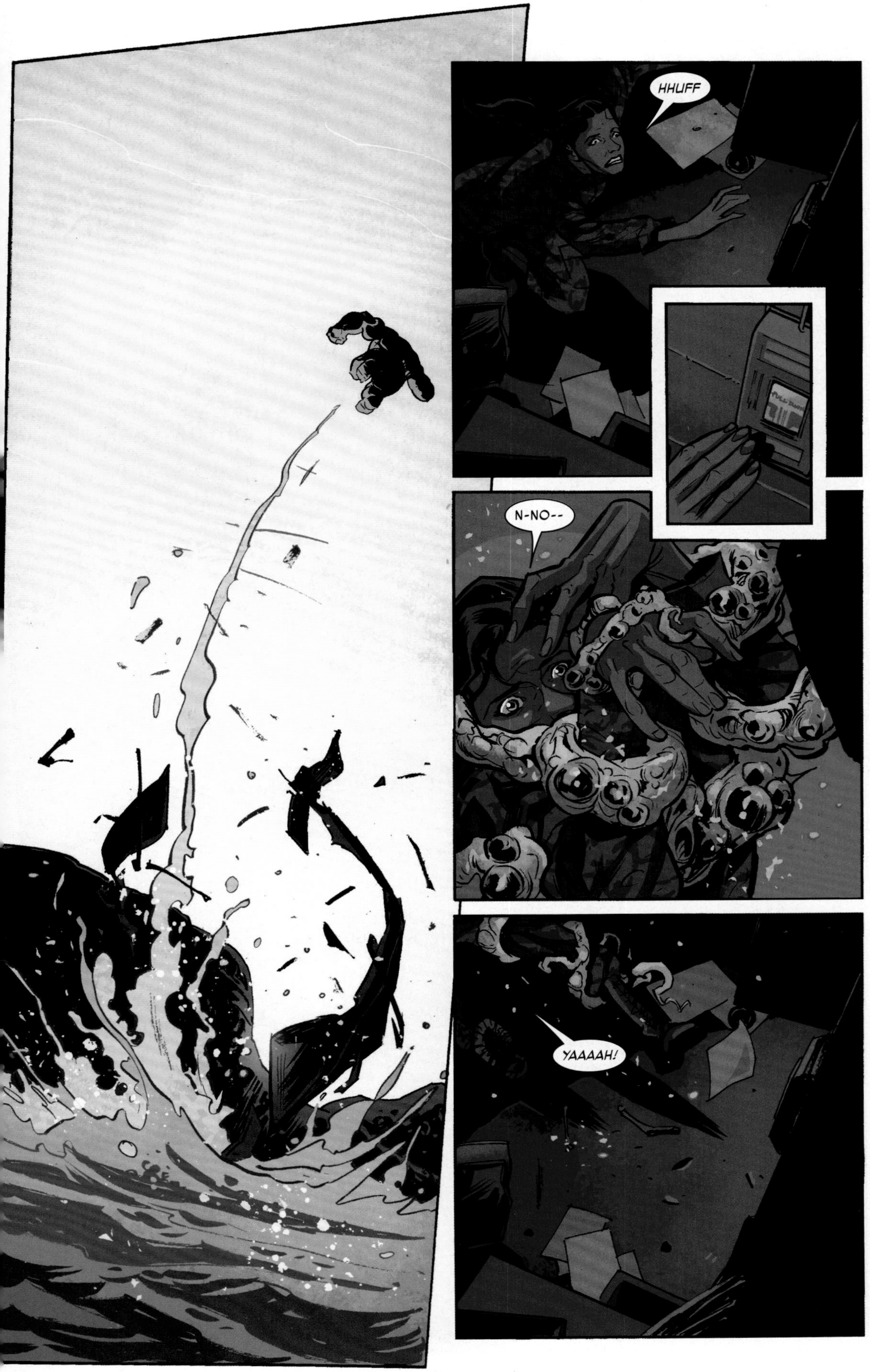
HHUFF
N-NO--
YAAAAH!

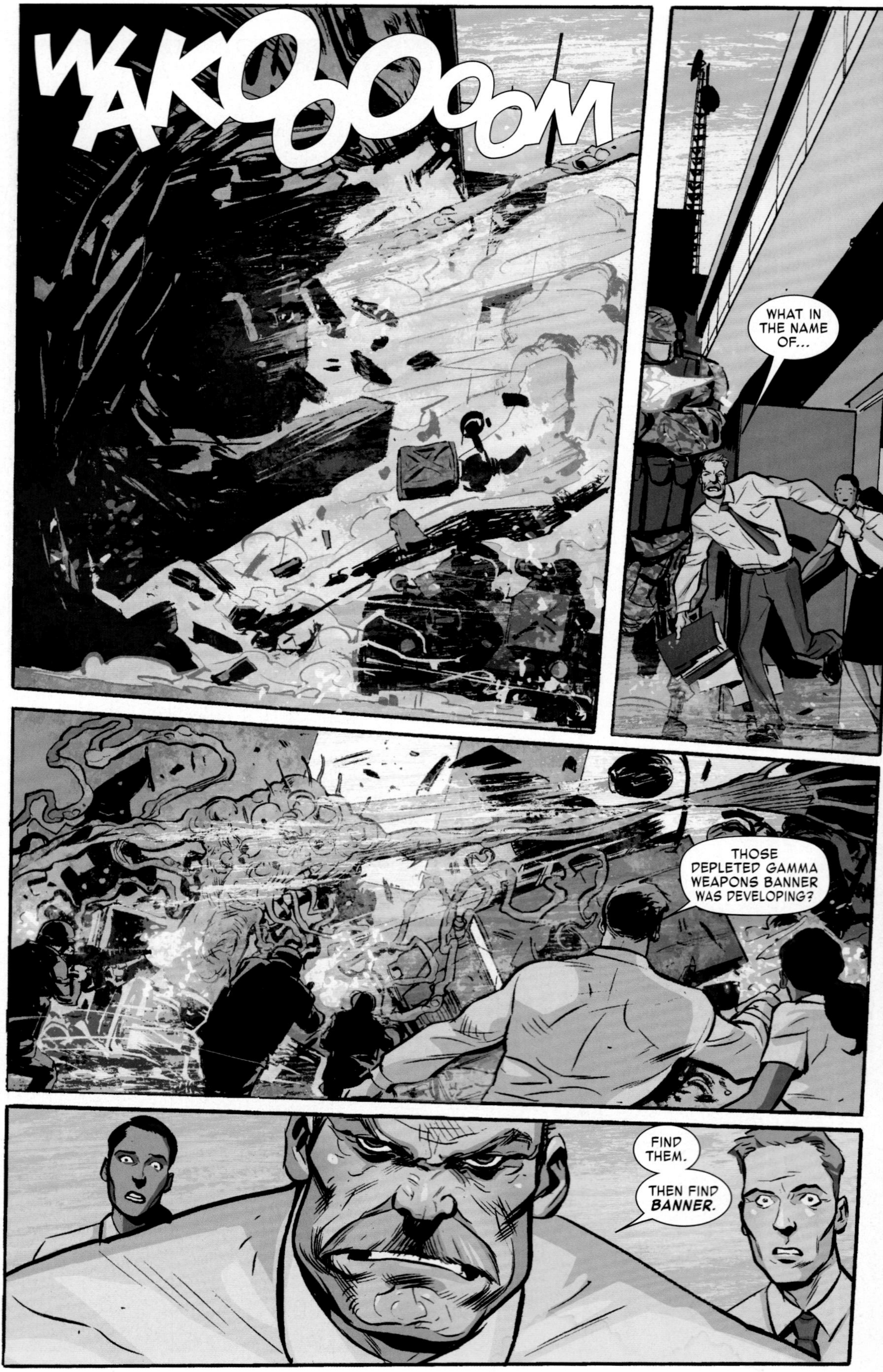
WAKOOOOOOM
WHAT IN THE NAME OF...
THOSE DEPLETED GAMMA WEAPONS BANNER WAS DEVELOPING?
FIND THEM.
THEN FIND BANNER.

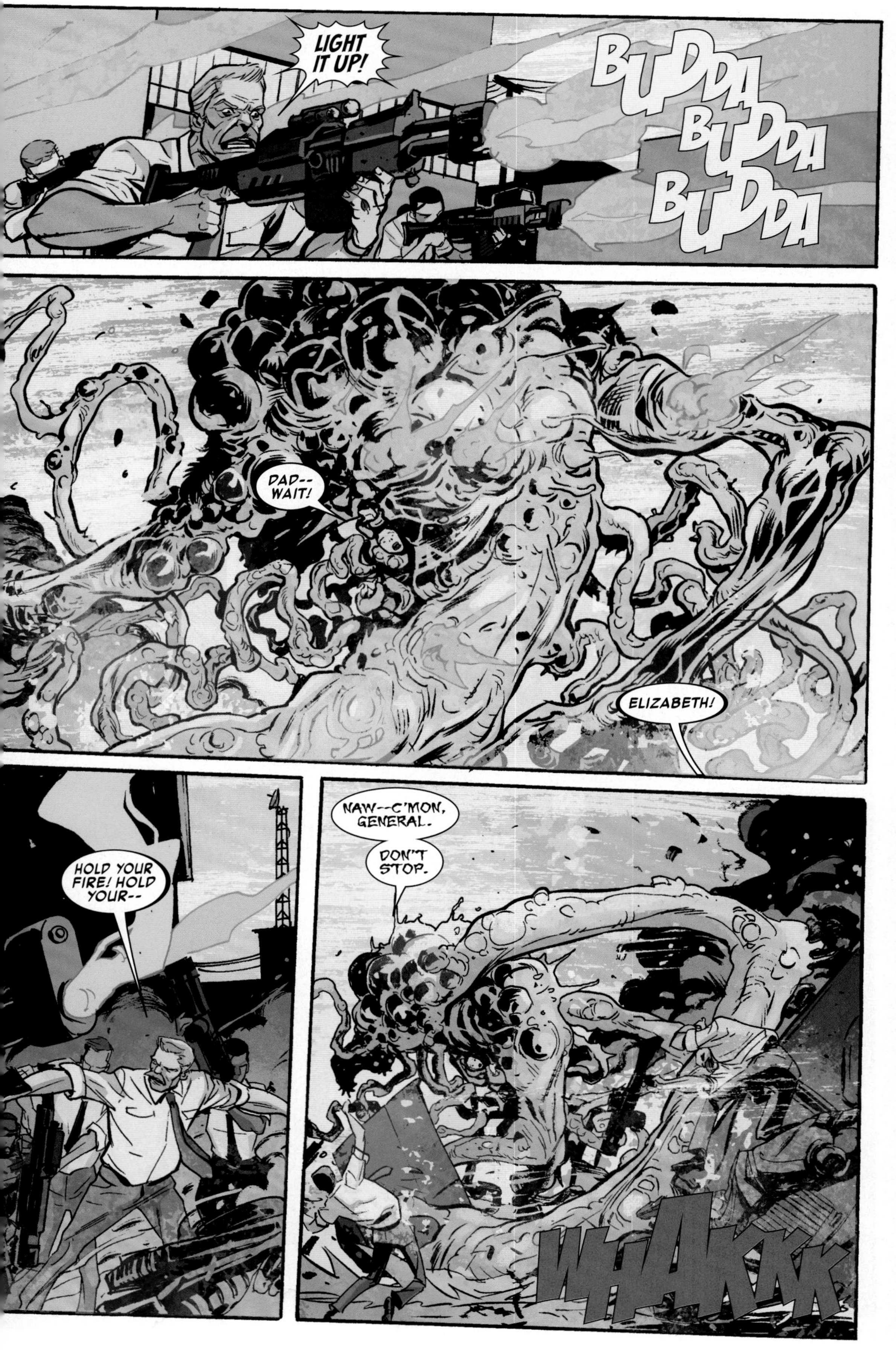
LIGHT IT UP!
BUDDA BUDDA BUDDA
DAD-- WAIT!
ELIZABETH!
HOLD YOUR FIRE! HOLD YOUR--
NAW--C'MON, GENERAL.
DON'T STOP.
WHAKKK

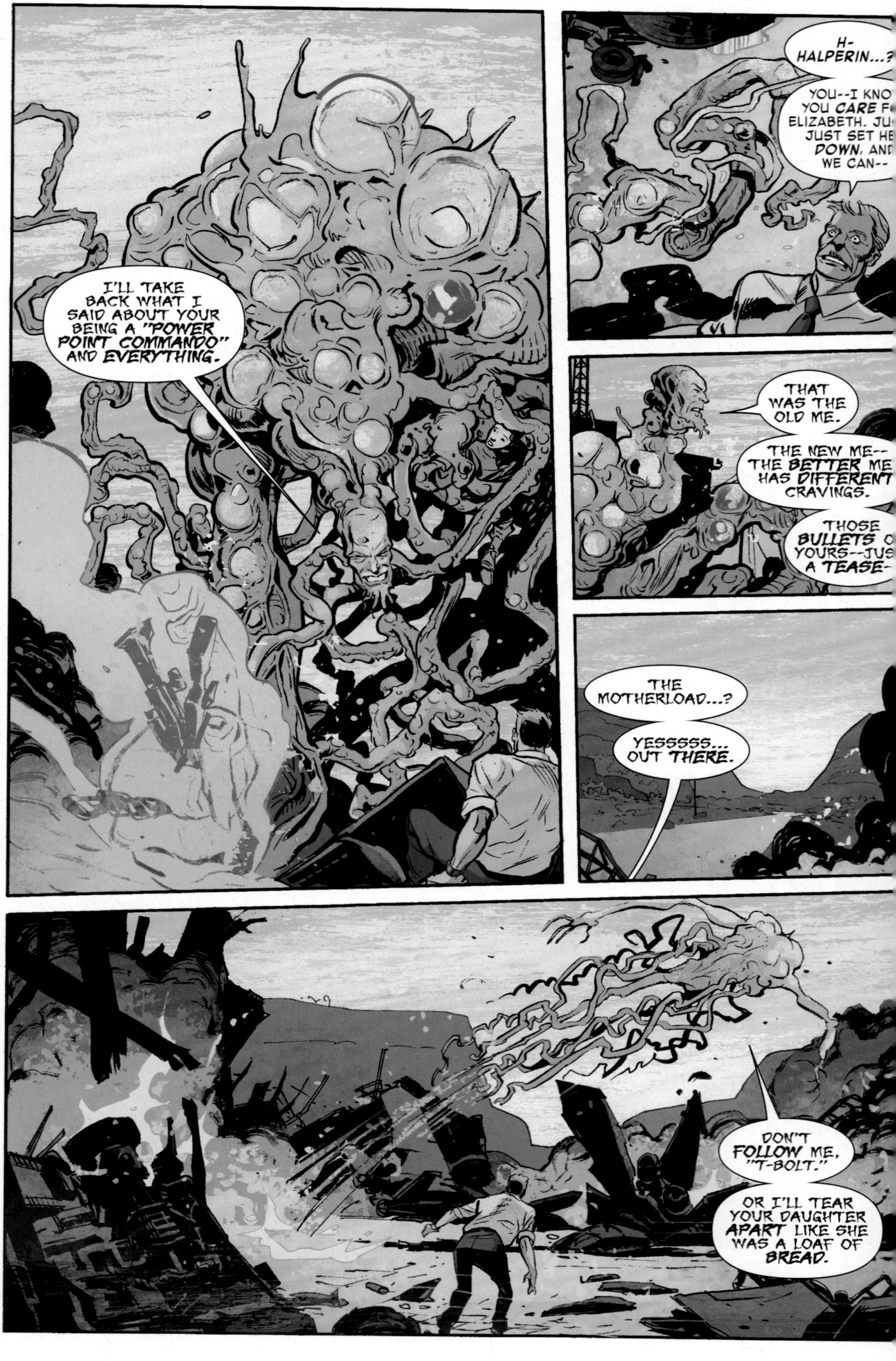

I'LL TAKE BACK WHAT I SAID ABOUT YOUR BEING A "POWER POINT COMMANDO" AND EVERYTHING.
H-HALPERIN...?
YOU--I KNO YOU CARE F ELIZABETH. JU JUST SET HE DOWN, AND WE CAN--
THAT WAS THE OLD ME.
THE NEW ME-- THE BETTER ME HAS DIFFERENT CRAVINGS.
THOSE BULLETS O YOURS--JUS A TEASE-
THE MOTHERLOAD...?
YESSSSS... OUT THERE.
DON'T FOLLOW ME, "T-BOLT."
OR I'LL TEAR YOUR DAUGHTER APART LIKE SHE WAS A LOAF OF BREAD.

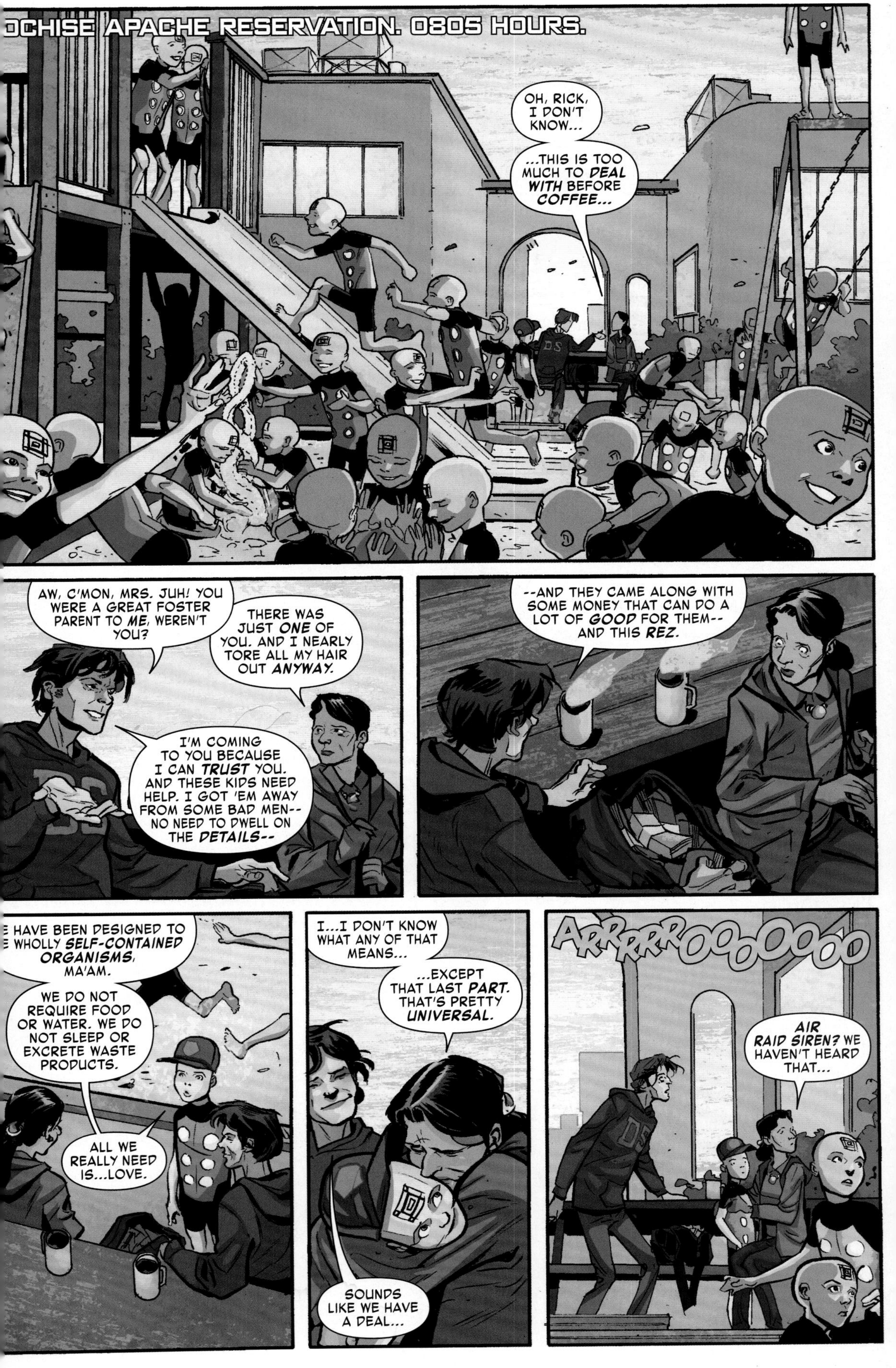
OCHISE APACHE RESERVATION. 0805 HOURS.
OH, RICK, I DON'T KNOW...
...THIS IS TOO MUCH TO DEAL WITH BEFORE COFFEE...
AW, C'MON, MRS. JUH! YOU WERE A GREAT FOSTER PARENT TO ME, WEREN'T YOU?
THERE WAS JUST ONE OF YOU. AND I NEARLY TORE ALL MY HAIR OUT ANYWAY.
I'M COMING TO YOU BECAUSE I CAN TRUST YOU. AND THESE KIDS NEED HELP. I GOT 'EM AWAY FROM SOME BAD MEN-- NO NEED TO DWELL ON THE DETAILS--
--AND THEY CAME ALONG WITH SOME MONEY THAT CAN DO A LOT OF GOOD FOR THEM-- AND THIS REZ.
E HAVE BEEN DESIGNED TO E WHOLLY SELF-CONTAINED ORGANISMS, MA'AM.
WE DO NOT REQUIRE FOOD OR WATER. WE DO NOT SLEEP OR EXCRETE WASTE PRODUCTS.
ALL WE REALLY NEED IS...LOVE.
I...I DON'T KNOW WHAT ANY OF THAT MEANS...
...EXCEPT THAT LAST PART. THAT'S PRETTY UNIVERSAL.
SOUNDS LIKE WE HAVE A DEAL...
ARRRRROOOOOOO
AIR RAID SIREN? WE HAVEN'T HEARD THAT...

"...SINCE THE *BASE* DID THEIR LAST *BOMB TEST*..."

ARRRROOOOOOOOOOOHHHH

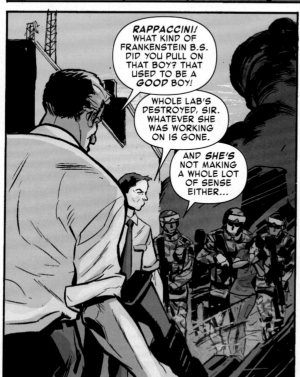

RAPPACCINI! WHAT KIND OF FRANKENSTEIN B.S. DID YOU PULL ON THAT BOY? THAT USED TO BE A *GOOD BOY!*

WHOLE LAB'S DESTROYED, SIR. WHATEVER SHE WAS WORKING ON IS GONE.

AND *SHE'S* NOT MAKING A WHOLE LOT OF SENSE EITHER...

A MORPHOGENIC NEOPLASM... OR...OR FULL-BODY *METAPLASIA*... THAT'S WHAT "HULKISM" IS...

...A LIVING, BREATHING *CANCER!* THE DRUG THERAPY *MUTATED* IT...COMBINED WITH HIS *ADDICTION*... A BAD MIX--

YOU'VE GOT TO *FIND* IT! YOU'VE GOT TO *FIND* IT AND *KILL* IT BEFORE IT INFECTS THE *REST* OF US!

EVACUATE GAMMA BASE--AND THE SURROUNDING TOWNS--GIMME A HUNDRED-CLICK PERIMETER!

B-BUT GENERAL--YOUR DAUGHTER--

DON'T TELL ME WHAT I ALREADY KNOW, AIRMAN!

GIVE THE ORDER! NOW!

CAN'T YOU SEE WHERE HALPERIN'S GONE?

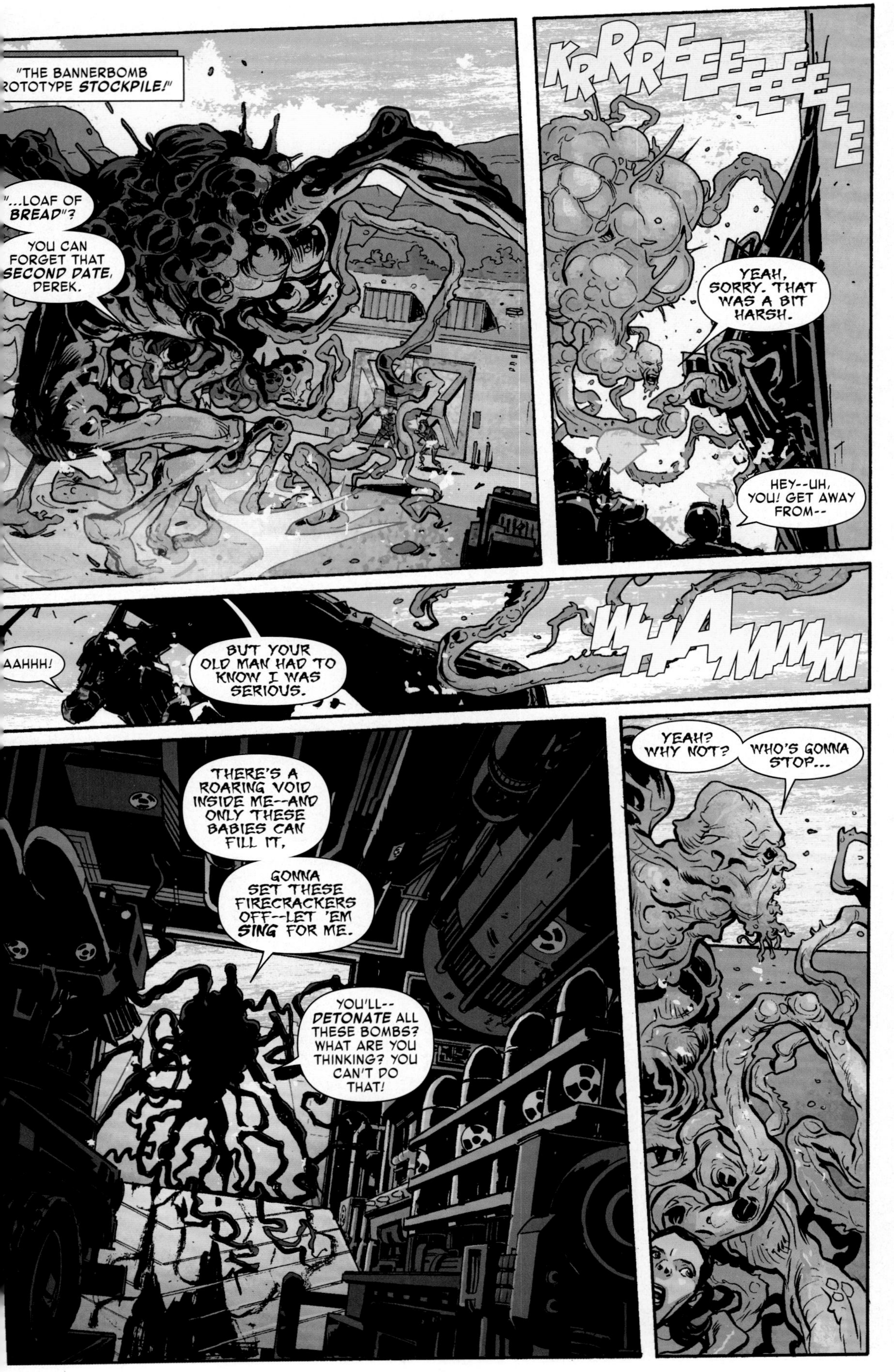
"THE BANNERBOMB
ROTOTYPE STOCKPILE!"
"...LOAF OF BREAD"?
YOU CAN FORGET THAT SECOND DATE, DEREK.
KRRREEEEEEEEEEE
YEAH, SORRY. THAT WAS A BIT HARSH.
HEY--UH, YOU! GET AWAY FROM--
AAHHH!
BUT YOUR OLD MAN HAD TO KNOW I WAS SERIOUS.
WHAMMMM
THERE'S A ROARING VOID INSIDE ME--AND ONLY THESE BABIES CAN FILL IT.
GONNA SET THESE FIRECRACKERS OFF--LET 'EM SING FOR ME.
YOU'LL--DETONATE ALL THESE BOMBS? WHAT ARE YOU THINKING? YOU CAN'T DO THAT!
YEAH? WHY NOT?
WHO'S GONNA STOP...

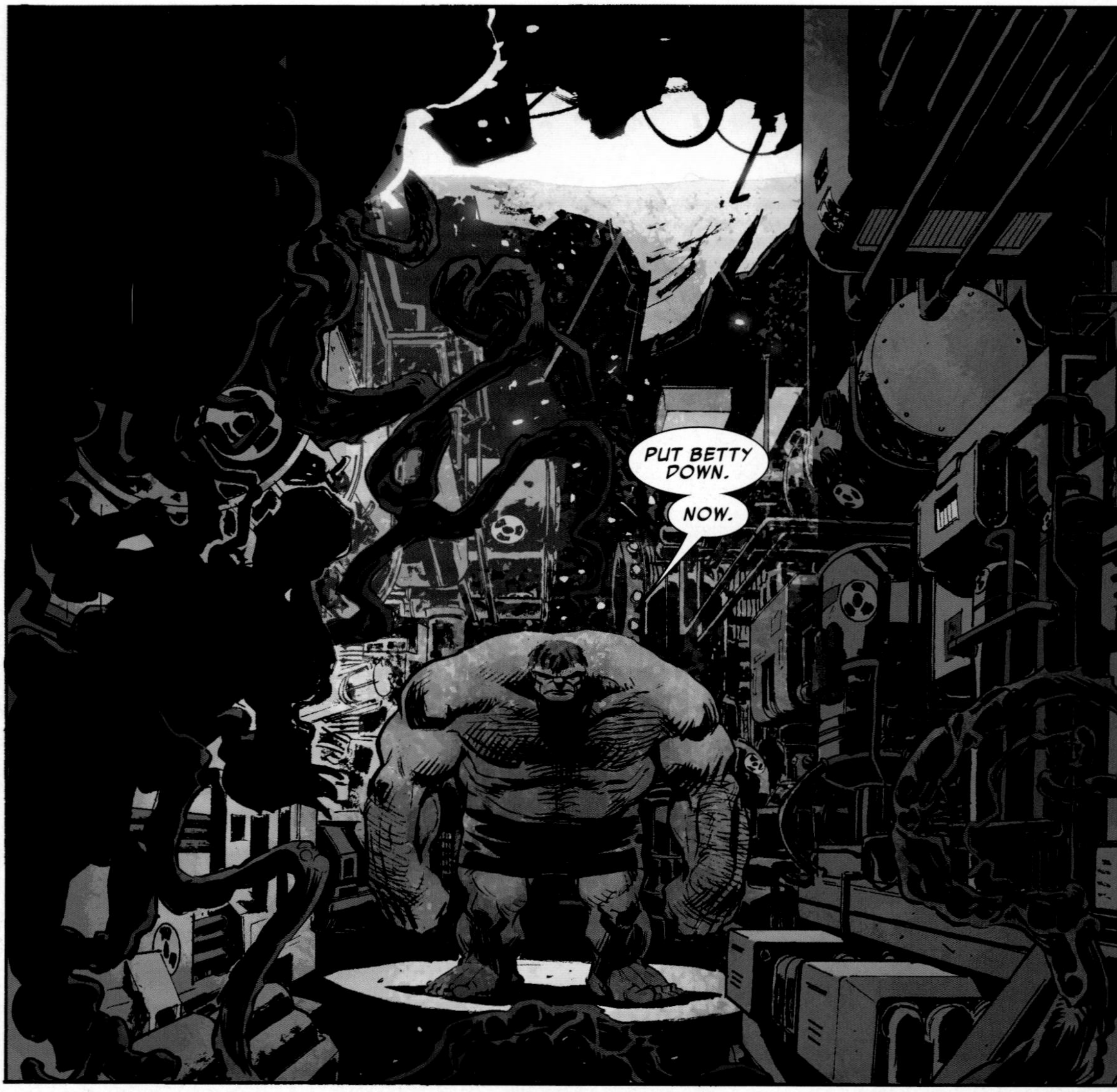
PUT BETTY DOWN.
NOW.

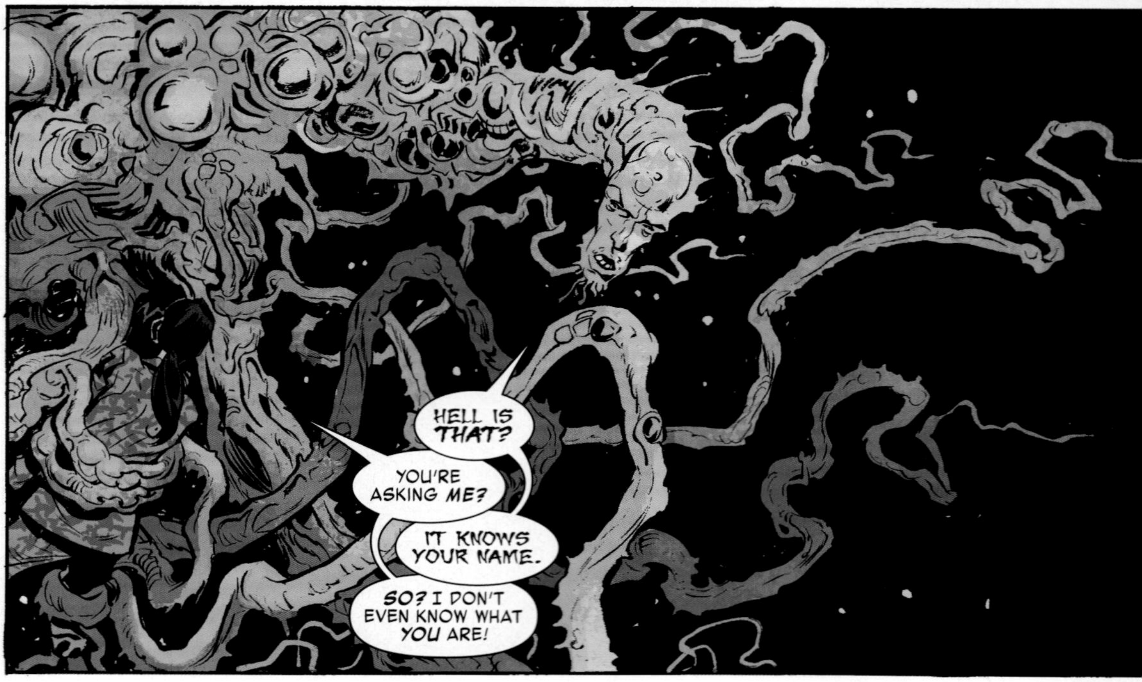
HELL IS THAT?
YOU'RE ASKING ME?
IT KNOWS YOUR NAME.
SO? I DON'T EVEN KNOW WHAT YOU ARE!

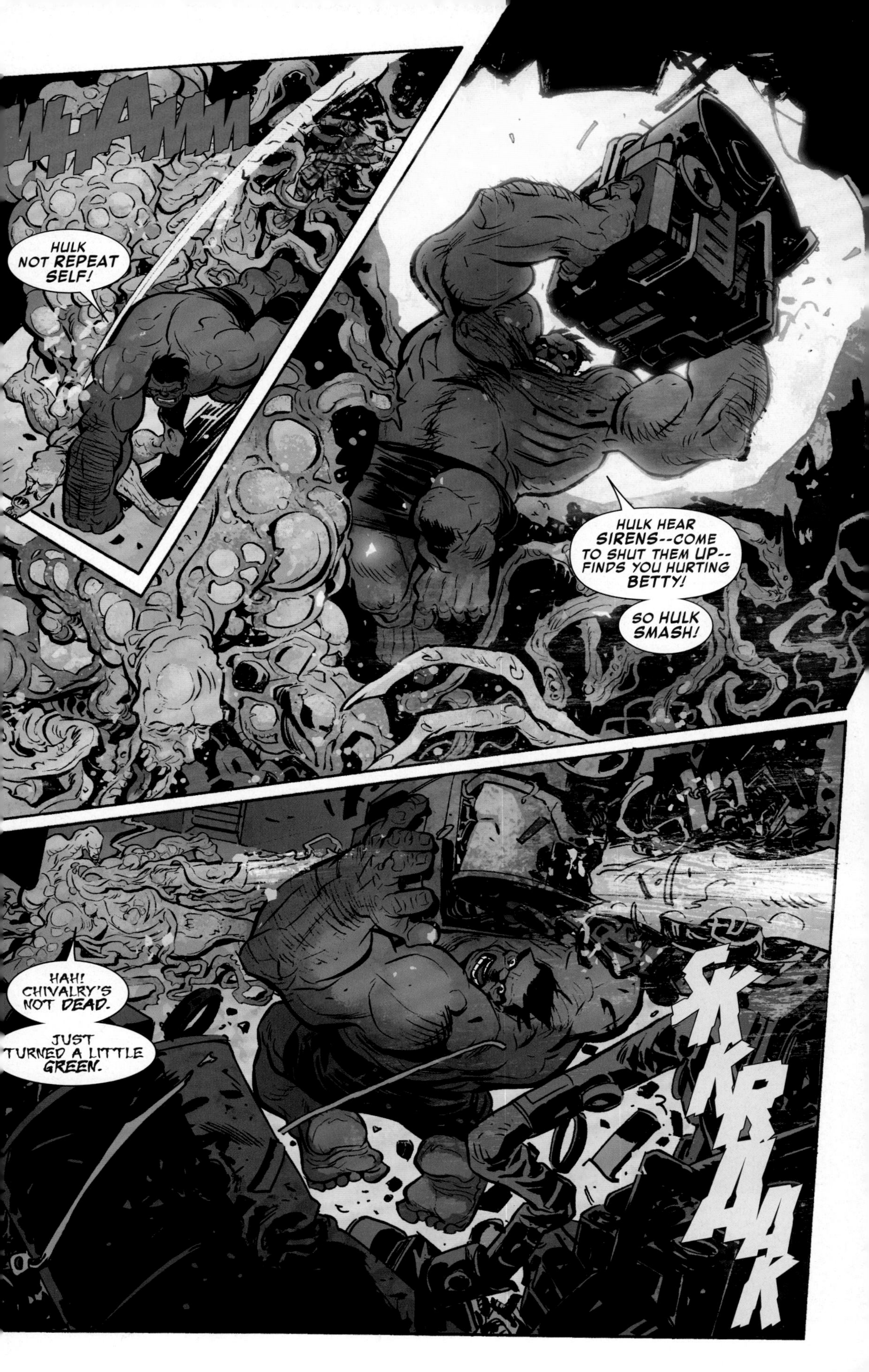
WHAMM
HULK NOT REPEAT SELF!
HULK HEAR SIRENS--COME TO SHUT THEM UP--FINDS YOU HURTING BETTY!
SO HULK SMASH!
HAH! CHIVALRY'S NOT DEAD.
JUST TURNED A LITTLE GREEN.
SKRAAAK

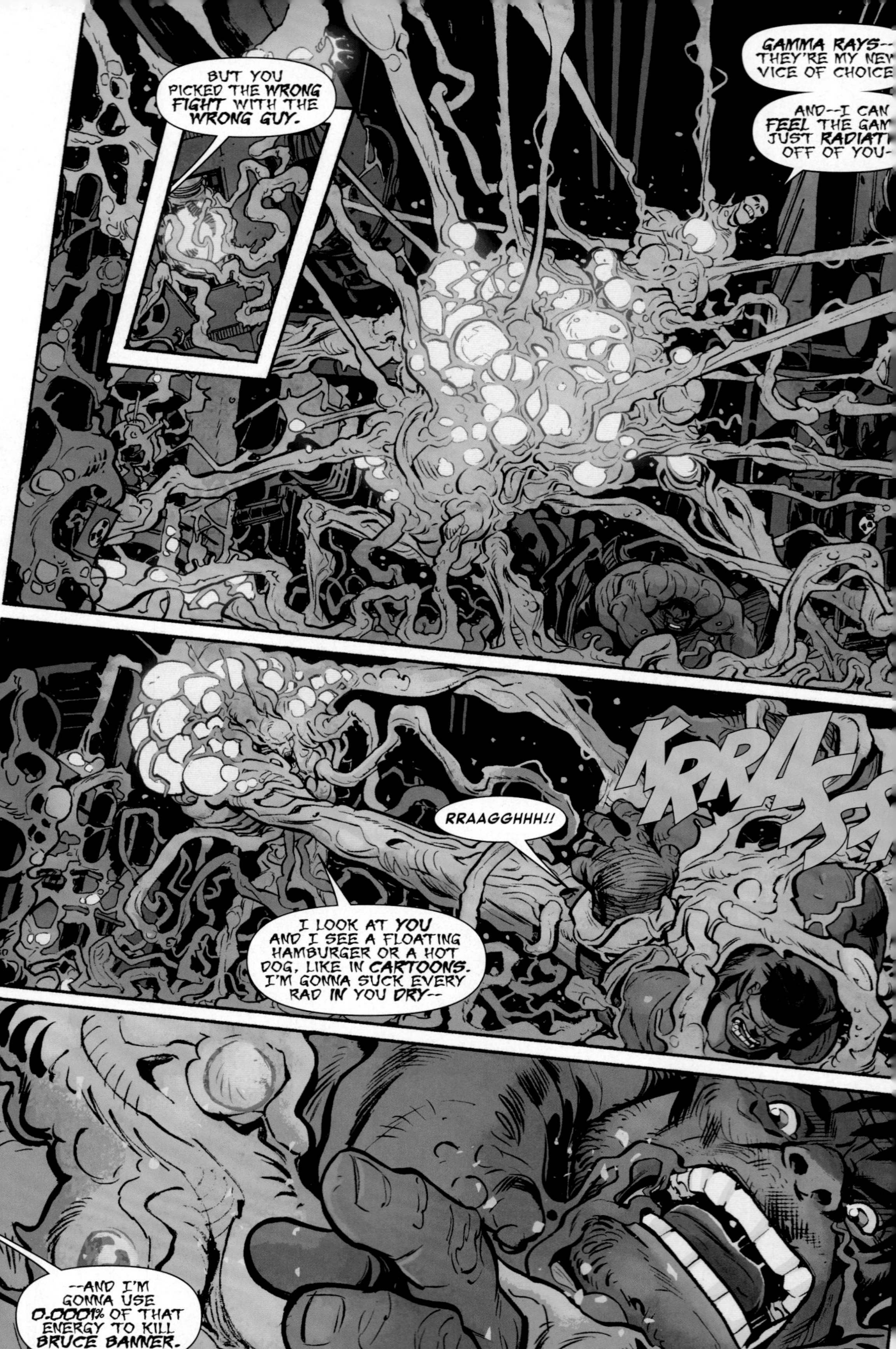
BUT YOU PICKED THE WRONG FIGHT WITH THE WRONG GUY.
GAMMA RAYS-- THEY'RE MY NEW VICE OF CHOICE
AND--I CAN FEEL THE GAM JUST RADIAT OFF OF YOU-
RRAAGGHHH!!
I LOOK AT YOU AND I SEE A FLOATING HAMBURGER OR A HOT DOG, LIKE IN CARTOONS. I'M GONNA SUCK EVERY RAD IN YOU DRY--
--AND I'M GONNA USE 0.0001% OF THAT ENERGY TO KILL BRUCE BANNER.

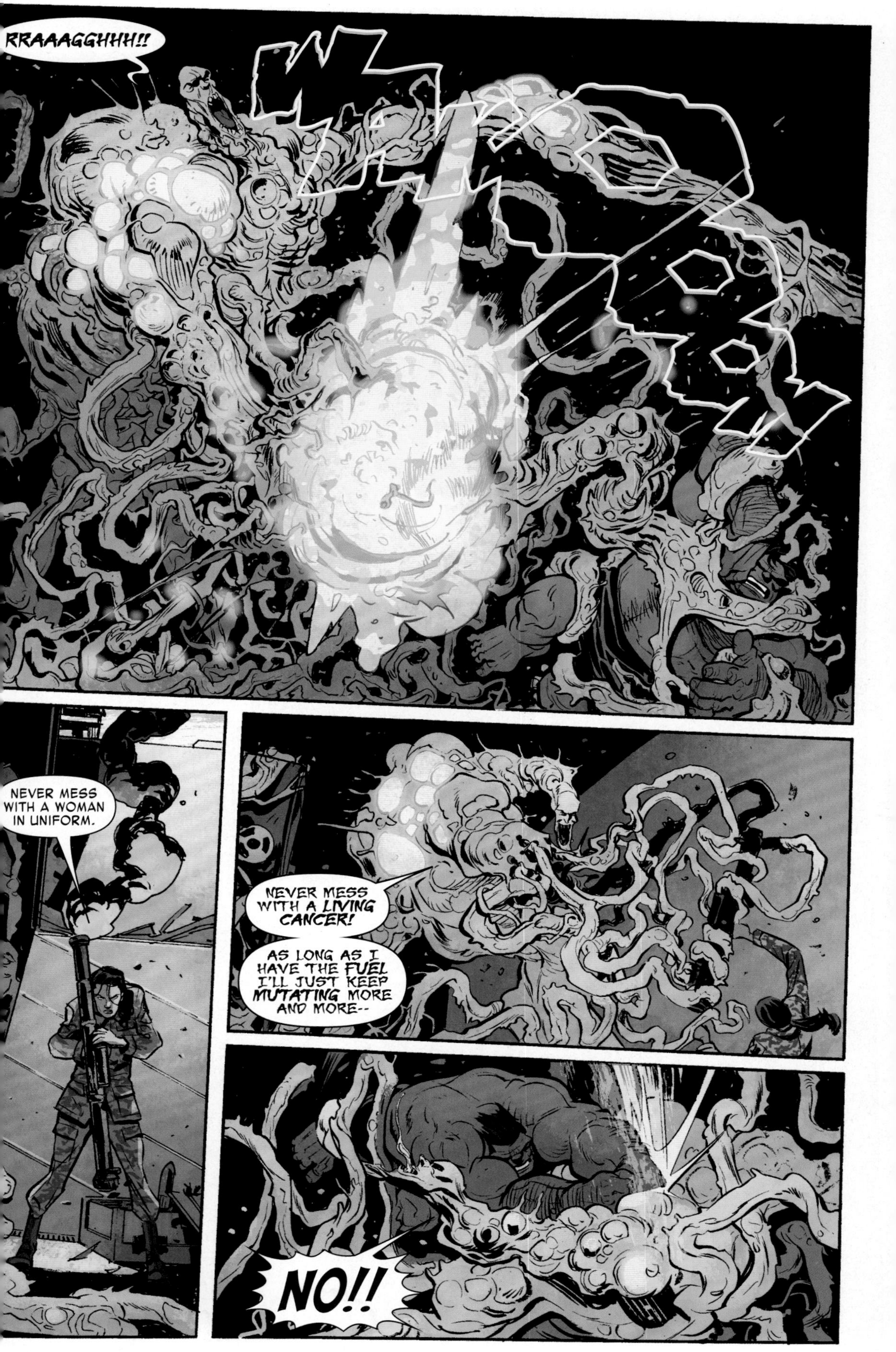

RRAAAGGHHH!!
NEVER MESS WITH A WOMAN IN UNIFORM.
NEVER MESS WITH A *LIVING CANCER!*
AS LONG AS I HAVE THE *FUEL* I'LL JUST KEEP *MUTATING* MORE AND MORE--
NO!!

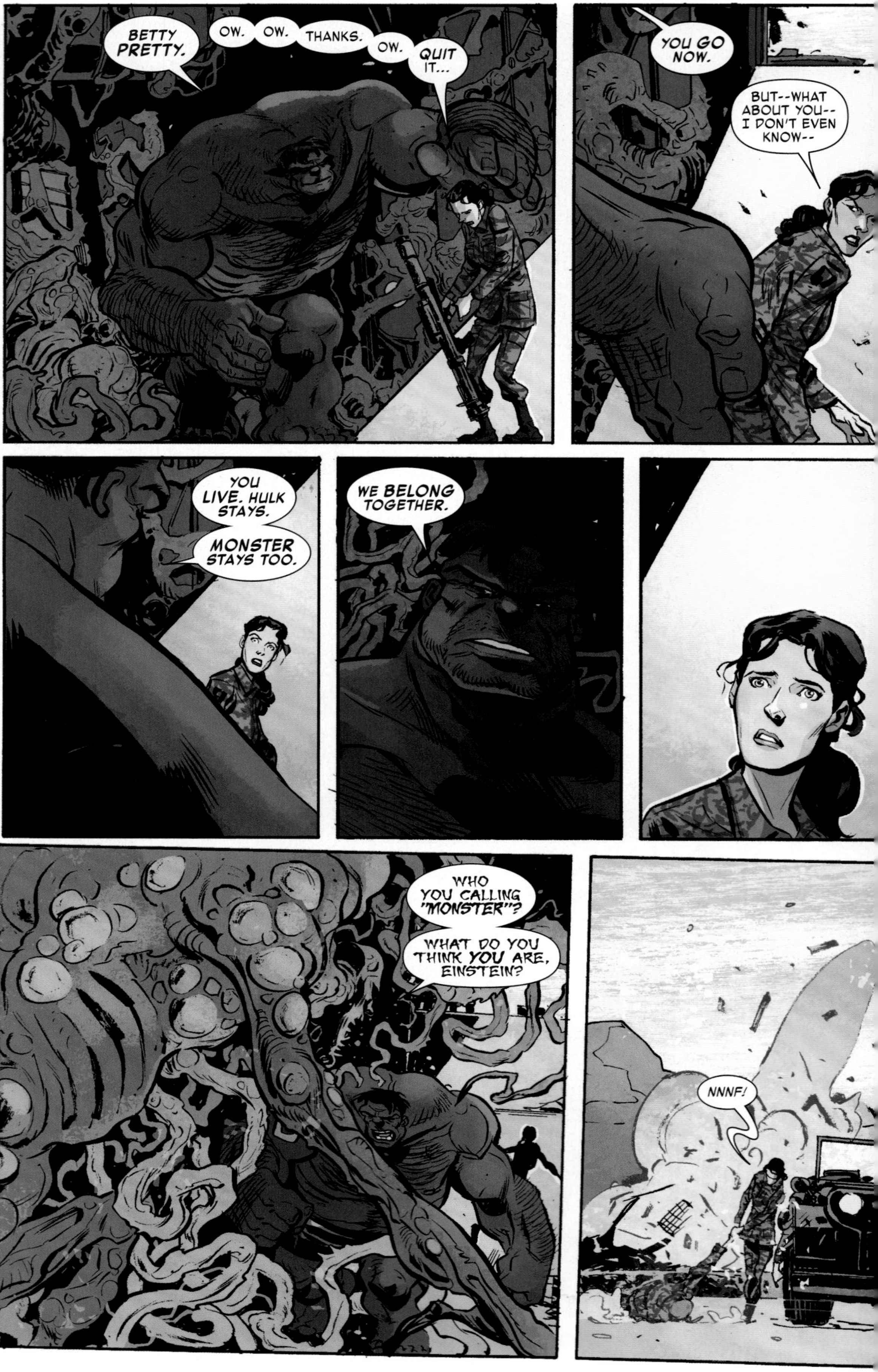
BETTY PRETTY.
OW.
OW.
THANKS.
OW.
QUIT IT...
YOU GO NOW.
BUT--WHAT ABOUT YOU-- I DON'T EVEN KNOW--
YOU LIVE. HULK STAYS.
MONSTER STAYS TOO.
WE BELONG TOGETHER.
WHO YOU CALLING "MONSTER"?
WHAT DO YOU THINK YOU ARE, EINSTEIN?
NNNF!

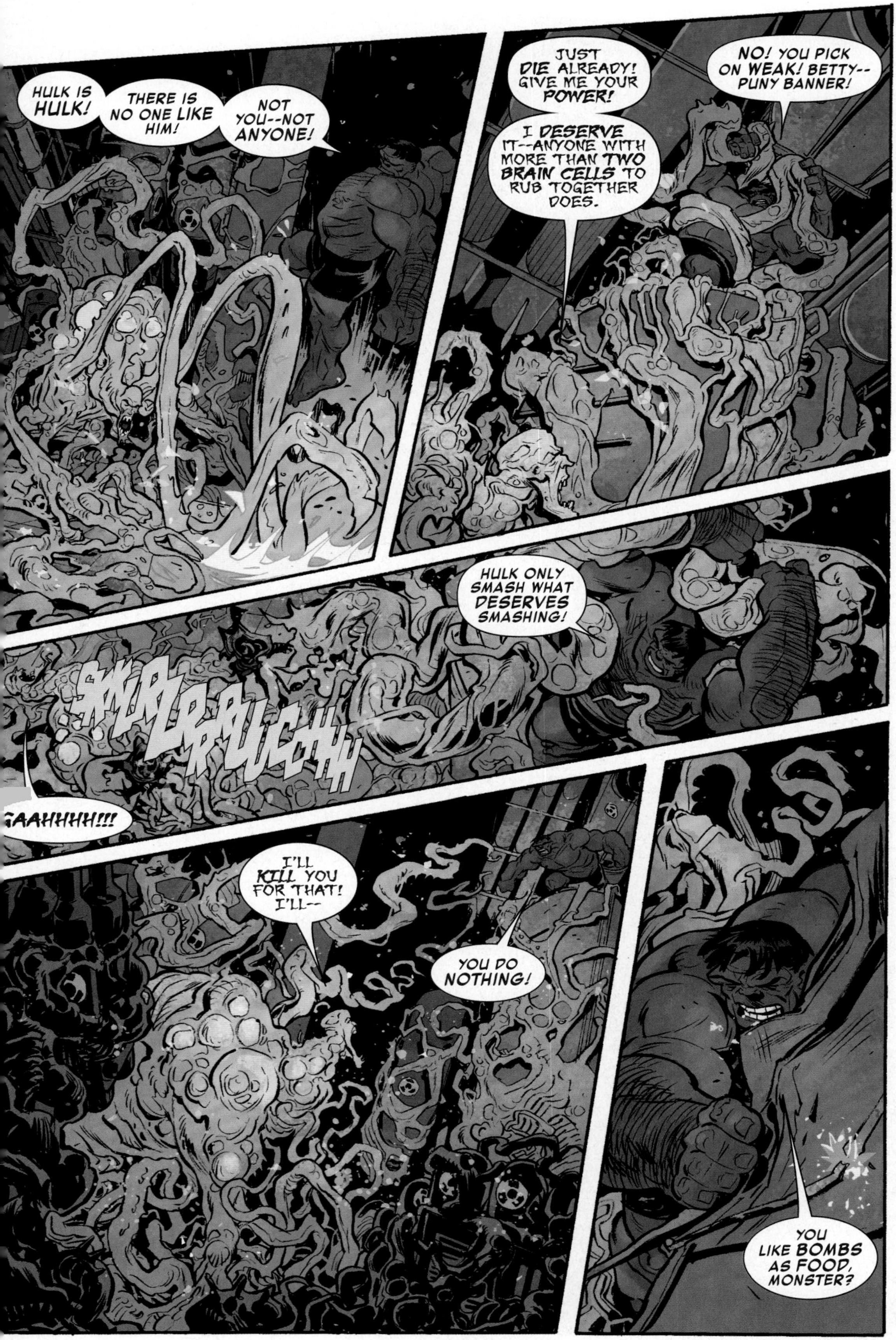
HULK IS HULK!
THERE IS NO ONE LIKE HIM!
NOT YOU--NOT ANYONE!
JUST DIE ALREADY! GIVE ME YOUR POWER!
I DESERVE IT--ANYONE WITH MORE THAN TWO BRAIN CELLS TO RUB TOGETHER DOES.
NO! YOU PICK ON WEAK! BETTY--PUNY BANNER!
HULK ONLY SMASH WHAT DESERVES SMASHING!
GAAHHHH!!!
I'LL KILL YOU FOR THAT! I'LL--
YOU DO NOTHING!
YOU LIKE BOMBS AS FOOD, MONSTER?

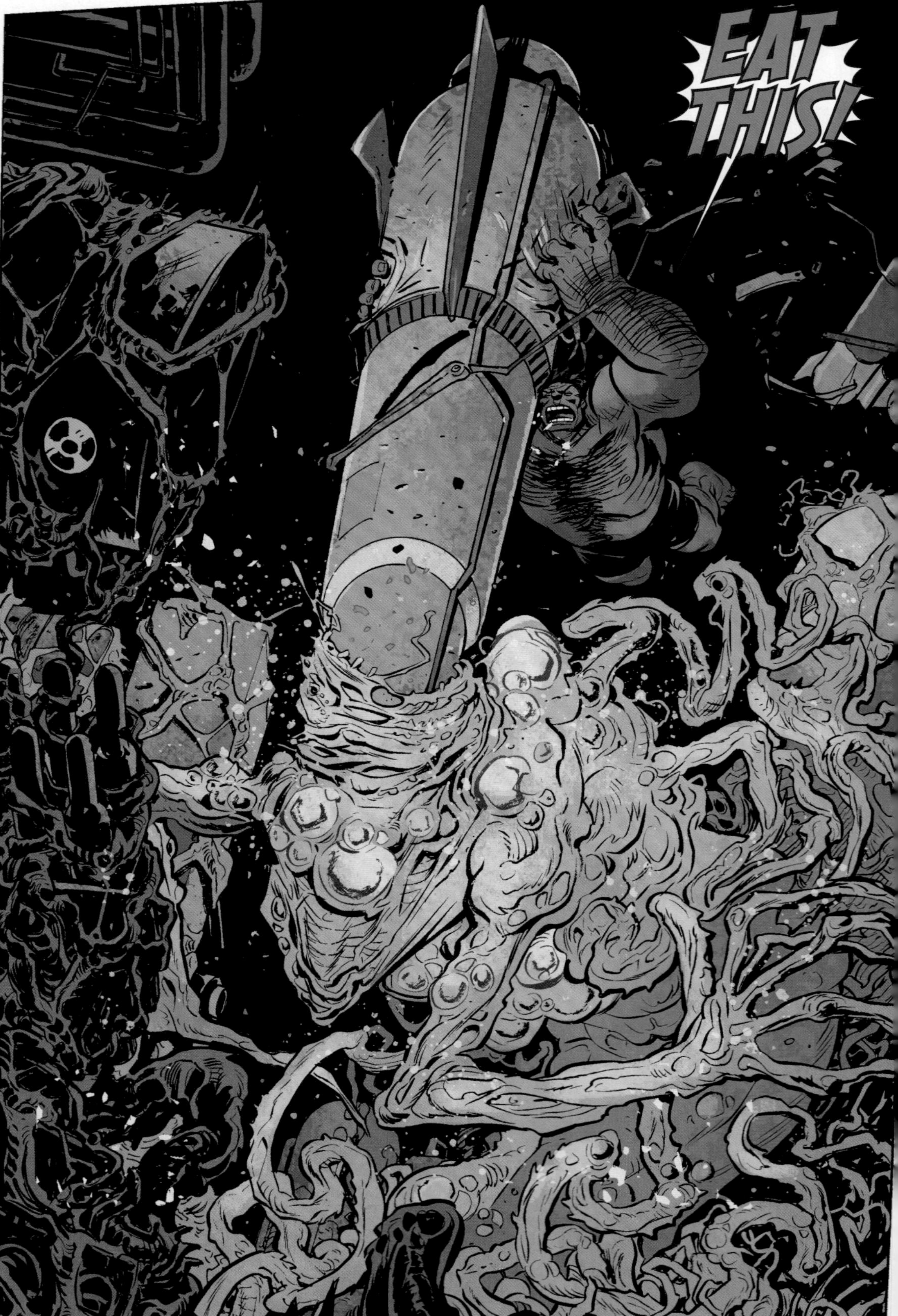
EAT THIS!

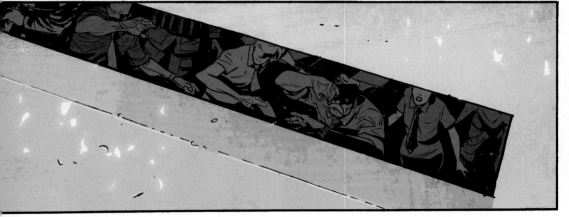

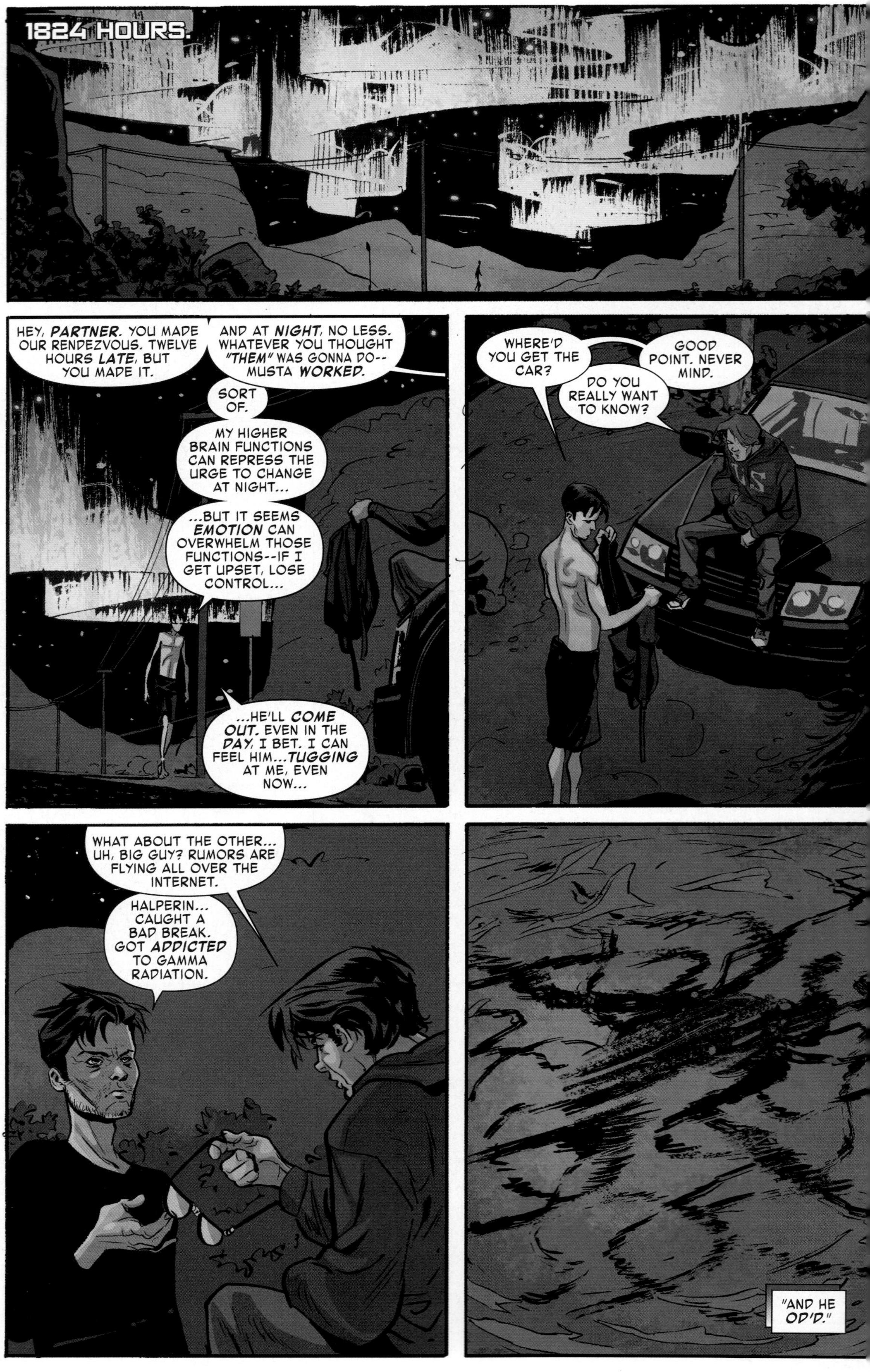
1824 HOURS.
HEY, PARTNER. YOU MADE OUR RENDEZVOUS. TWELVE HOURS LATE, BUT YOU MADE IT.
AND AT NIGHT, NO LESS. WHATEVER YOU THOUGHT "THEM" WAS GONNA DO--MUSTA WORKED.
SORT OF.
MY HIGHER BRAIN FUNCTIONS CAN REPRESS THE URGE TO CHANGE AT NIGHT...
...BUT IT SEEMS EMOTION CAN OVERWHELM THOSE FUNCTIONS--IF I GET UPSET, LOSE CONTROL...
...HE'LL COME OUT. EVEN IN THE DAY, I BET. I CAN FEEL HIM...TUGGING AT ME, EVEN NOW...
WHERE'D YOU GET THE CAR?
DO YOU REALLY WANT TO KNOW?
GOOD POINT. NEVER MIND.
WHAT ABOUT THE OTHER... UH, BIG GUY? RUMORS ARE FLYING ALL OVER THE INTERNET.
HALPERIN... CAUGHT A BAD BREAK. GOT ADDICTED TO GAMMA RADIATION.
"AND HE OD'D."

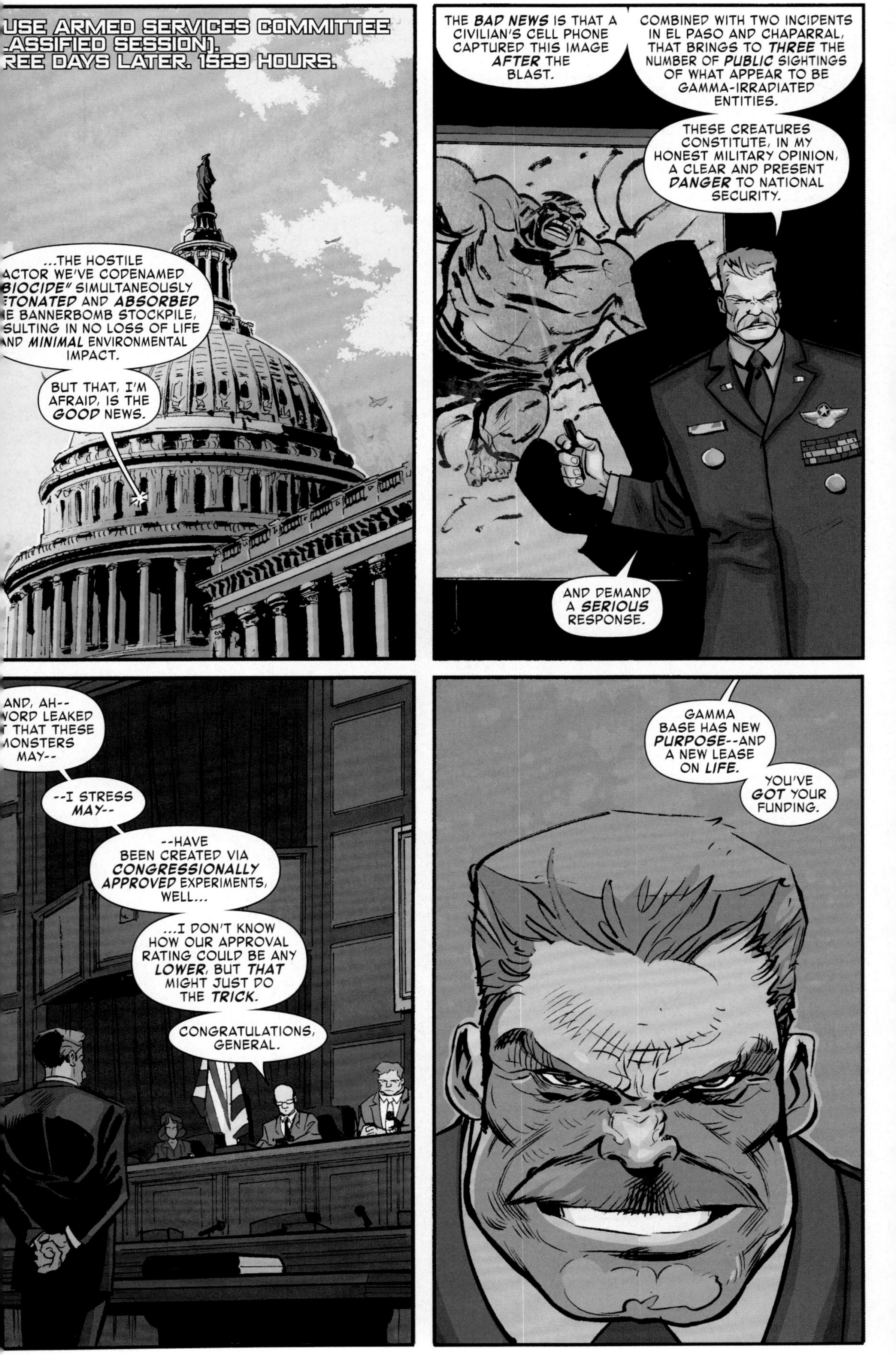
USE ARMED SERVICES COMMITTEE
LASSIFIED SESSION).
REE DAYS LATER. 1529 HOURS.
...THE HOSTILE ACTOR WE'VE CODENAMED "BIOCIDE" SIMULTANEOUSLY ETONATED AND ABSORBED IE BANNERBOMB STOCKPILE, SULTING IN NO LOSS OF LIFE AND MINIMAL ENVIRONMENTAL IMPACT.
BUT THAT, I'M AFRAID, IS THE GOOD NEWS.
THE BAD NEWS IS THAT A CIVILIAN'S CELL PHONE CAPTURED THIS IMAGE AFTER THE BLAST.
COMBINED WITH TWO INCIDENTS IN EL PASO AND CHAPARRAL, THAT BRINGS TO THREE THE NUMBER OF PUBLIC SIGHTINGS OF WHAT APPEAR TO BE GAMMA-IRRADIATED ENTITIES.
THESE CREATURES CONSTITUTE, IN MY HONEST MILITARY OPINION, A CLEAR AND PRESENT DANGER TO NATIONAL SECURITY.
AND DEMAND A SERIOUS RESPONSE.
AND, AH-- WORD LEAKED T THAT THESE MONSTERS MAY--
--I STRESS MAY--
--HAVE BEEN CREATED VIA CONGRESSIONALLY APPROVED EXPERIMENTS, WELL...
...I DON'T KNOW HOW OUR APPROVAL RATING COULD BE ANY LOWER, BUT THAT MIGHT JUST DO THE TRICK.
CONGRATULATIONS, GENERAL.
GAMMA BASE HAS NEW PURPOSE--AND A NEW LEASE ON LIFE.
YOU'VE GOT YOUR FUNDING.

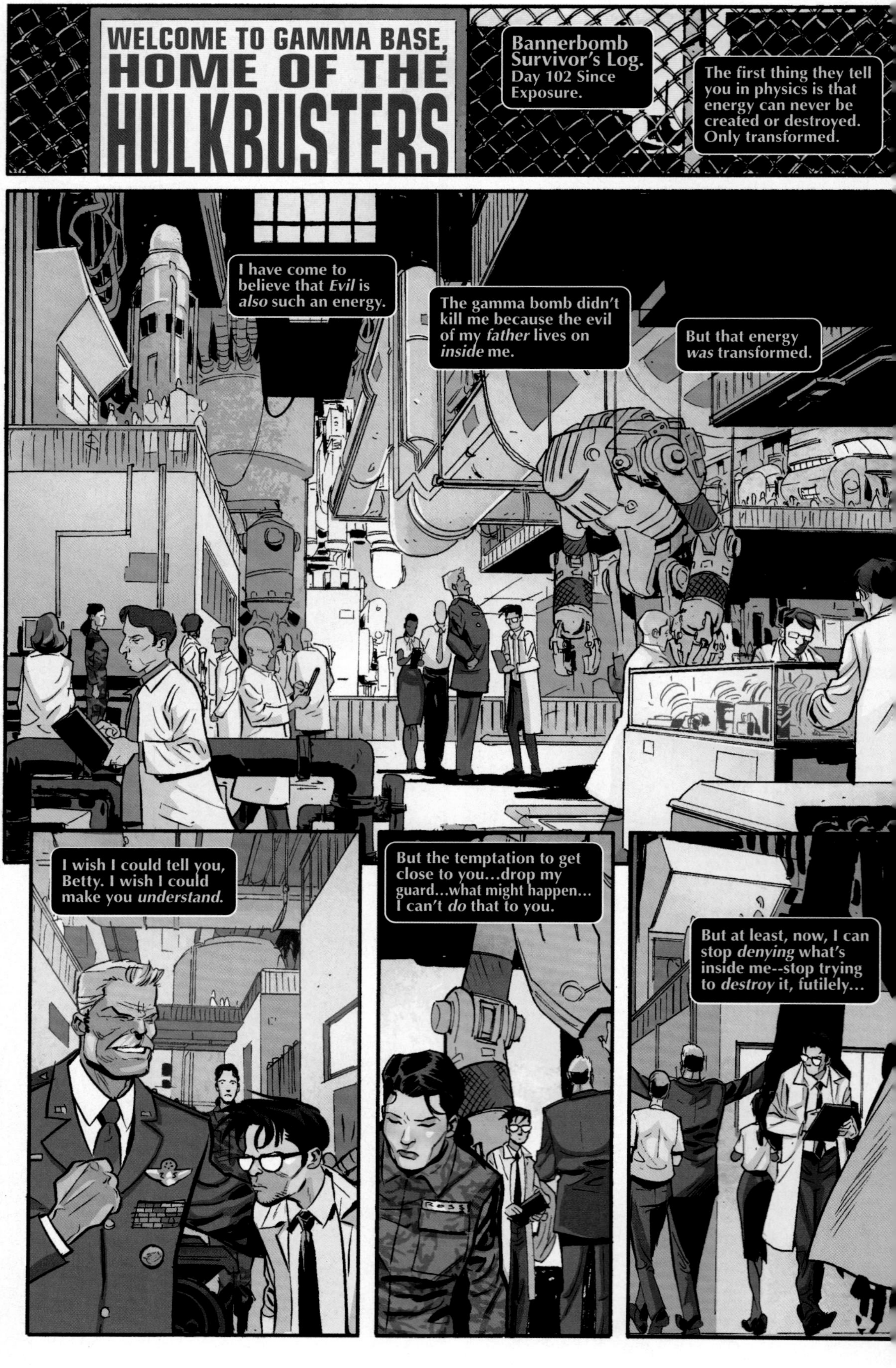
WELCOME TO GAMMA BASE, HOME OF THE HULKBUSTERS
Bannerbomb Survivor's Log. Day 102 Since Exposure.
The first thing they tell you in physics is that energy can never be created or destroyed. Only transformed.
I have come to believe that *Evil* is *also* such an energy.
The gamma bomb didn't kill me because the evil of my *father* lives on *inside* me.
But that energy *was* transformed.
I wish I could tell you, Betty. I wish I could make you *understand.*
But the temptation to get close to you…drop my guard…what might happen… I can't *do* that to you.
But at least, now, I can stop *denying* what's inside me--stop trying to *destroy* it, futilely…

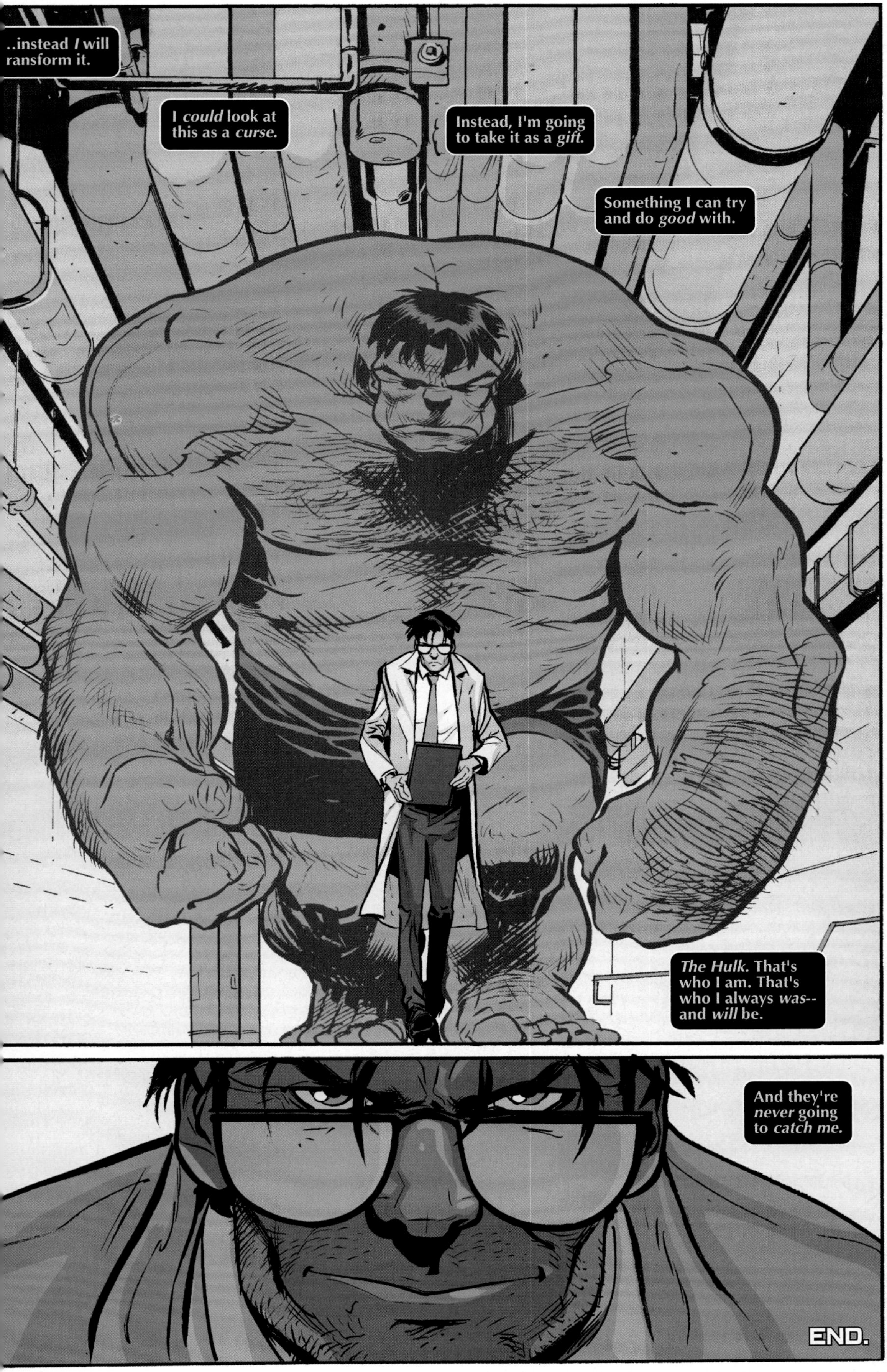
..instead I will
ransform it.
I *could* look at this as a *curse.*
Instead, I'm going to take it as a *gift.*
Something I can try and do *good* with.
The Hulk. That's who I am. That's who I always *was*-- and *will* be.
And they're *never* going to *catch me.*
END.

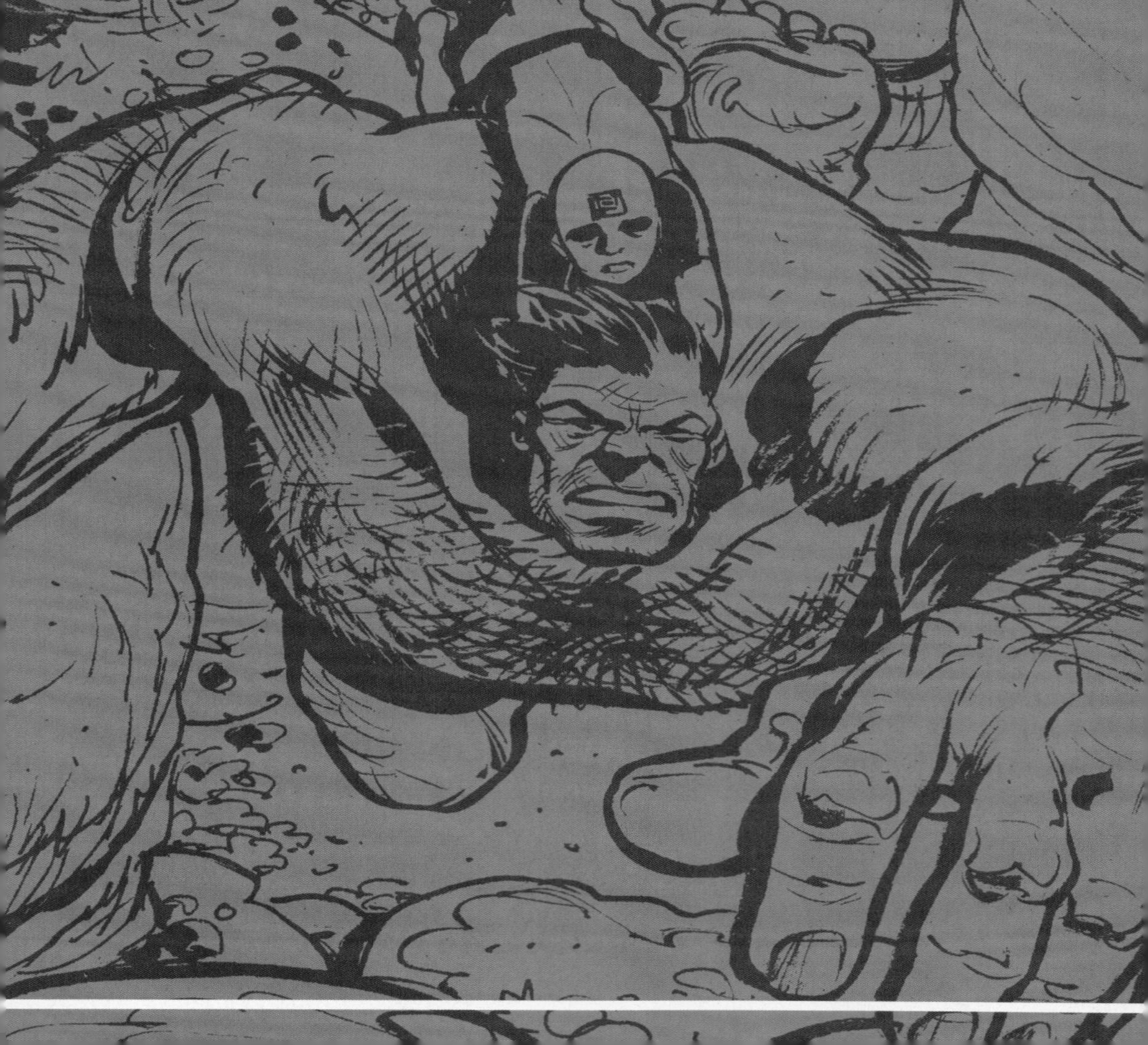

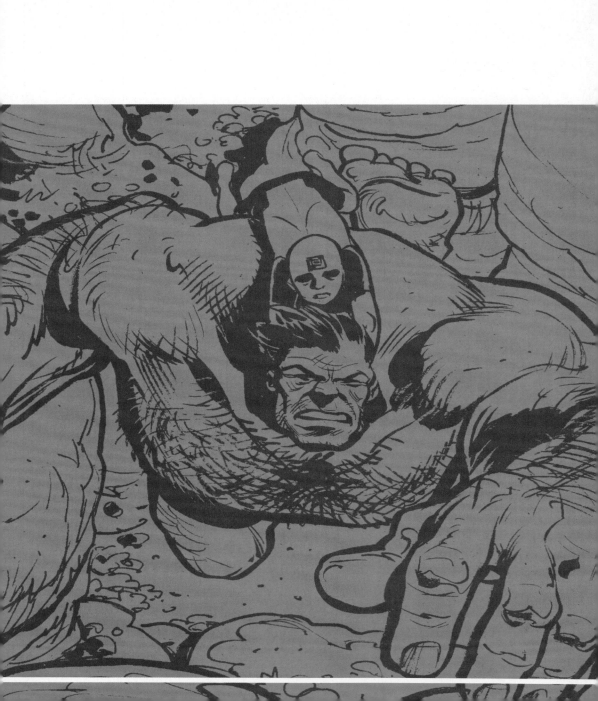

IMMORTAL HULK #1 (2018) BRUCE BANNER HAS RETURNED FROM THE DEAD, BUT HE DIDN'T COME BACK ALONE. WHEN NIGHT FALLS, IT IS TIME FOR THE HORROR KNOWN AS THE IMMORTAL HULK TO RISE.

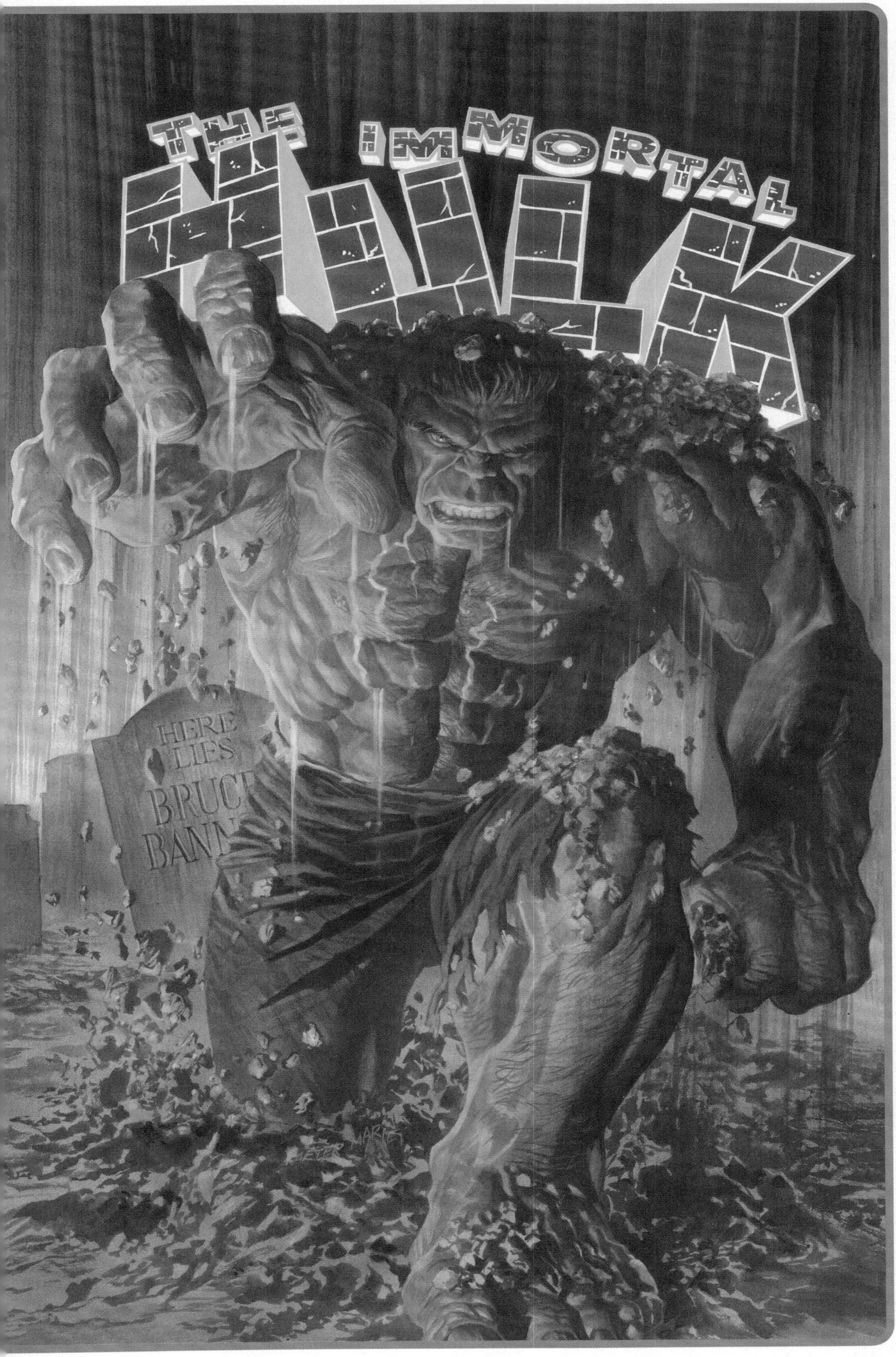
THE IMMORTAL HULK
HERE LIES BRUCE BANN

"**MAN IS, ON THE WHOLE, LESS GOOD THAN HE IMAGINES HIMSELF OR WANTS TO BE.**"

– CARL GUSTAV JUNG
PSYCHOLOGY AND RELIGION

HERE ARE TWO PEOPLE IN EVERY MIRROR.

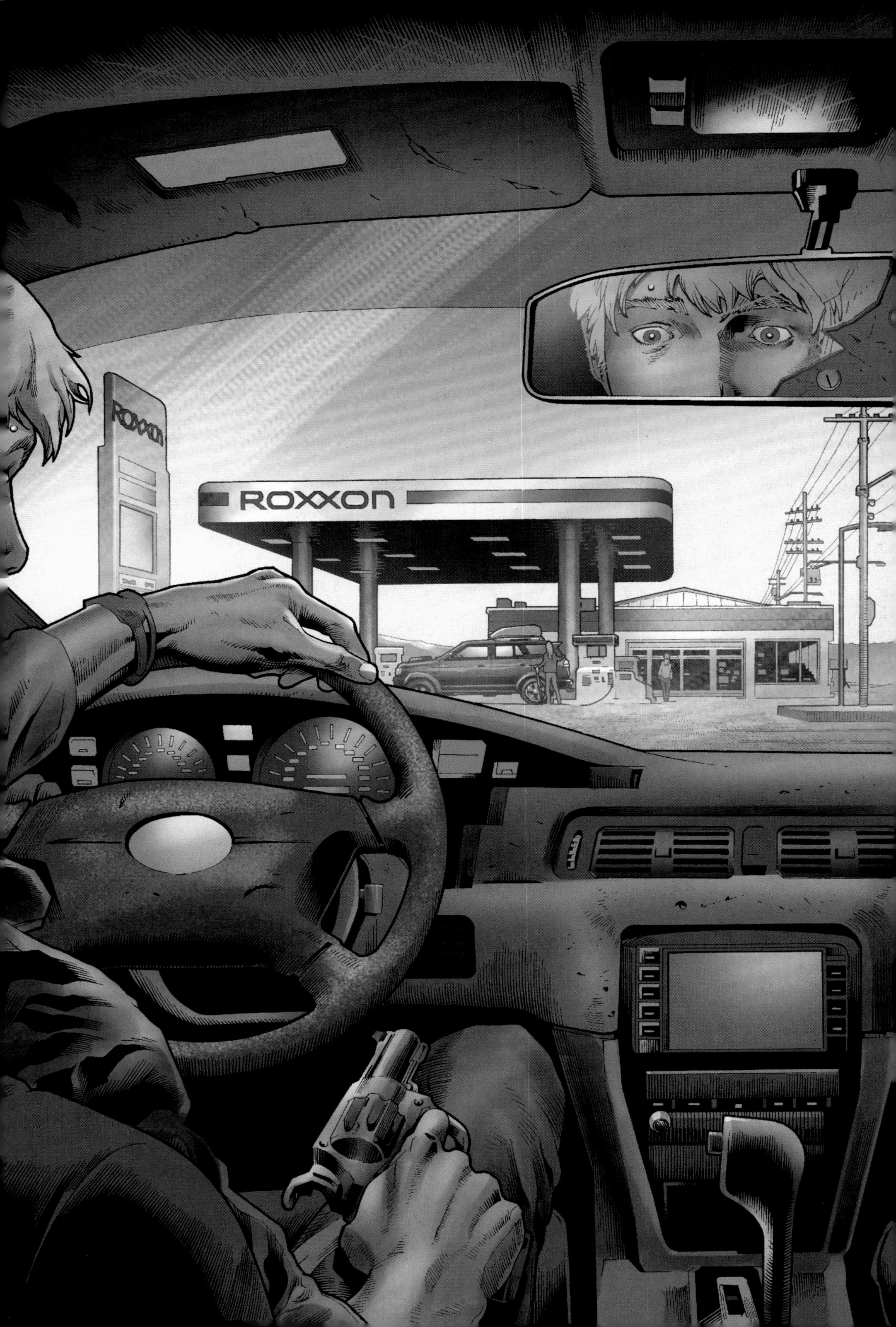
ROXXON
ROXXON

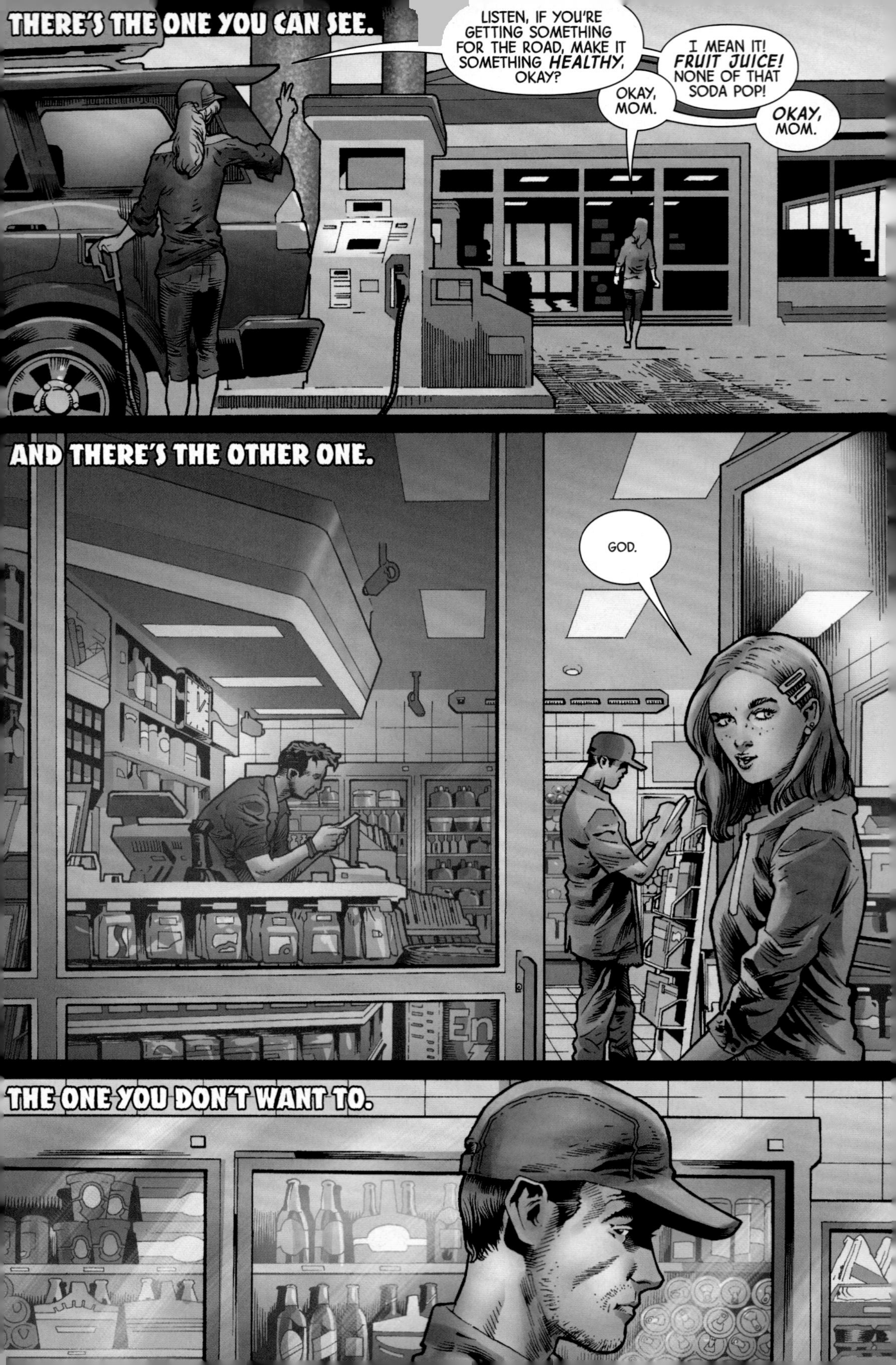
THERE'S THE ONE YOU CAN SEE.
LISTEN, IF YOU'RE GETTING SOMETHING FOR THE ROAD, MAKE IT SOMETHING HEALTHY, OKAY?
OKAY, MOM.
I MEAN IT! FRUIT JUICE! NONE OF THAT SODA POP!
OKAY, MOM.
AND THERE'S THE OTHER ONE.
GOD.
THE ONE YOU DON'T WANT TO.

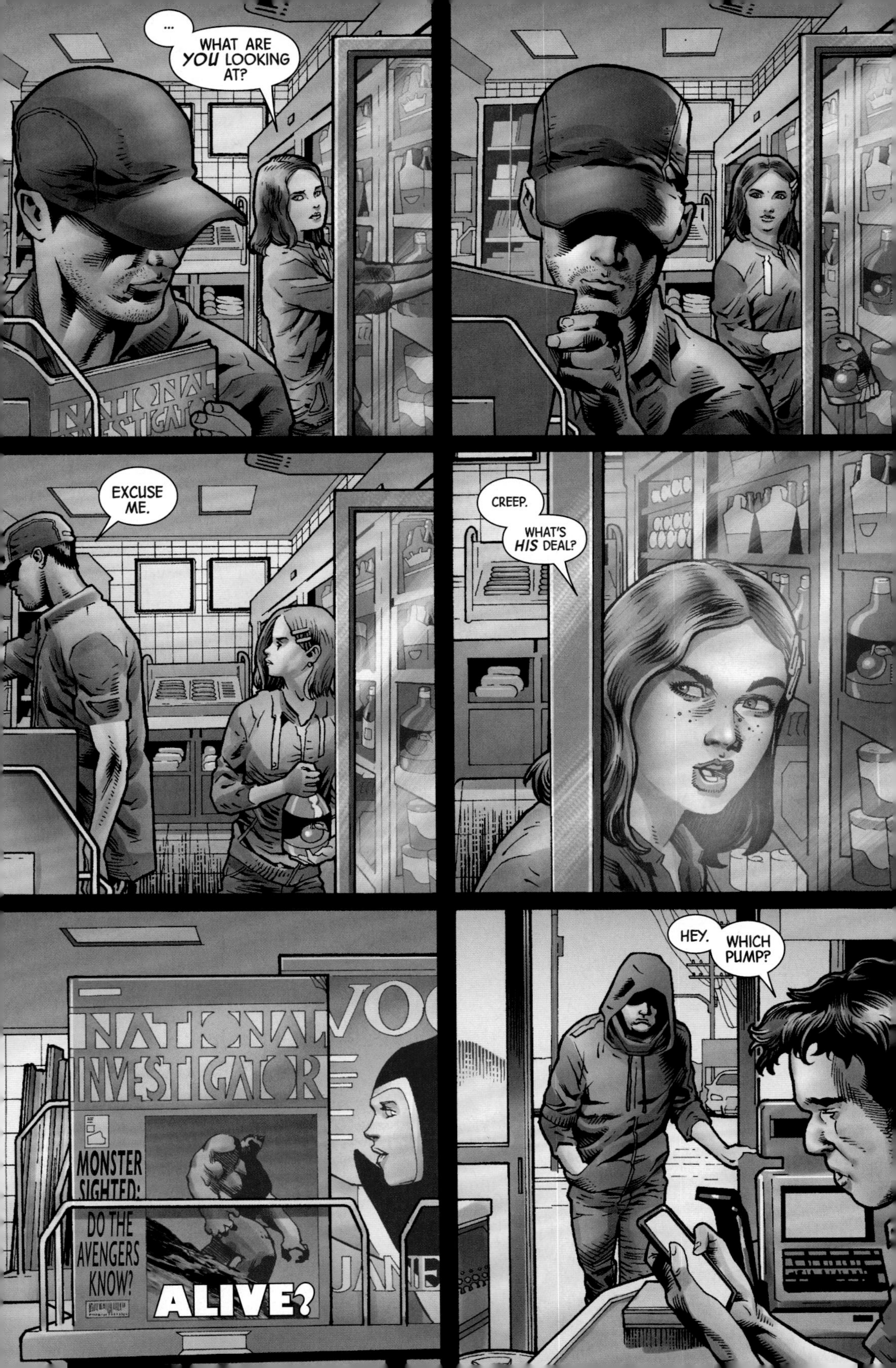
...
WHAT ARE YOU LOOKING AT?
EXCUSE ME.
CREEP.
WHAT'S HIS DEAL?
NATIONAL INVESTIGATOR
MONSTER SIGHTED:
DO THE AVENGERS KNOW?
ALIVE?
HEY.
WHICH PUMP?

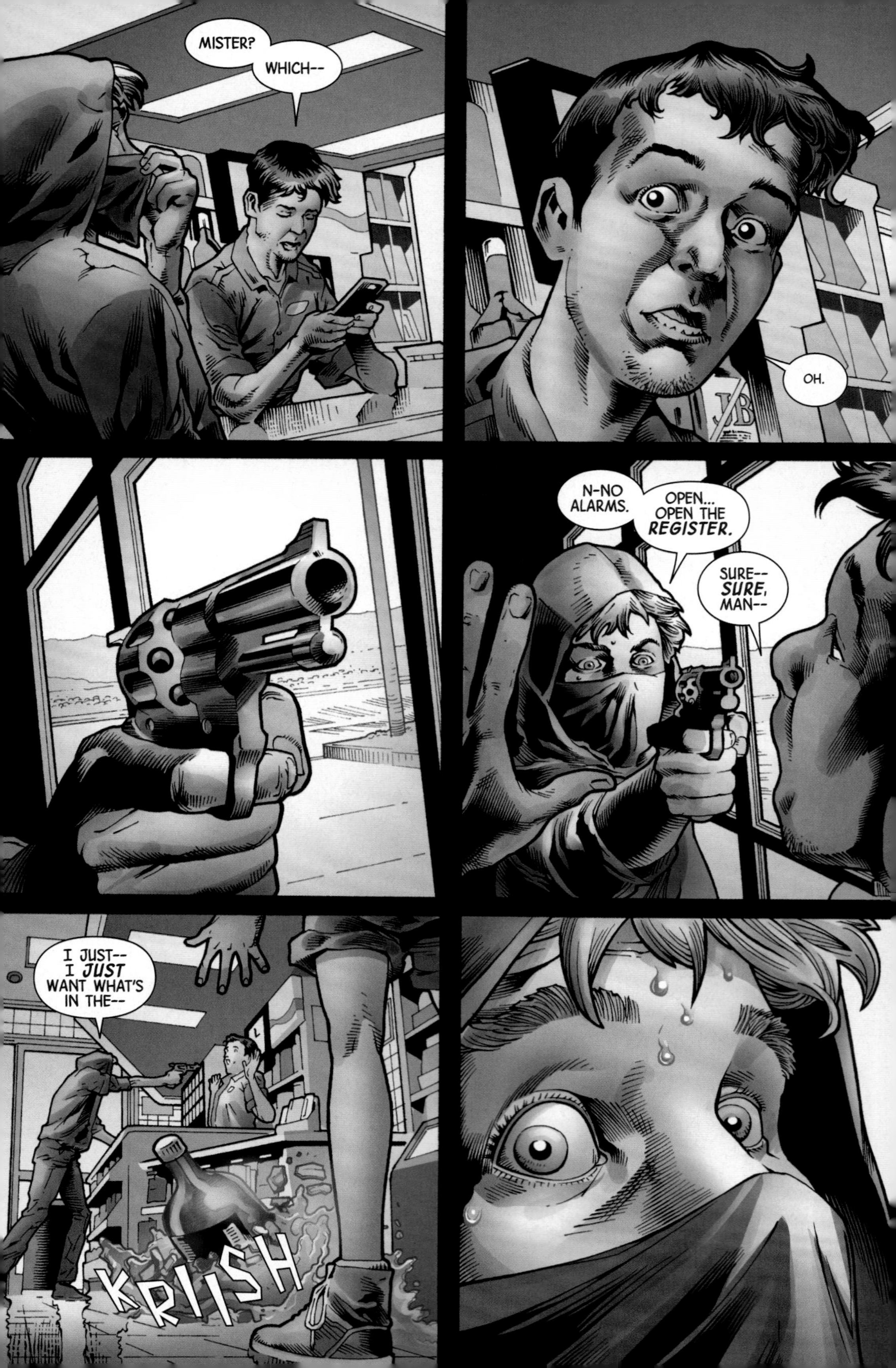
MISTER?
WHICH--
OH.
N-NO ALARMS.
OPEN... OPEN THE REGISTER.
SURE-- SURE, MAN--
I JUST-- I JUST WANT WHAT'S IN THE--
KRIISH

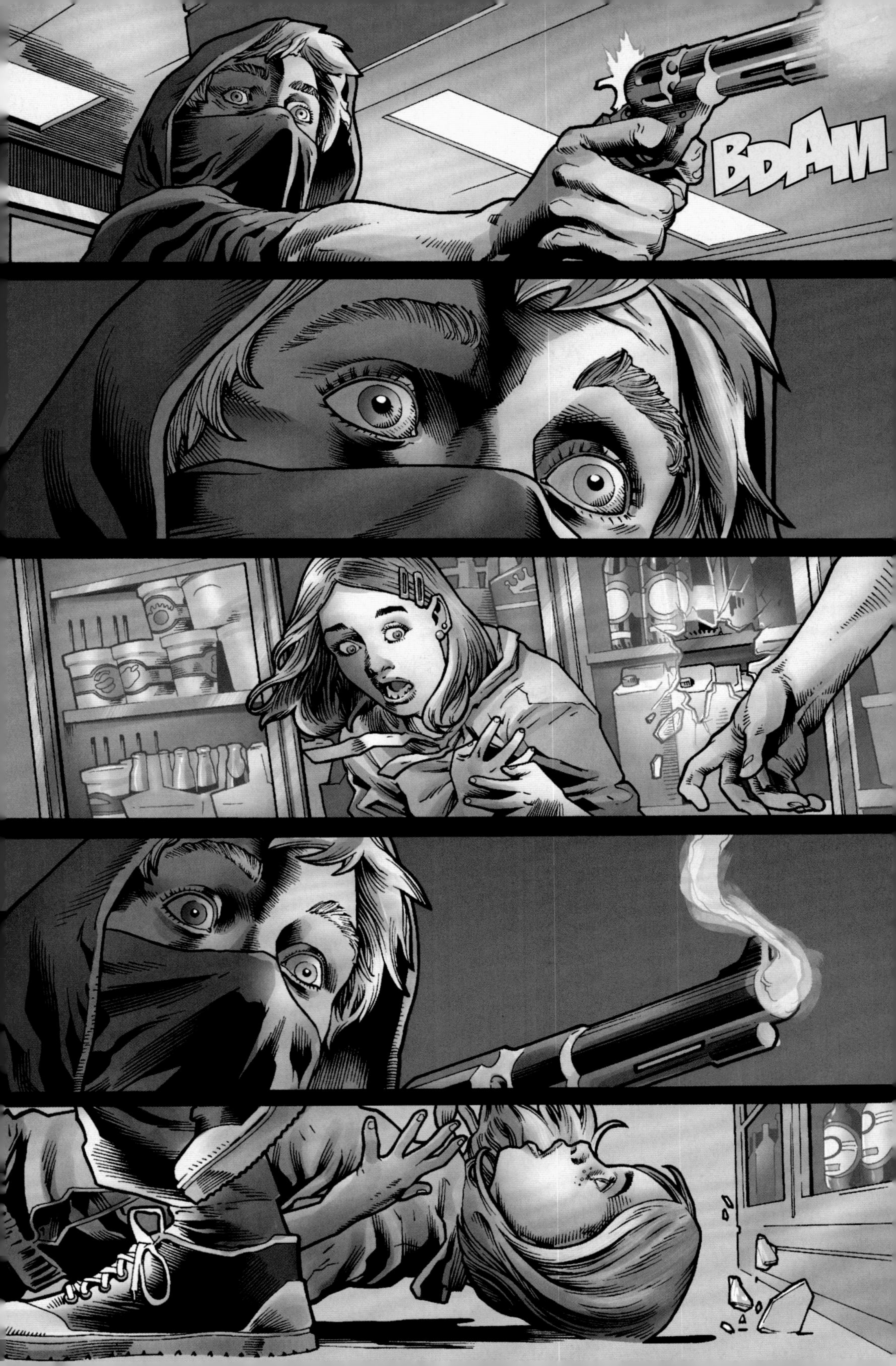
BDAM

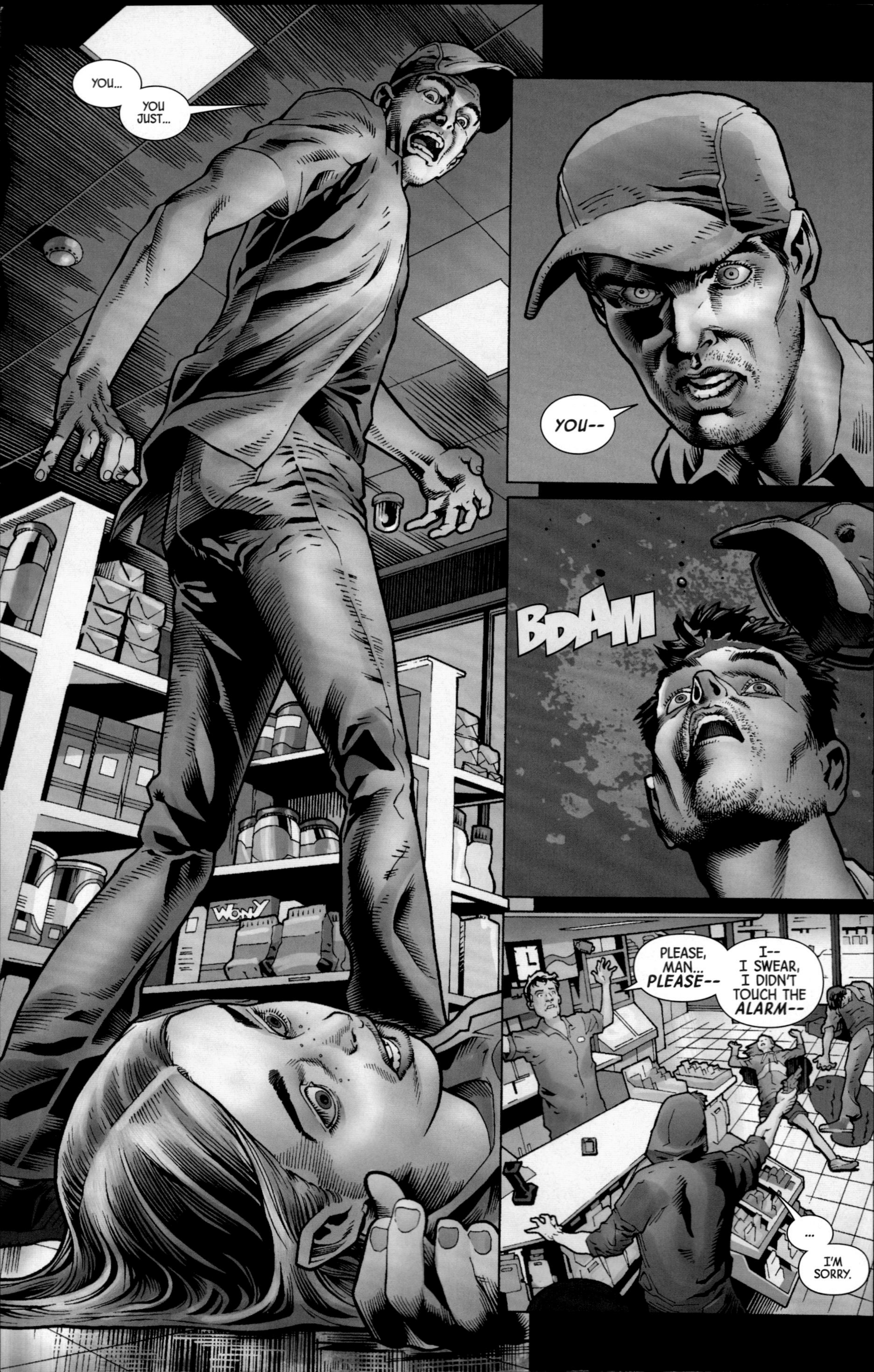
YOU...
YOU JUST...
YOU--
BDAM
PLEASE, MAN... PLEASE--
I-- I SWEAR, I DIDN'T TOUCH THE ALARM--
...
I'M SORRY.

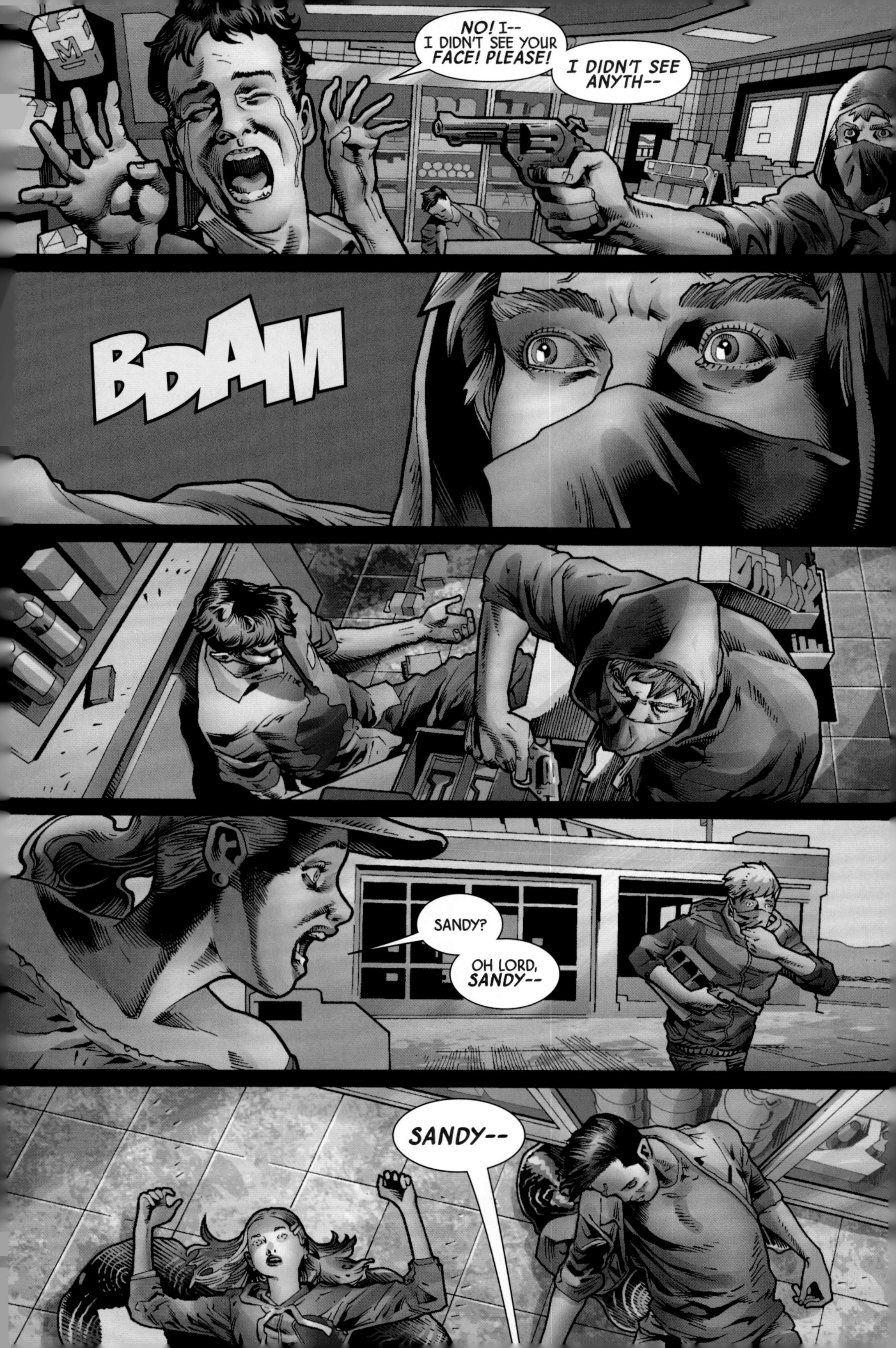
NO! I-- I DIDN'T SEE YOUR FACE! PLEASE!
I DIDN'T SEE ANYTH--
BDAM
SANDY?
OH LORD, SANDY--
SANDY--

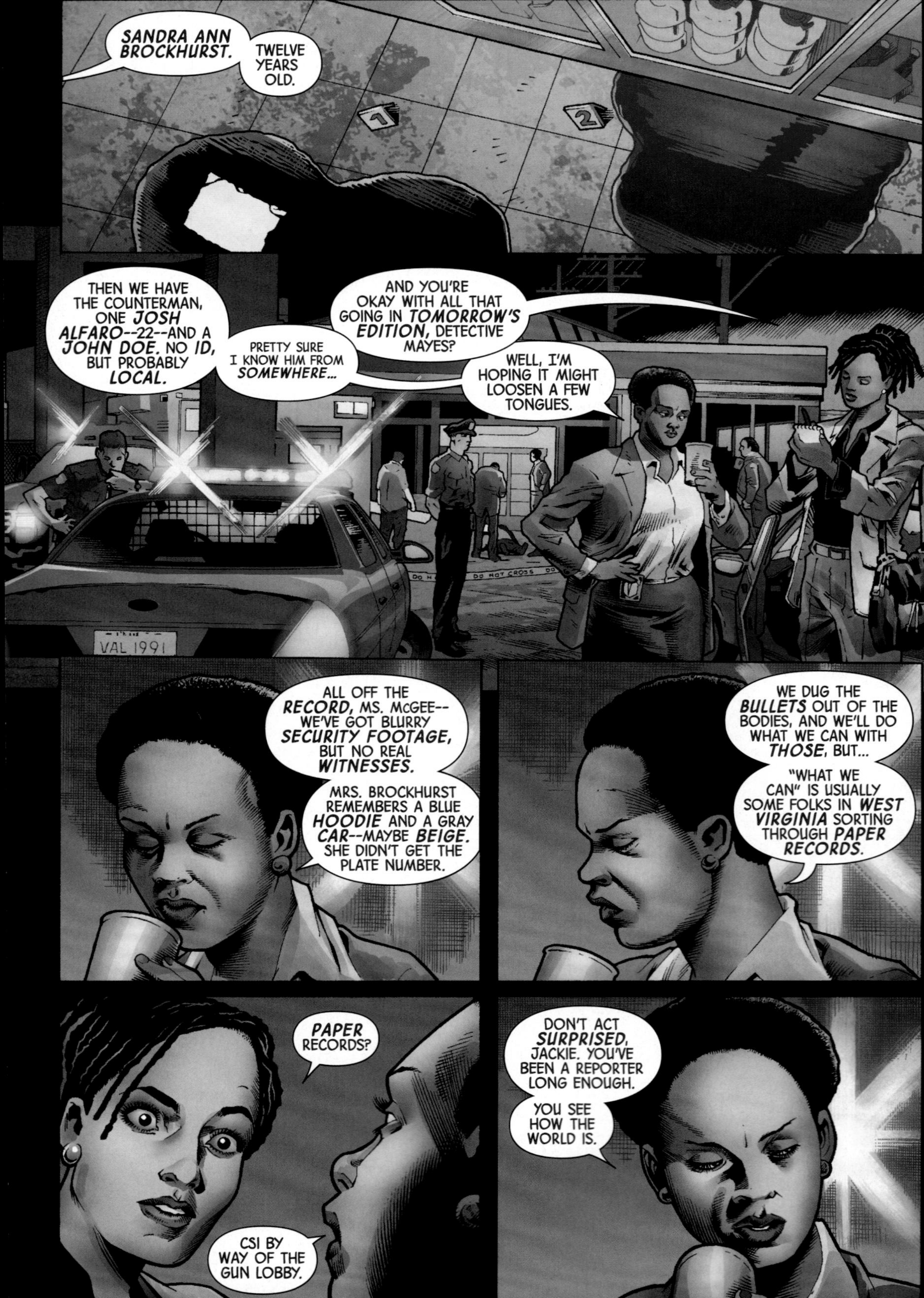
SANDRA ANN BROCKHURST.
TWELVE YEARS OLD.
THEN WE HAVE THE COUNTERMAN, ONE JOSH ALFARO--22--AND A JOHN DOE. NO ID, BUT PROBABLY LOCAL.
PRETTY SURE I KNOW HIM FROM SOMEWHERE...
AND YOU'RE OKAY WITH ALL THAT GOING IN TOMORROW'S EDITION, DETECTIVE MAYES?
WELL, I'M HOPING IT MIGHT LOOSEN A FEW TONGUES.
DO NOT CROSS
VAL 1991
ALL OFF THE RECORD, MS. McGEE--WE'VE GOT BLURRY SECURITY FOOTAGE, BUT NO REAL WITNESSES.
MRS. BROCKHURST REMEMBERS A BLUE HOODIE AND A GRAY CAR--MAYBE BEIGE. SHE DIDN'T GET THE PLATE NUMBER.
WE DUG THE BULLETS OUT OF THE BODIES, AND WE'LL DO WHAT WE CAN WITH THOSE, BUT...
"WHAT WE CAN" IS USUALLY SOME FOLKS IN WEST VIRGINIA SORTING THROUGH PAPER RECORDS.
PAPER RECORDS?
CSI BY WAY OF THE GUN LOBBY.
DON'T ACT SURPRISED, JACKIE. YOU'VE BEEN A REPORTER LONG ENOUGH.
YOU SEE HOW THE WORLD IS.

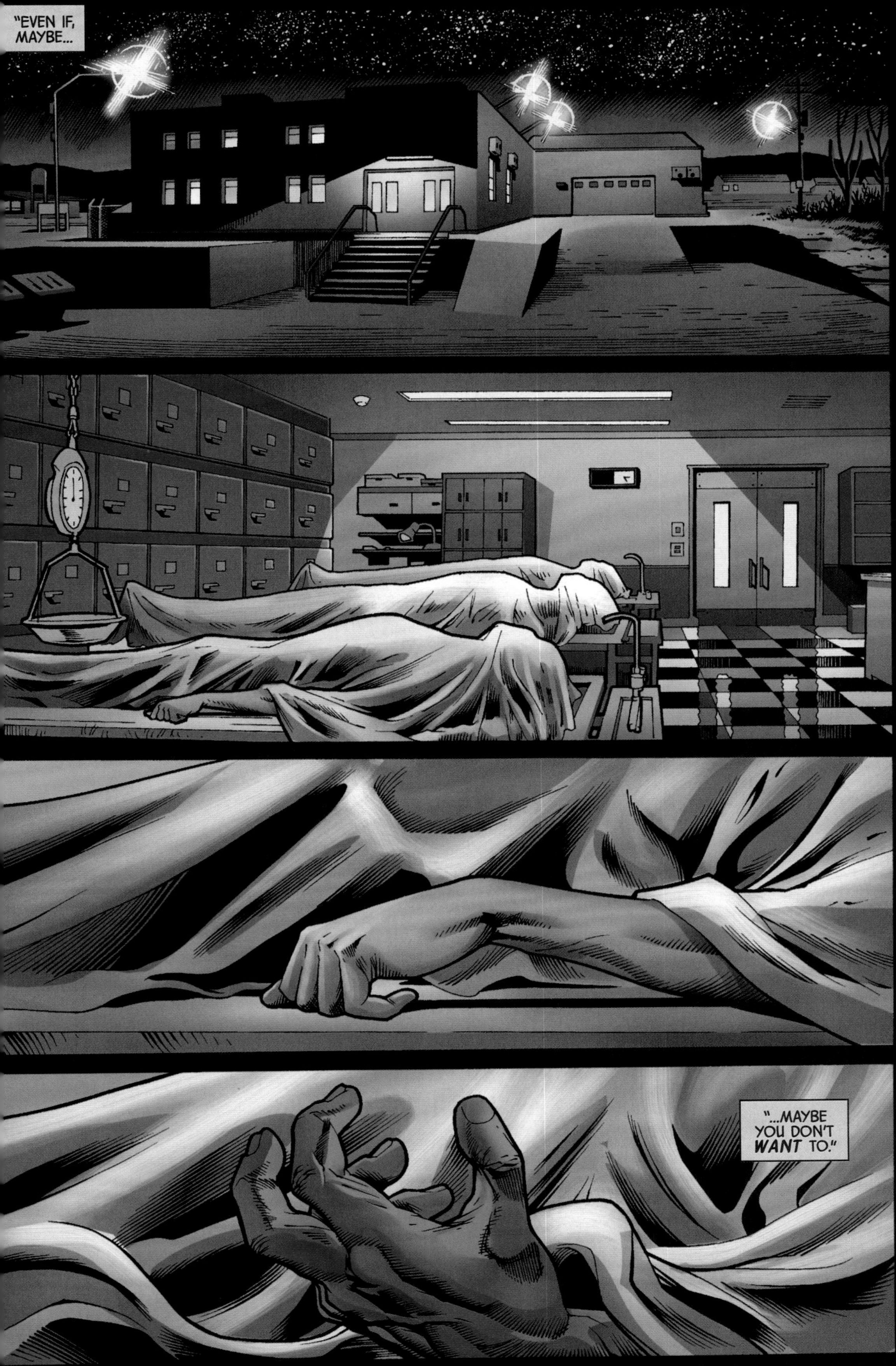
"EVEN IF, MAYBE...
"...MAYBE YOU DON'T *WANT* TO."

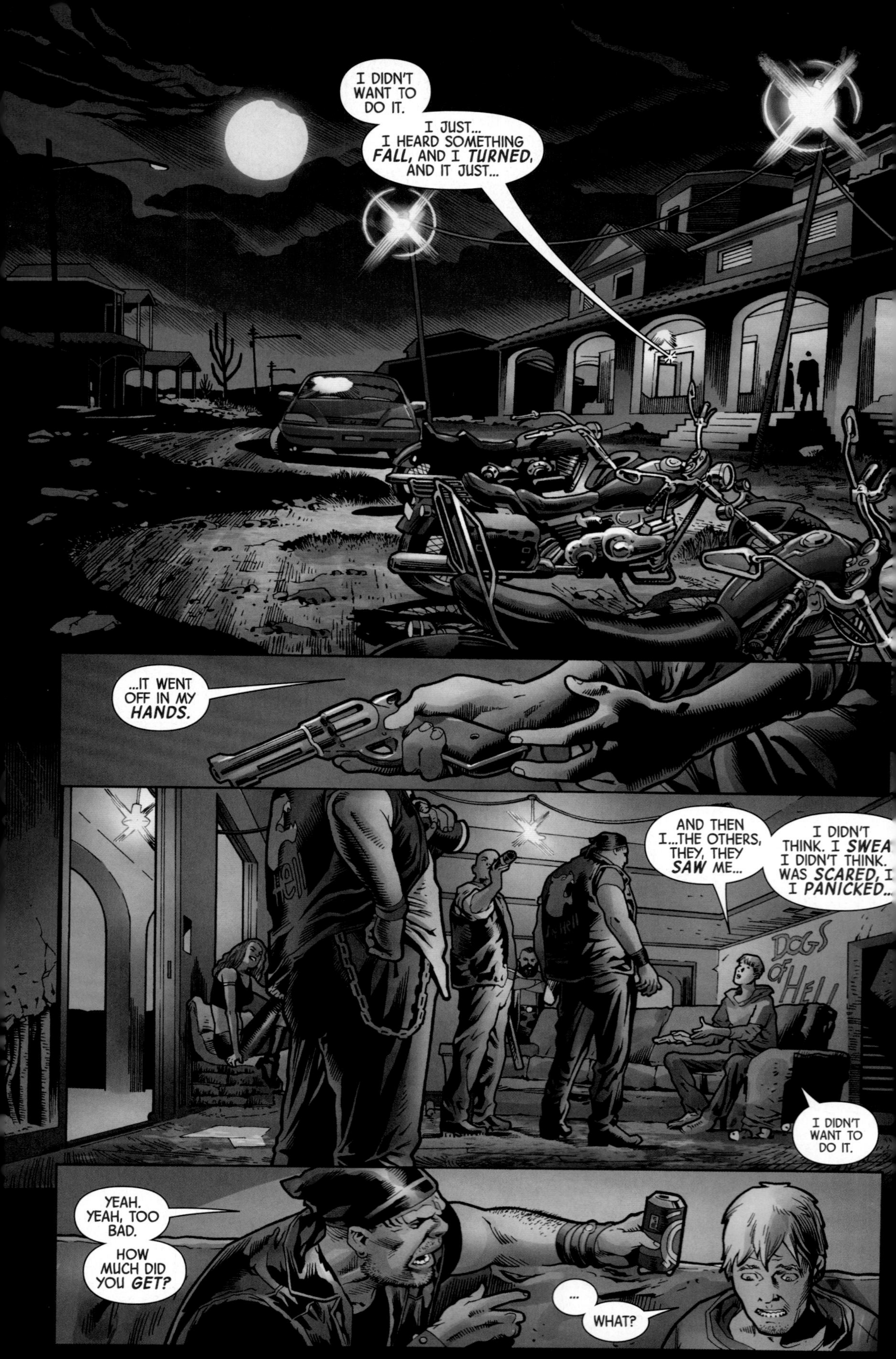
I DIDN'T WANT TO DO IT.
I JUST... I HEARD SOMETHING FALL, AND I TURNED, AND IT JUST...
...IT WENT OFF IN MY HANDS.
AND THEN I...THE OTHERS, THEY, THEY SAW ME...
I DIDN'T THINK. I SWEA I DIDN'T THINK. WAS SCARED, I I PANICKED...
DOGS OF HELL
I DIDN'T WANT TO DO IT.
YEAH. YEAH, TOO BAD.
HOW MUCH DID YOU GET?
...
WHAT?

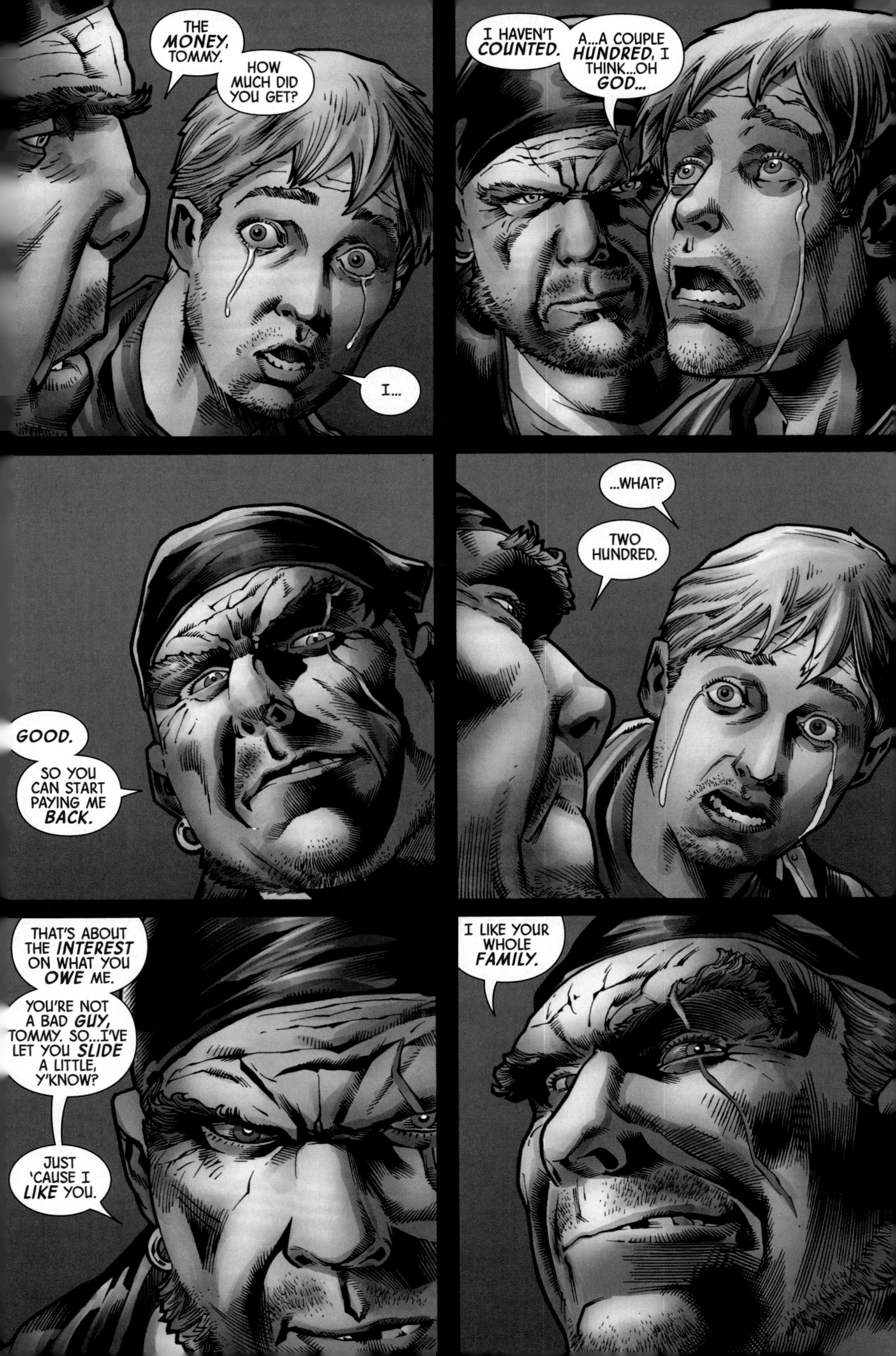
THE *MONEY*, TOMMY.
HOW MUCH DID YOU GET?
I...
I HAVEN'T *COUNTED.*
A...A COUPLE *HUNDRED*, I THINK...OH *GOD...*
GOOD.
SO YOU CAN START PAYING ME *BACK.*
...WHAT?
TWO HUNDRED.
THAT'S ABOUT THE *INTEREST* ON WHAT YOU *OWE* ME.
YOU'RE NOT A BAD *GUY*, TOMMY. SO...I'VE LET YOU *SLIDE* A LITTLE, Y'KNOW?
JUST 'CAUSE I *LIKE* YOU.
I LIKE YOUR WHOLE *FAMILY.*

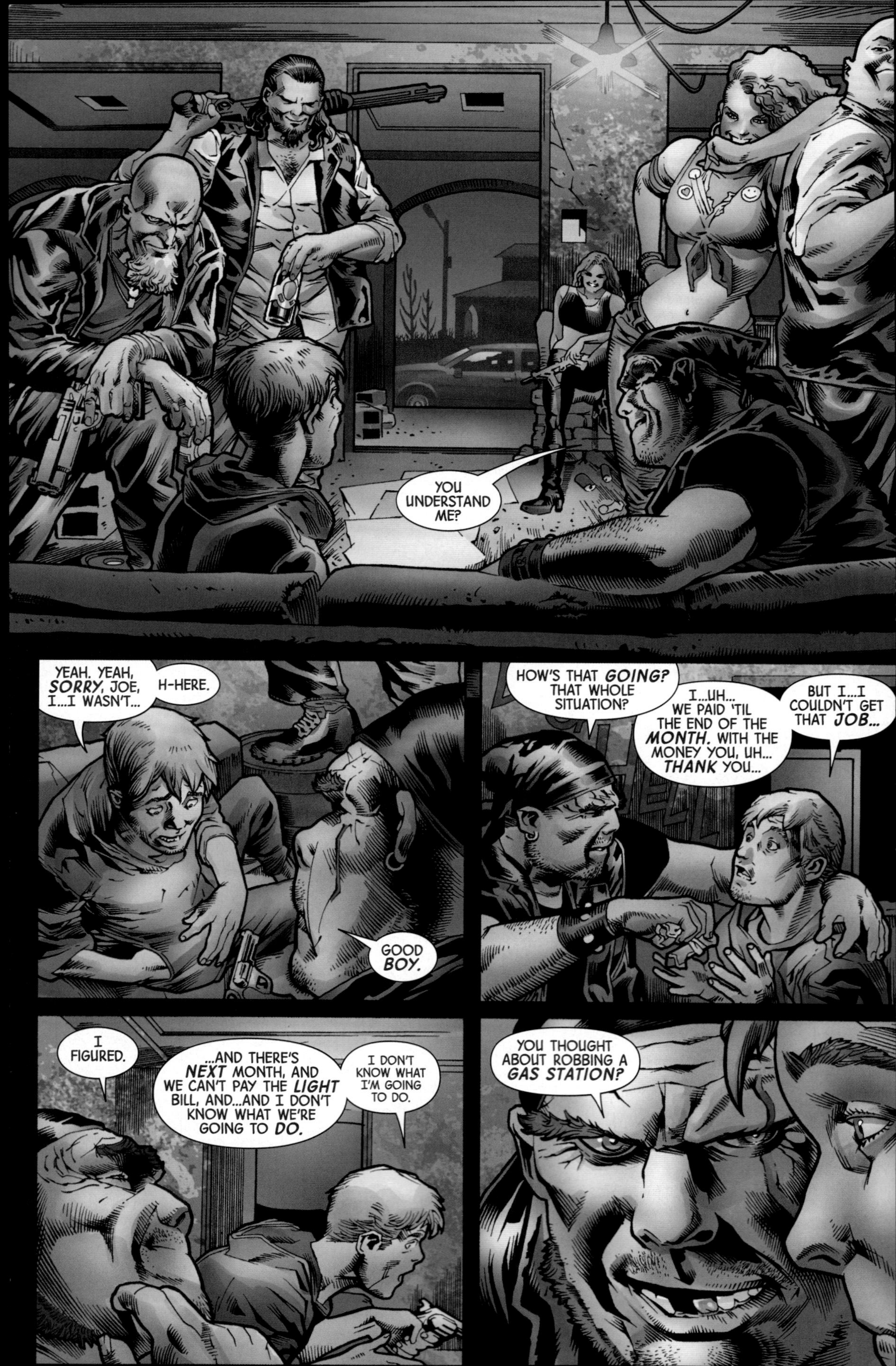

YOU UNDERSTAND ME?
YEAH. YEAH, SORRY, JOE, I...I WASN'T...
H-HERE.
GOOD BOY.
HOW'S THAT GOING? THAT WHOLE SITUATION?
I...UH... WE PAID 'TIL THE END OF THE MONTH. WITH THE MONEY YOU, UH... THANK YOU...
BUT I...I COULDN'T GET THAT JOB...
I FIGURED.
...AND THERE'S NEXT MONTH, AND WE CAN'T PAY THE LIGHT BILL, AND...AND I DON'T KNOW WHAT WE'RE GOING TO DO.
I DON'T KNOW WHAT I'M GOING TO DO.
YOU THOUGHT ABOUT ROBBING A GAS STATION?

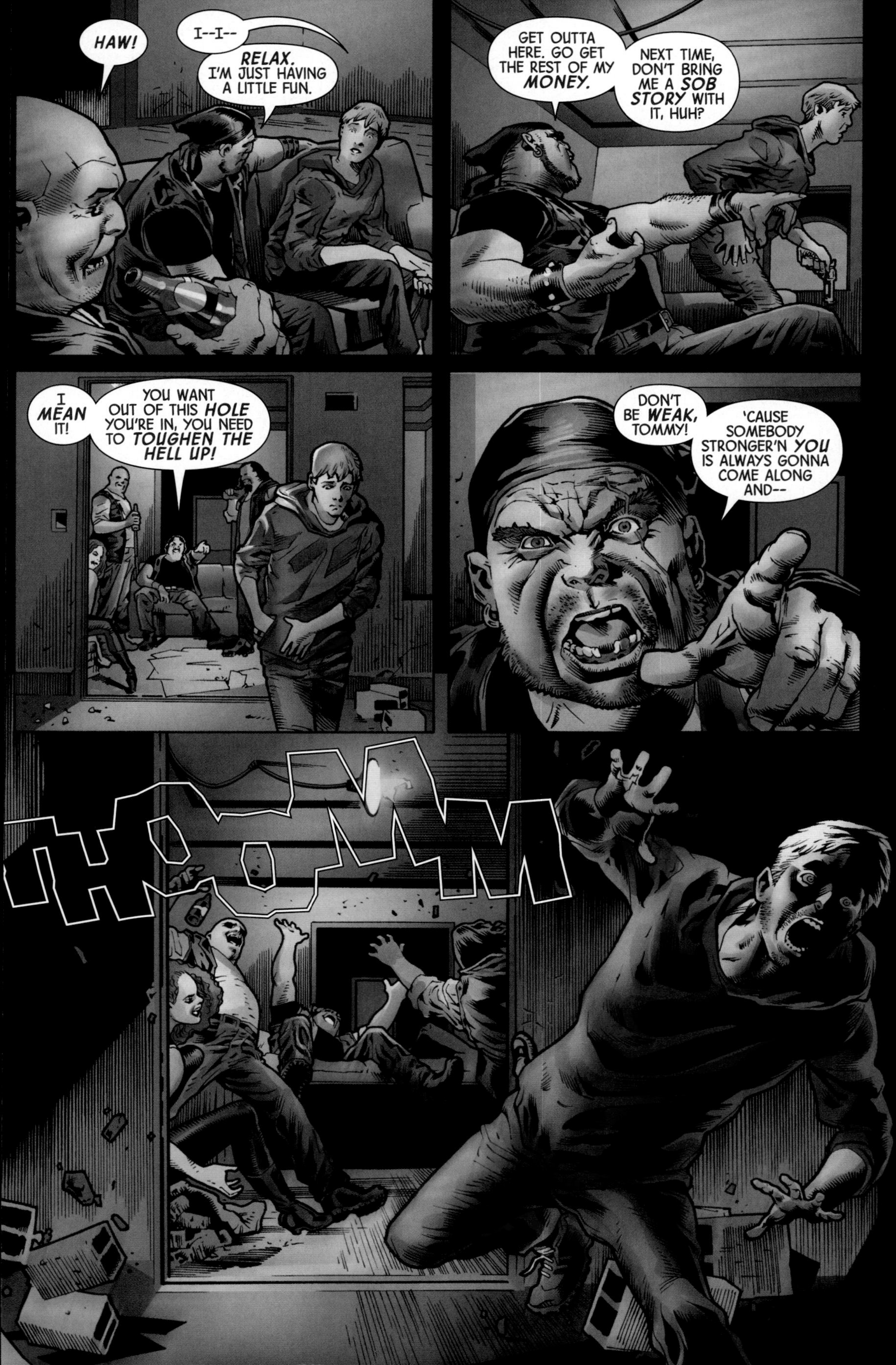
HAW!
I--I--
RELAX. I'M JUST HAVING A LITTLE FUN.
GET OUTTA HERE. GO GET THE REST OF MY MONEY.
NEXT TIME, DON'T BRING ME A SOB STORY WITH IT, HUH?
I MEAN IT!
YOU WANT OUT OF THIS HOLE YOU'RE IN, YOU NEED TO TOUGHEN THE HELL UP!
DON'T BE WEAK, TOMMY!
'CAUSE SOMEBODY STRONGER'N YOU IS ALWAYS GONNA COME ALONG AND--
THOOMM

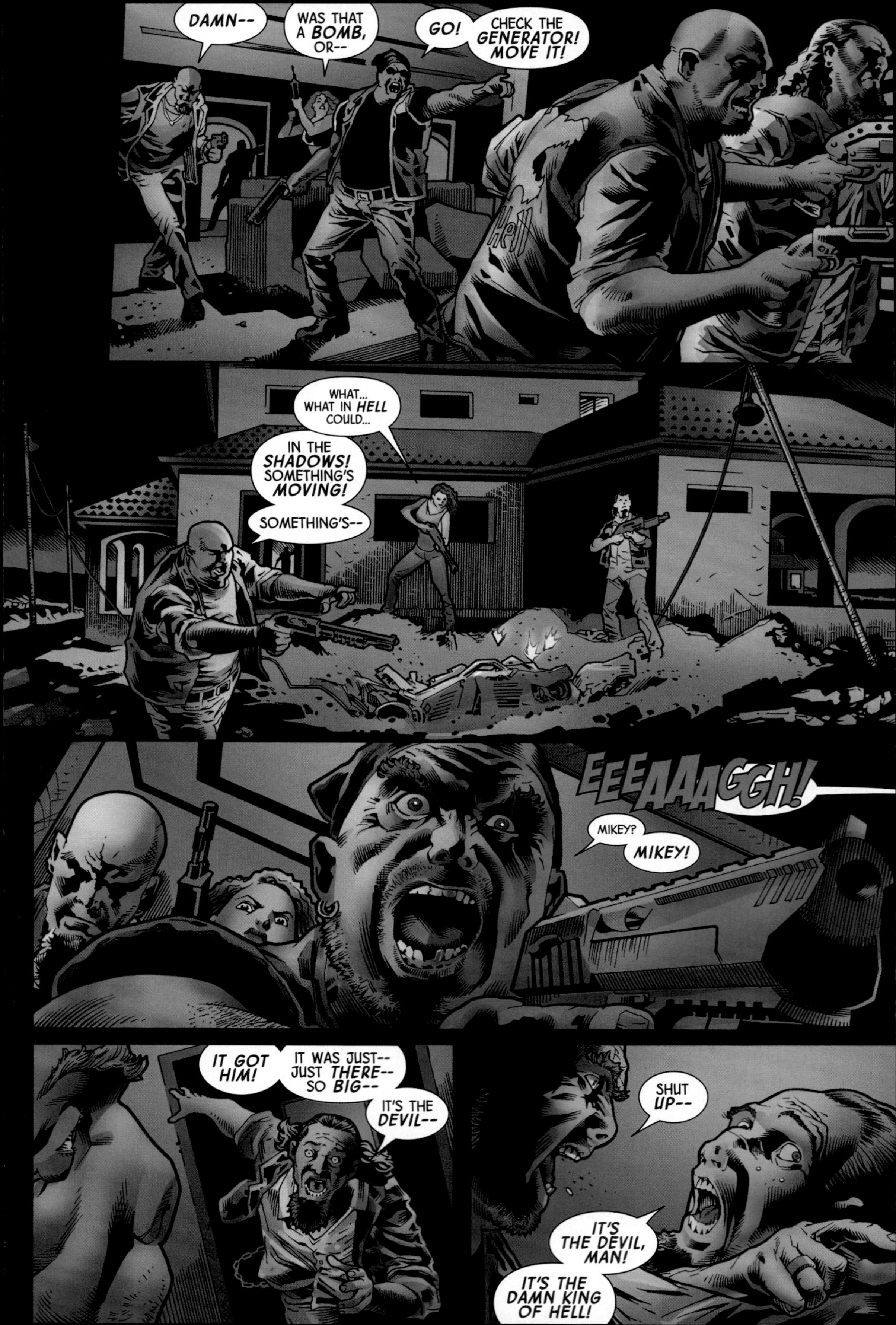
DAMN--
WAS THAT A BOMB, OR--
GO!
CHECK THE GENERATOR! MOVE IT!
Hell
WHAT... WHAT IN HELL COULD...
IN THE SHADOWS! SOMETHING'S MOVING!
SOMETHING'S--
EEEAAAGGH!
MIKEY?
MIKEY!
IT GOT HIM!
IT WAS JUST-- JUST THERE-- SO BIG--
IT'S THE DEVIL--
SHUT UP--
IT'S THE DEVIL, MAN!
IT'S THE DAMN KING OF HELL!

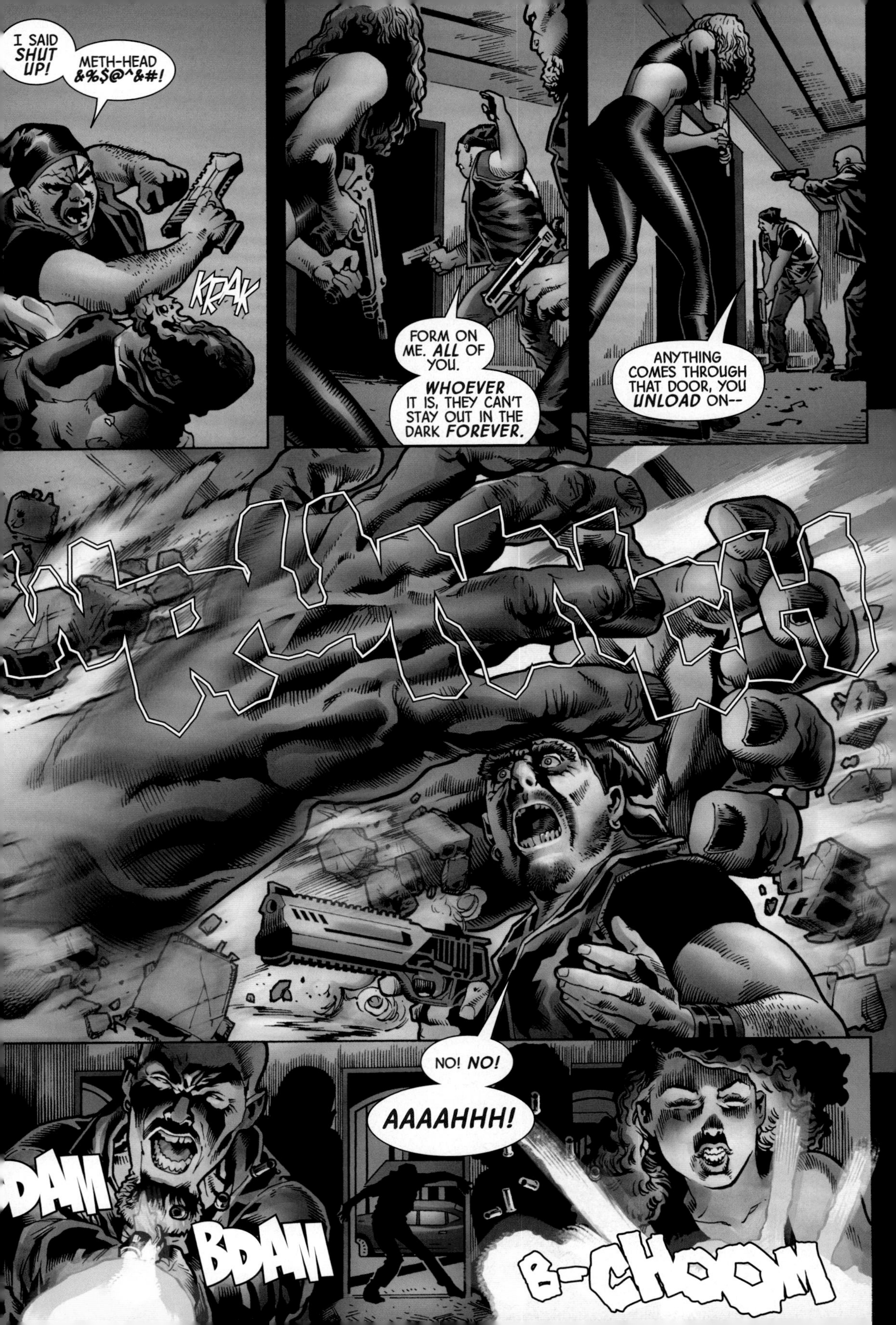

I SAID SHUT UP!
METH-HEAD &%$@^&#!
KRAK
FORM ON ME. ALL OF YOU.
WHOEVER IT IS, THEY CAN'T STAY OUT IN THE DARK FOREVER.
ANYTHING COMES THROUGH THAT DOOR, YOU UNLOAD ON--
NO! NO!
AAAAHHH!
DAM
BDAM
B-CHOOM

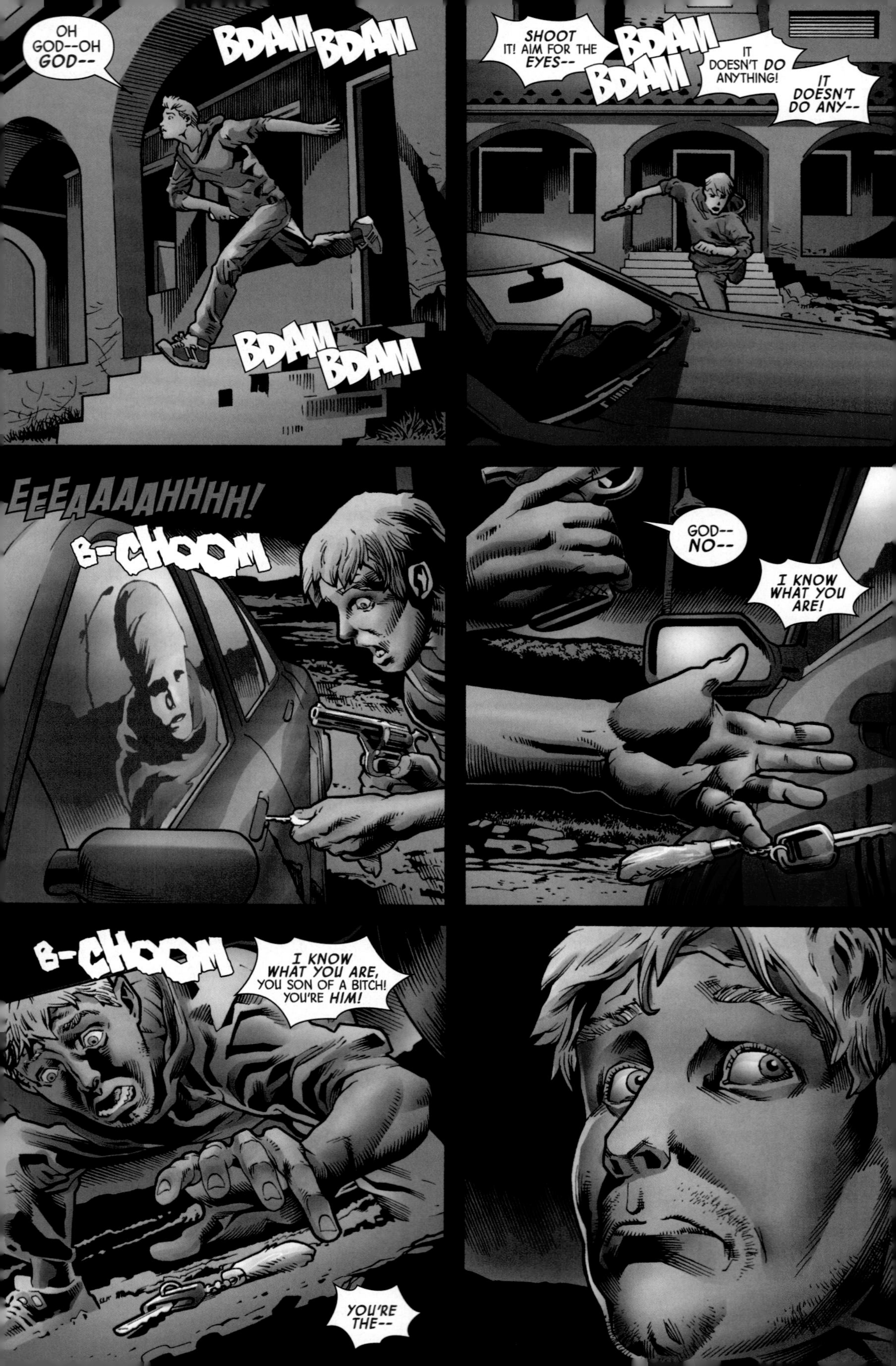
OH GOD--OH GOD--
BDAM BDAM
BDAM BDAM
SHOOT IT! AIM FOR THE EYES--
BDAM BDAM
IT DOESN'T DO ANYTHING!
IT DOESN'T DO ANY--
EEEAAAAHHHH!
B-CHOOM
GOD-- NO--
I KNOW WHAT YOU ARE!
B-CHOOM
I KNOW WHAT YOU ARE, YOU SON OF A BITCH! YOU'RE HIM!
YOU'RE THE--

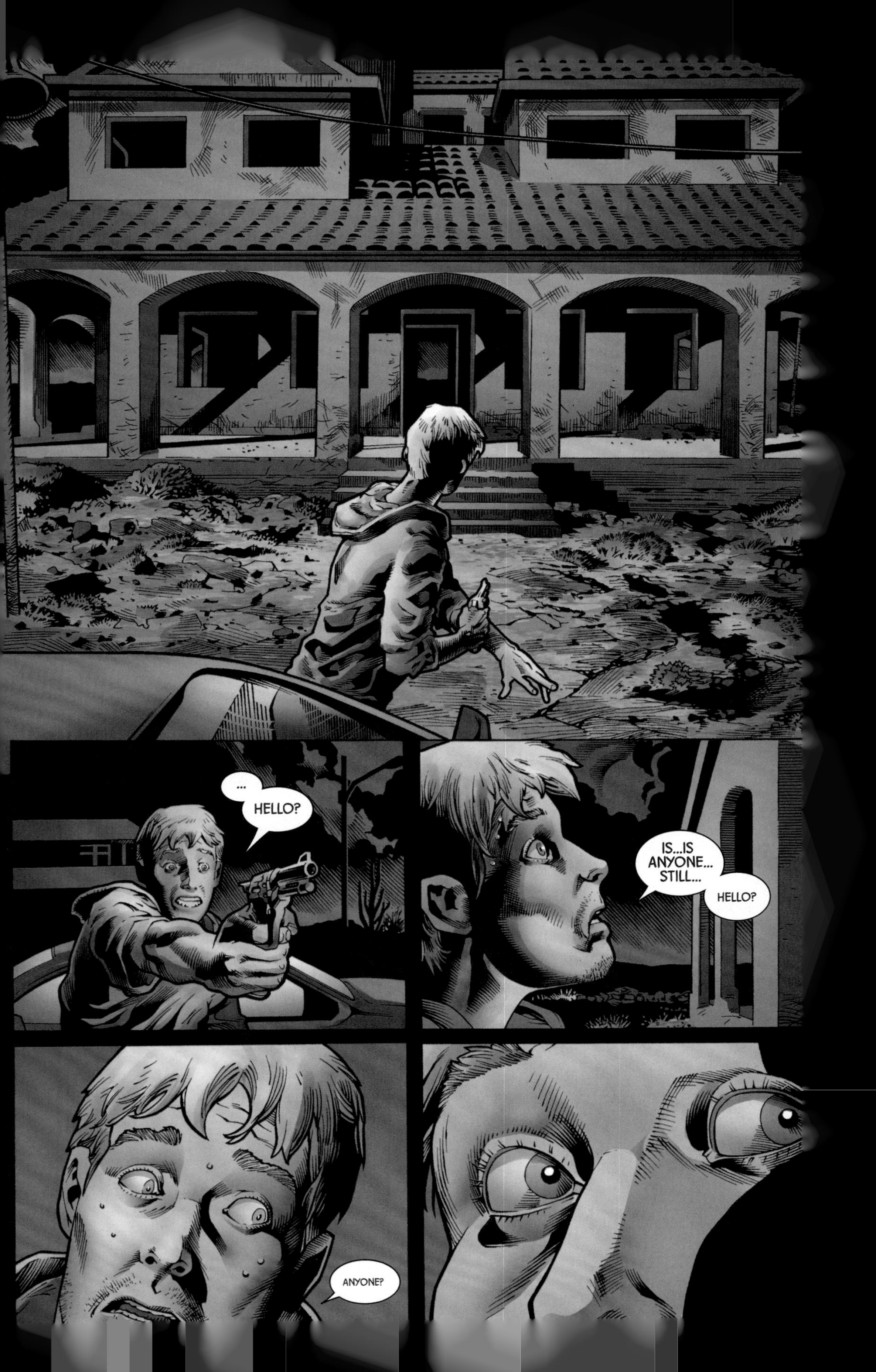
...
HELLO?
IS...IS ANYONE... STILL...
HELLO?
ANYONE?

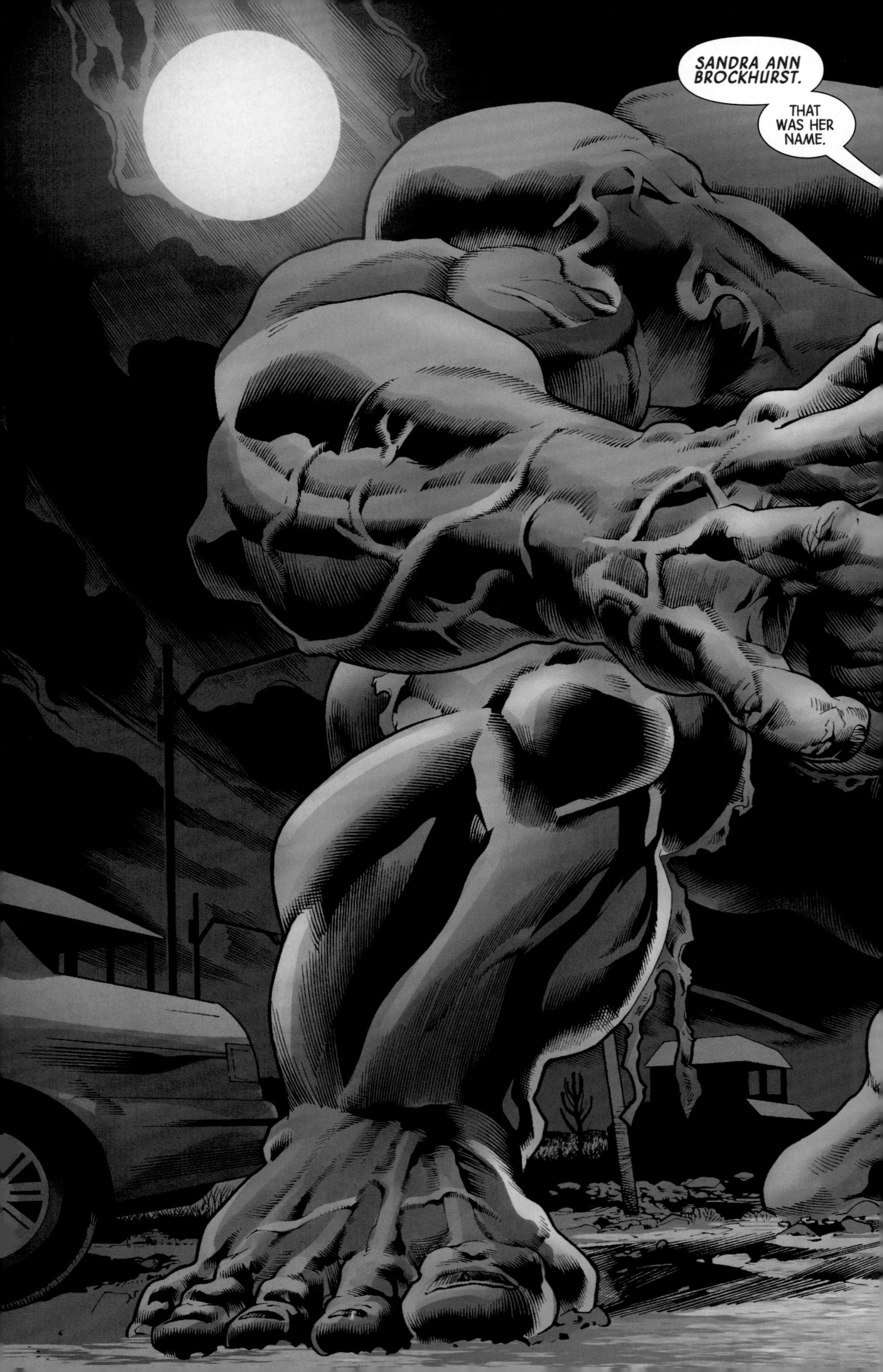
SANDRA ANN BROCKHURST.
THAT WAS HER NAME.

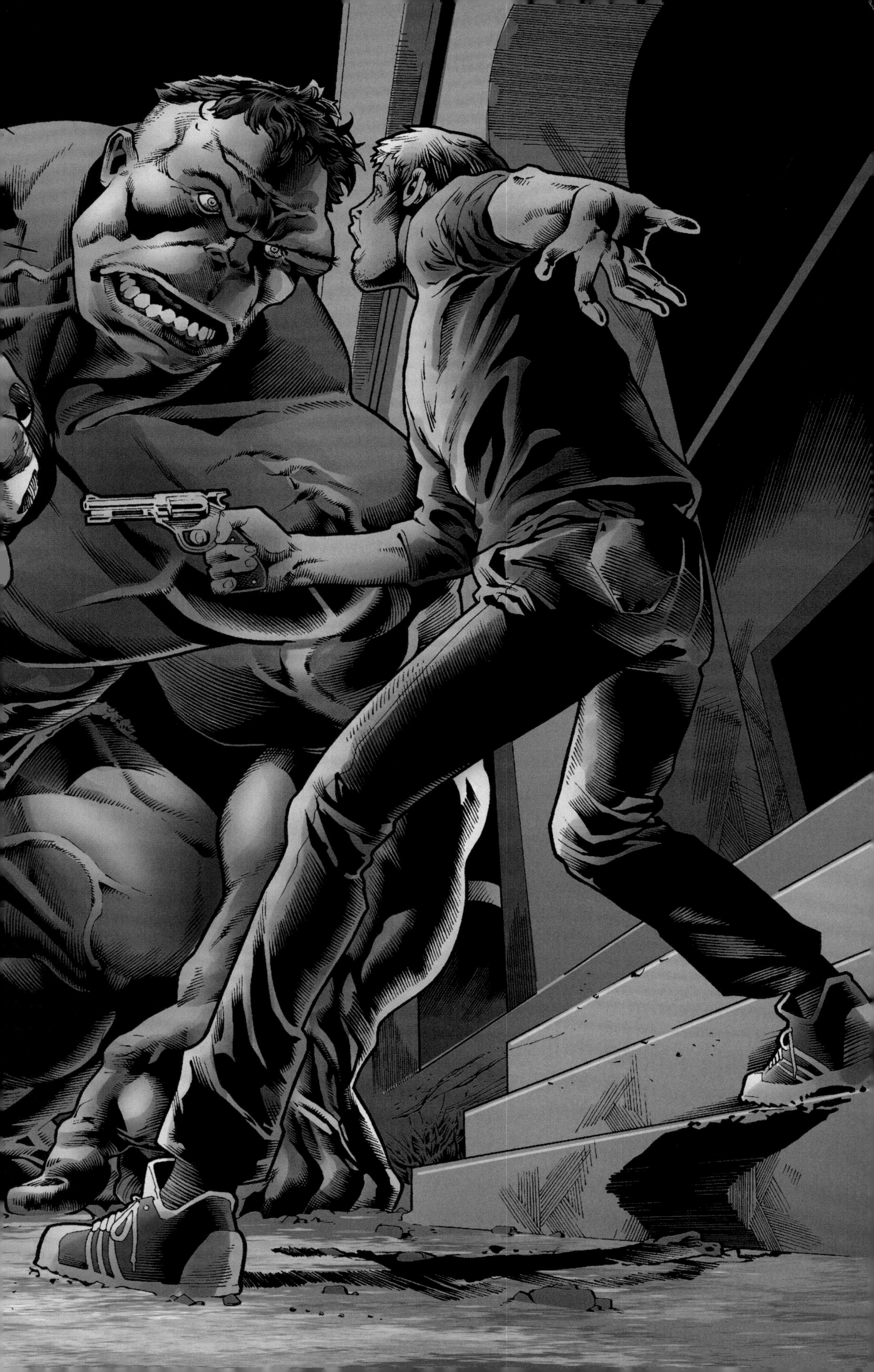

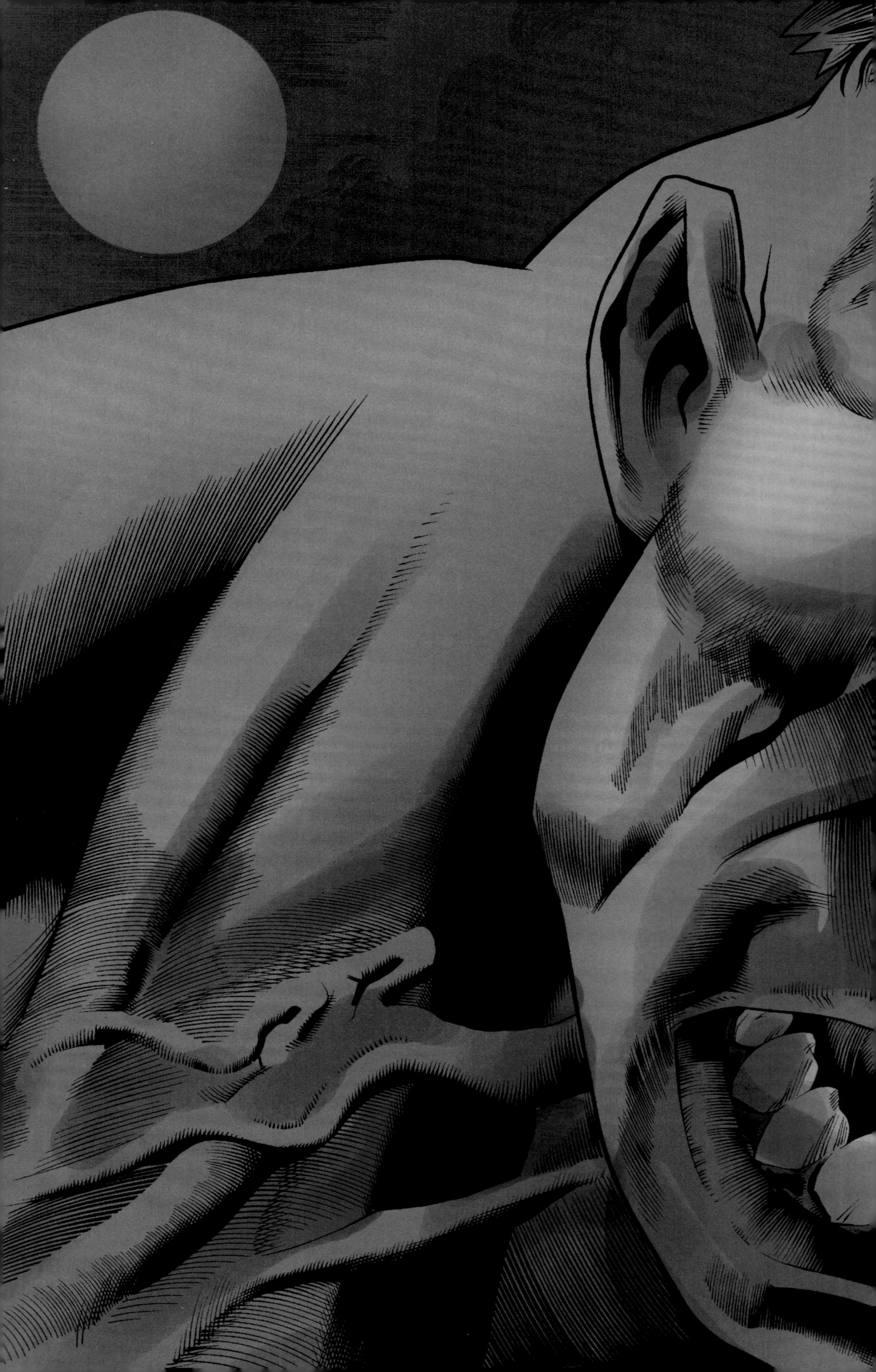

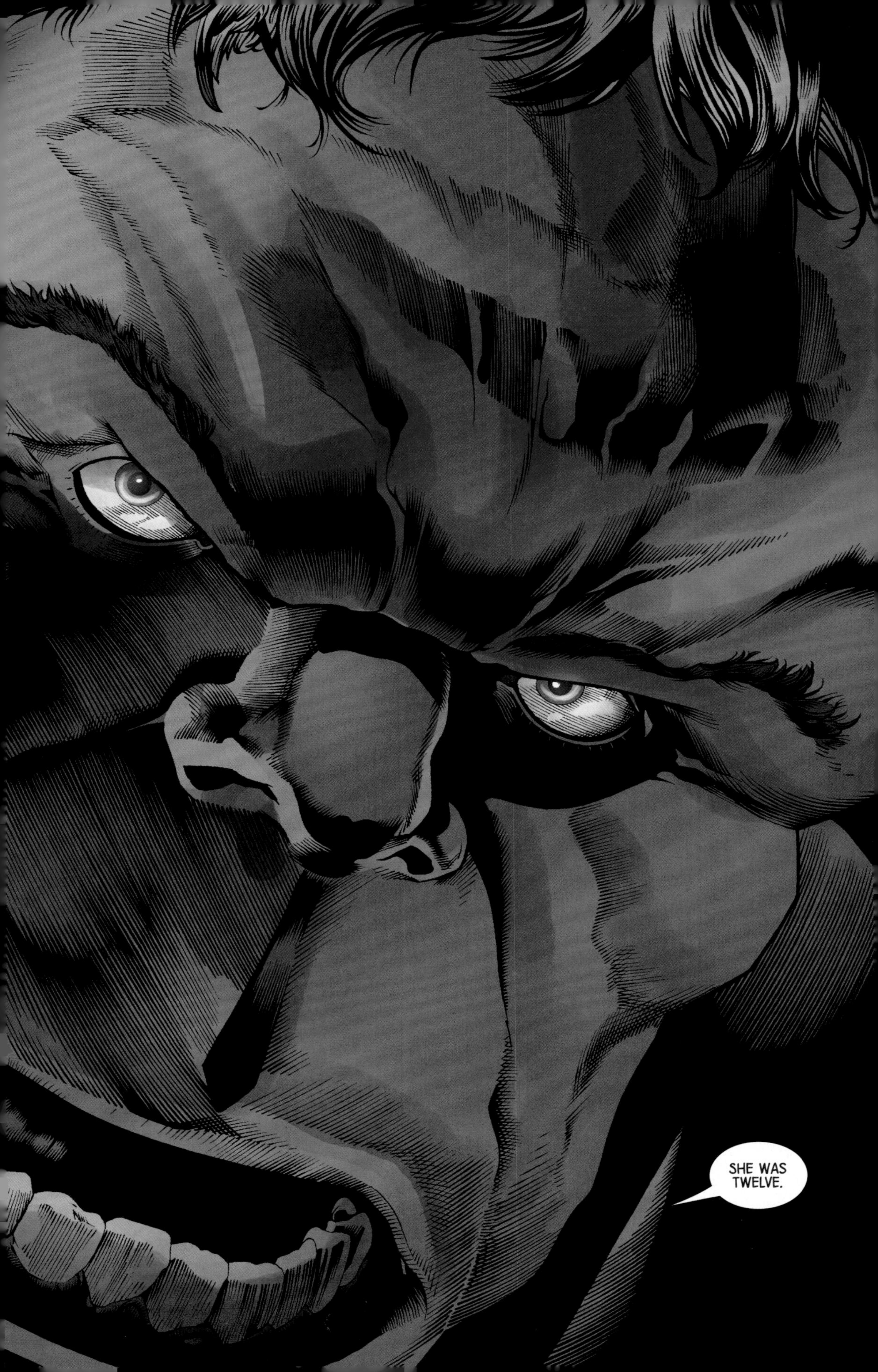
SHE WAS TWELVE.

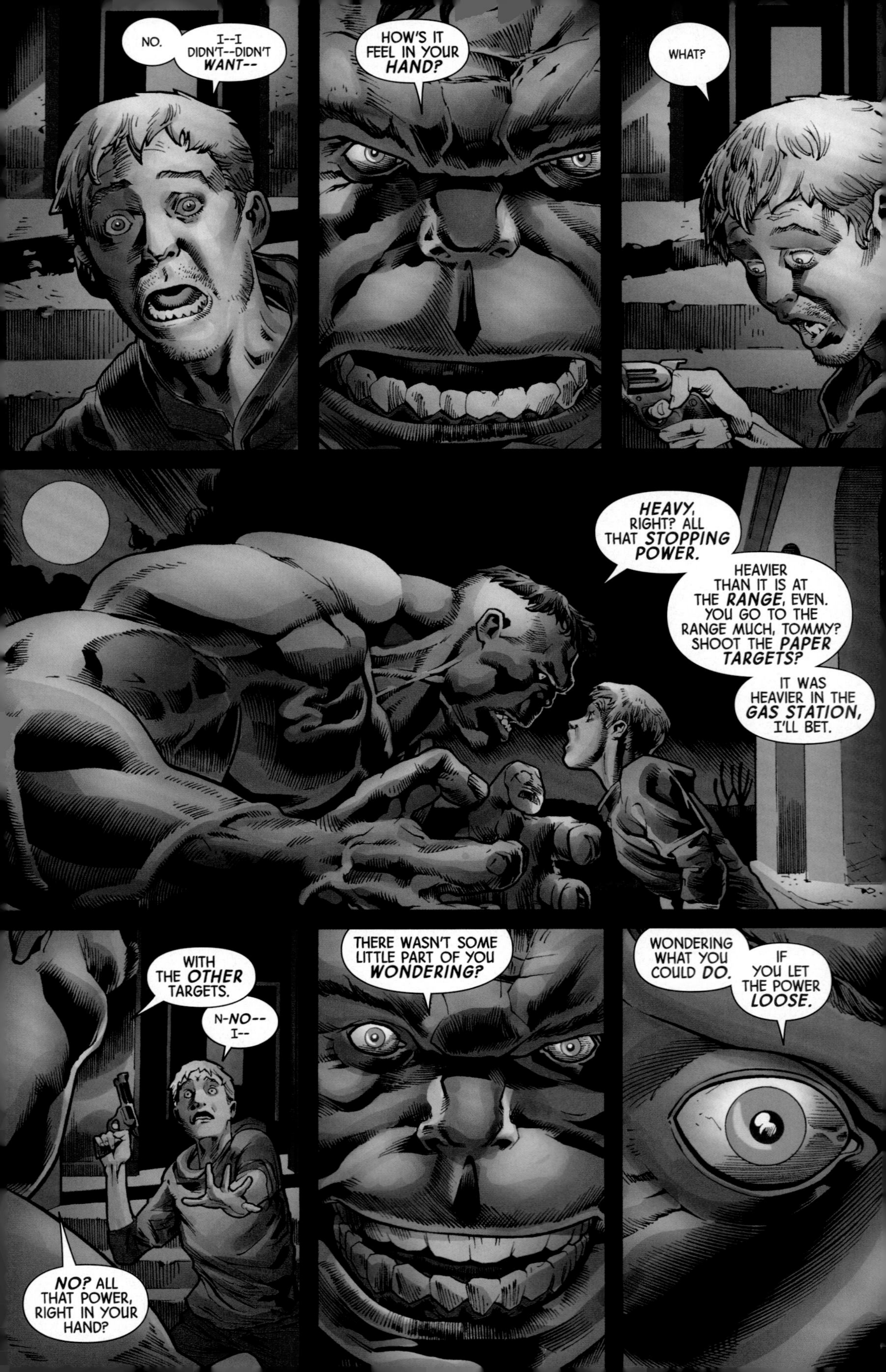
NO.
I--I DIDN'T--DIDN'T WANT--
HOW'S IT FEEL IN YOUR HAND?
WHAT?
HEAVY, RIGHT? ALL THAT STOPPING POWER.
HEAVIER THAN IT IS AT THE RANGE, EVEN. YOU GO TO THE RANGE MUCH, TOMMY? SHOOT THE PAPER TARGETS?
IT WAS HEAVIER IN THE GAS STATION, I'LL BET.
WITH THE OTHER TARGETS.
N-NO-- I--
NO? ALL THAT POWER, RIGHT IN YOUR HAND?
THERE WASN'T SOME LITTLE PART OF YOU WONDERING?
WONDERING WHAT YOU COULD DO.
IF YOU LET THE POWER LOOSE.

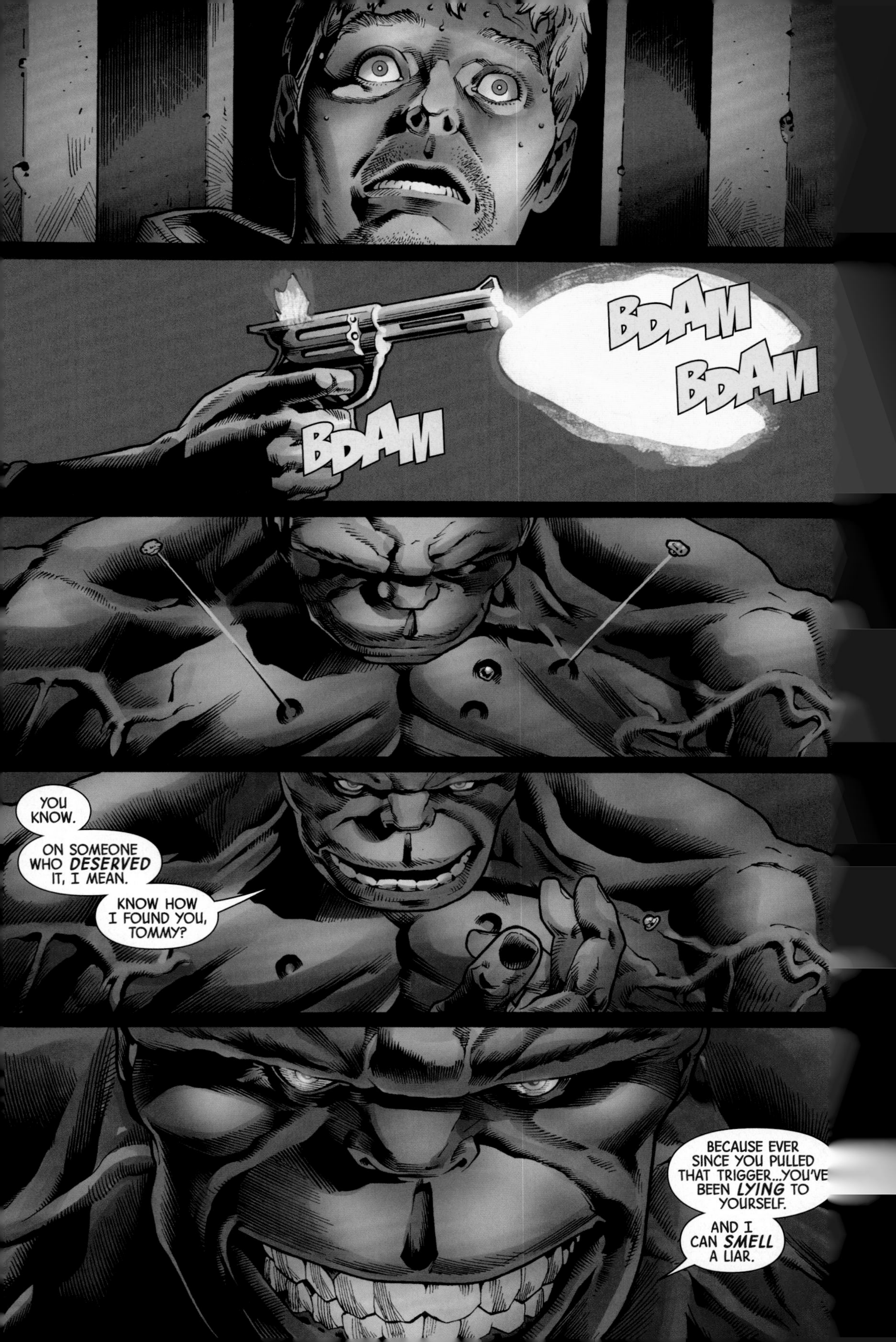

BDAM
BDAM
BDAM
YOU KNOW.
ON SOMEONE WHO DESERVED IT, I MEAN.
KNOW HOW I FOUND YOU, TOMMY?
BECAUSE EVER SINCE YOU PULLED THAT TRIGGER...YOU'VE BEEN LYING TO YOURSELF.
AND I CAN SMELL A LIAR.

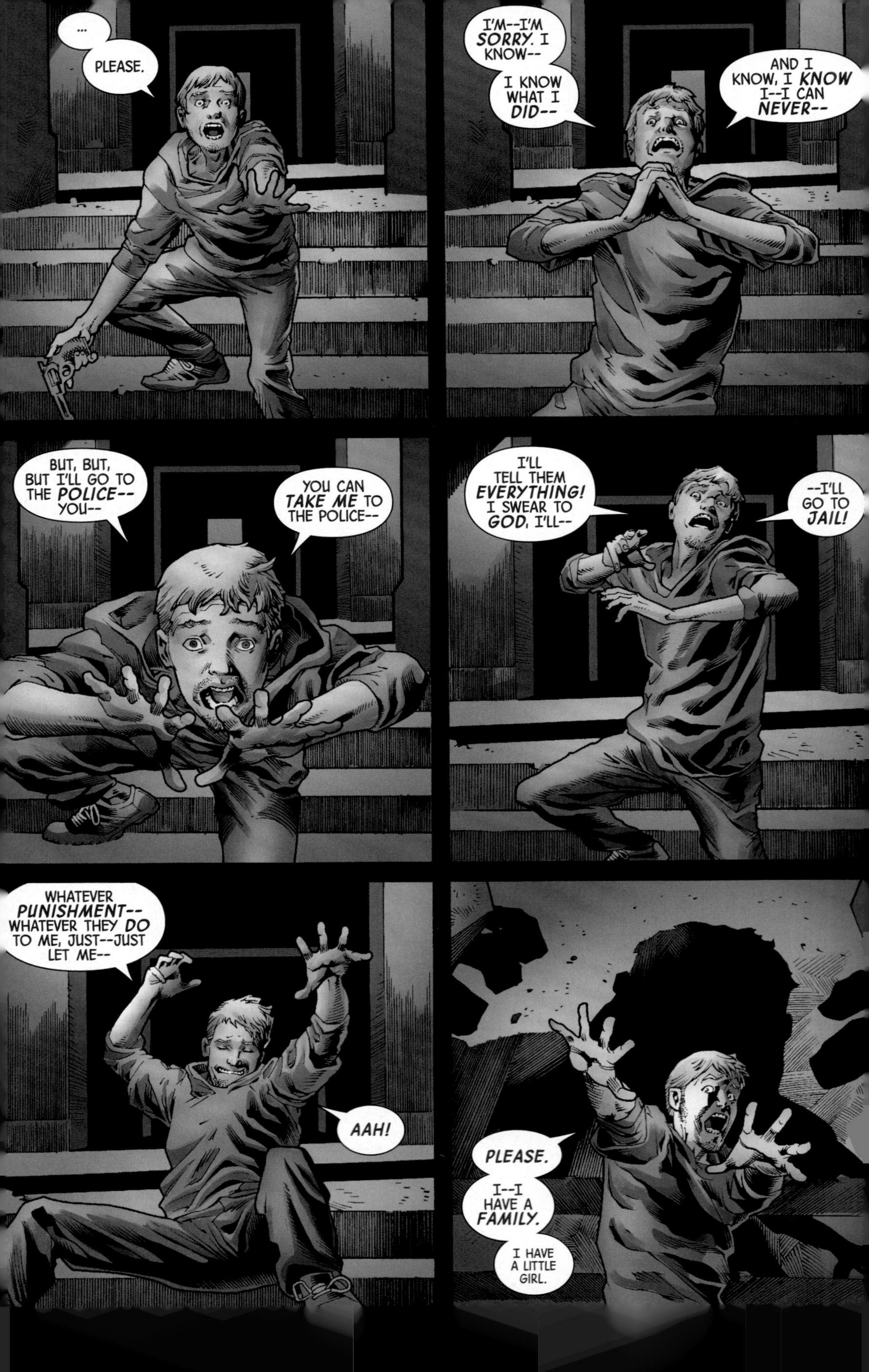
...
PLEASE.
I'M--I'M SORRY. I KNOW--
I KNOW WHAT I DID--
AND I KNOW, I KNOW I--I CAN NEVER--
BUT, BUT, BUT I'LL GO TO THE POLICE-- YOU--
YOU CAN TAKE ME TO THE POLICE--
I'LL TELL THEM EVERYTHING! I SWEAR TO GOD, I'LL--
--I'LL GO TO JAIL!
WHATEVER PUNISHMENT-- WHATEVER THEY DO TO ME, JUST--JUST LET ME--
AAH!
PLEASE.
I--I HAVE A FAMILY.
I HAVE A LITTLE GIRL.

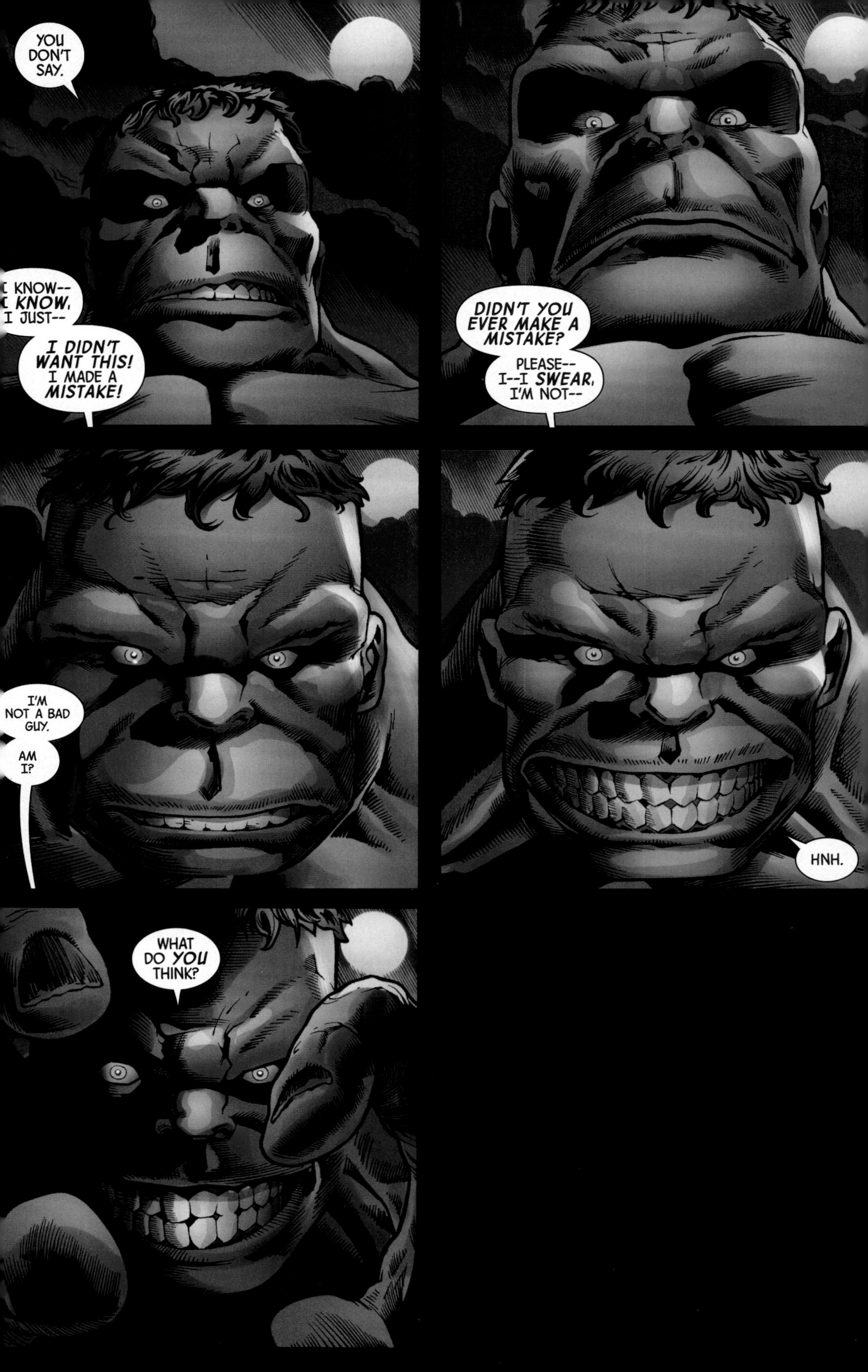

YOU DON'T SAY.
I KNOW-- I KNOW, I JUST--
I DIDN'T WANT THIS! I MADE A MISTAKE!
DIDN'T YOU EVER MAKE A MISTAKE?
PLEASE-- I--I SWEAR, I'M NOT--
I'M NOT A BAD GUY.
AM I?
HNH.
WHAT DO YOU THINK?

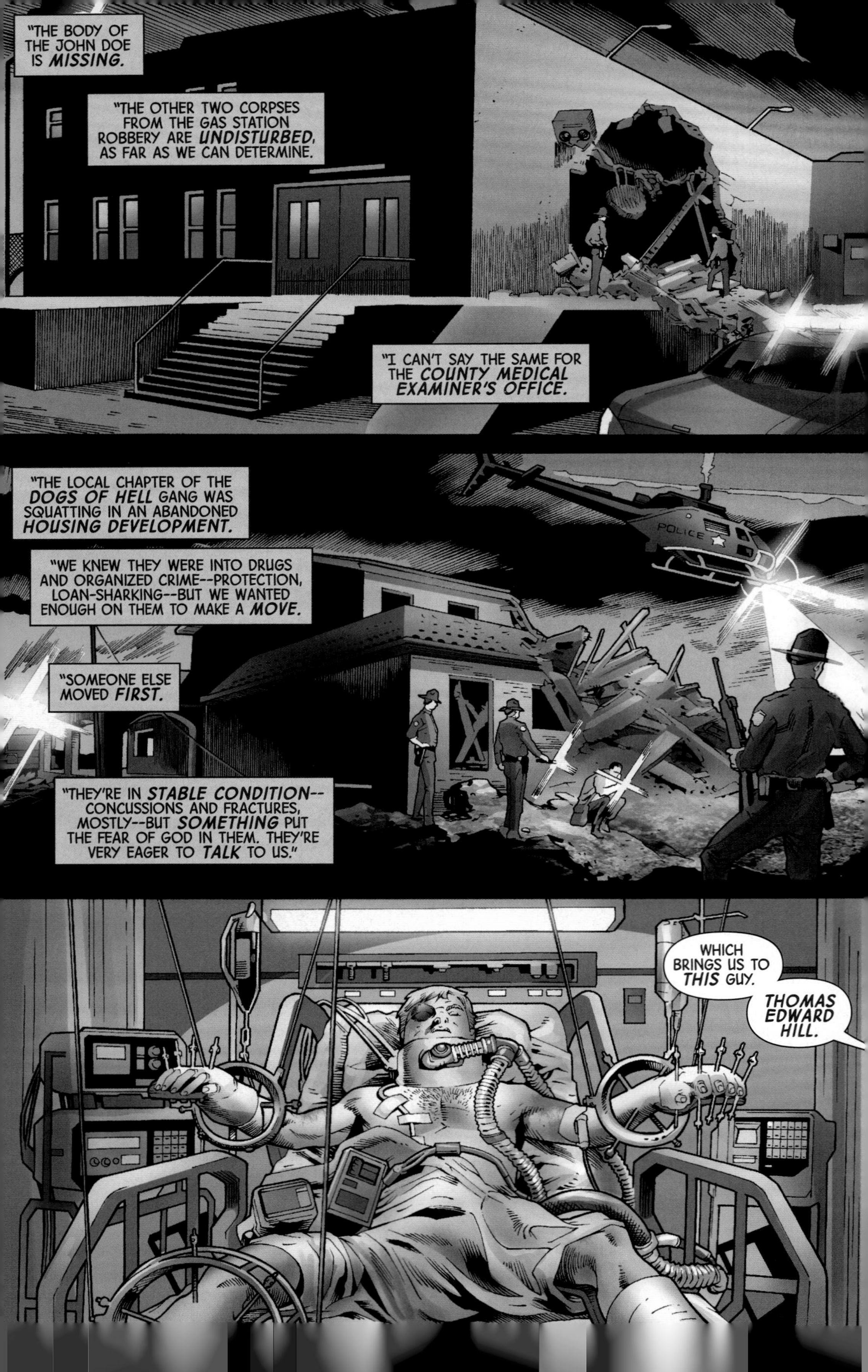
"THE BODY OF THE JOHN DOE IS MISSING.
"THE OTHER TWO CORPSES FROM THE GAS STATION ROBBERY ARE UNDISTURBED, AS FAR AS WE CAN DETERMINE.
"I CAN'T SAY THE SAME FOR THE COUNTY MEDICAL EXAMINER'S OFFICE.
"THE LOCAL CHAPTER OF THE DOGS OF HELL GANG WAS SQUATTING IN AN ABANDONED HOUSING DEVELOPMENT.
POLICE
"WE KNEW THEY WERE INTO DRUGS AND ORGANIZED CRIME--PROTECTION, LOAN-SHARKING--BUT WE WANTED ENOUGH ON THEM TO MAKE A MOVE.
"SOMEONE ELSE MOVED FIRST.
"THEY'RE IN STABLE CONDITION--CONCUSSIONS AND FRACTURES, MOSTLY--BUT SOMETHING PUT THE FEAR OF GOD IN THEM. THEY'RE VERY EAGER TO TALK TO US."
WHICH BRINGS US TO THIS GUY.
THOMAS EDWARD HILL.

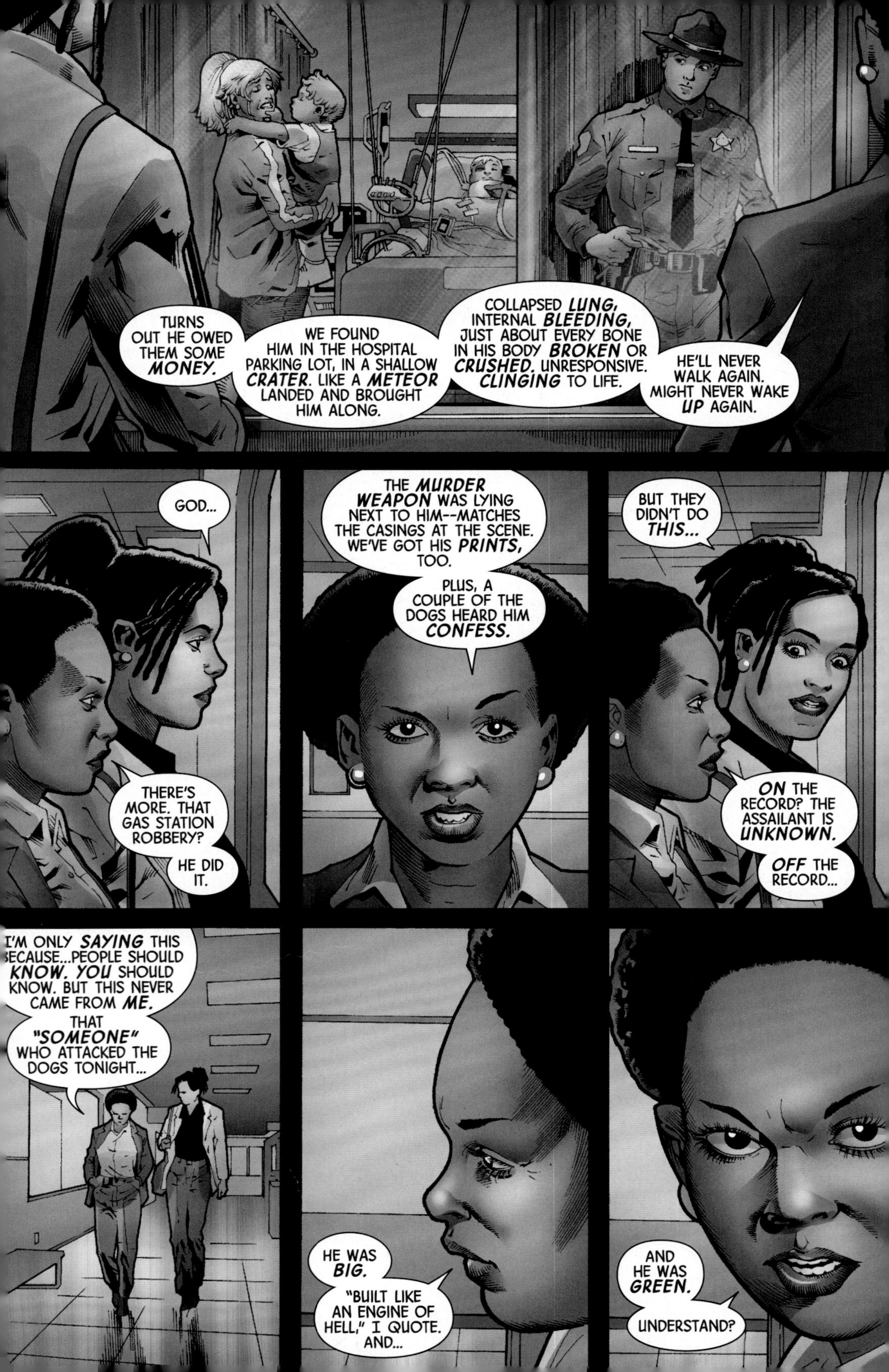

TURNS OUT HE OWED THEM SOME MONEY.
WE FOUND HIM IN THE HOSPITAL PARKING LOT, IN A SHALLOW CRATER. LIKE A METEOR LANDED AND BROUGHT HIM ALONG.
COLLAPSED LUNG, INTERNAL BLEEDING, JUST ABOUT EVERY BONE IN HIS BODY BROKEN OR CRUSHED. UNRESPONSIVE. CLINGING TO LIFE.
HE'LL NEVER WALK AGAIN. MIGHT NEVER WAKE UP AGAIN.
GOD...
THERE'S MORE. THAT GAS STATION ROBBERY?
HE DID IT.
THE MURDER WEAPON WAS LYING NEXT TO HIM--MATCHES THE CASINGS AT THE SCENE. WE'VE GOT HIS PRINTS, TOO.
PLUS, A COUPLE OF THE DOGS HEARD HIM CONFESS.
BUT THEY DIDN'T DO THIS...
ON THE RECORD? THE ASSAILANT IS UNKNOWN.
OFF THE RECORD...
I'M ONLY SAYING THIS BECAUSE...PEOPLE SHOULD KNOW. YOU SHOULD KNOW. BUT THIS NEVER CAME FROM ME.
THAT "SOMEONE" WHO ATTACKED THE DOGS TONIGHT...
HE WAS BIG.
"BUILT LIKE AN ENGINE OF HELL," I QUOTE. AND...
AND HE WAS GREEN.
UNDERSTAND?

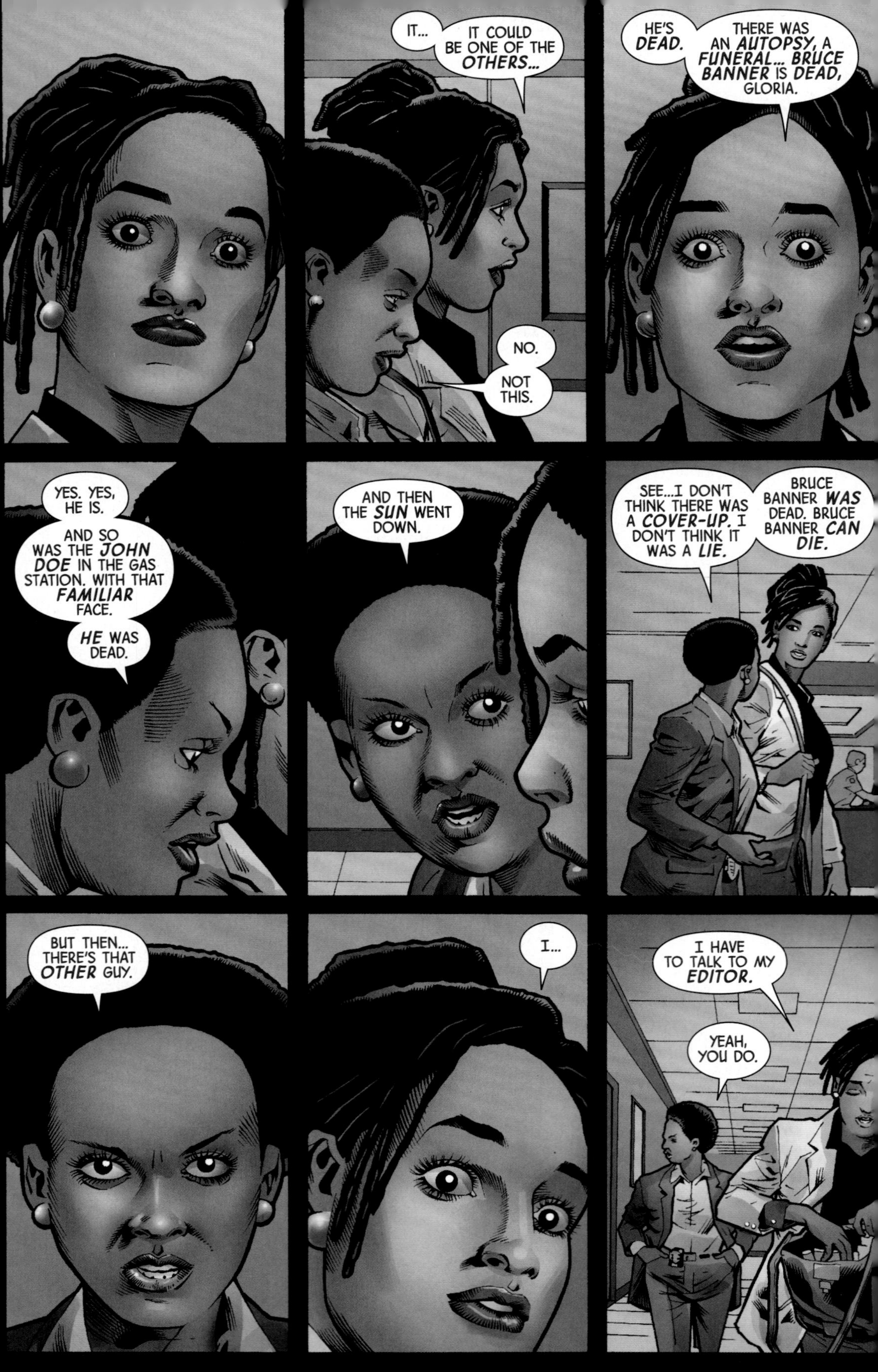
IT...
IT COULD BE ONE OF THE OTHERS...
NO.
NOT THIS.
HE'S DEAD.
THERE WAS AN AUTOPSY, A FUNERAL... BRUCE BANNER IS DEAD, GLORIA.
YES. YES, HE IS.
AND SO WAS THE JOHN DOE IN THE GAS STATION. WITH THAT FAMILIAR FACE.
HE WAS DEAD.
AND THEN THE SUN WENT DOWN.
SEE...I DON'T THINK THERE WAS A COVER-UP. I DON'T THINK IT WAS A LIE.
BRUCE BANNER WAS DEAD. BRUCE BANNER CAN DIE.
BUT THEN... THERE'S THAT OTHER GUY.
I...
I HAVE TO TALK TO MY EDITOR.
YEAH, YOU DO.

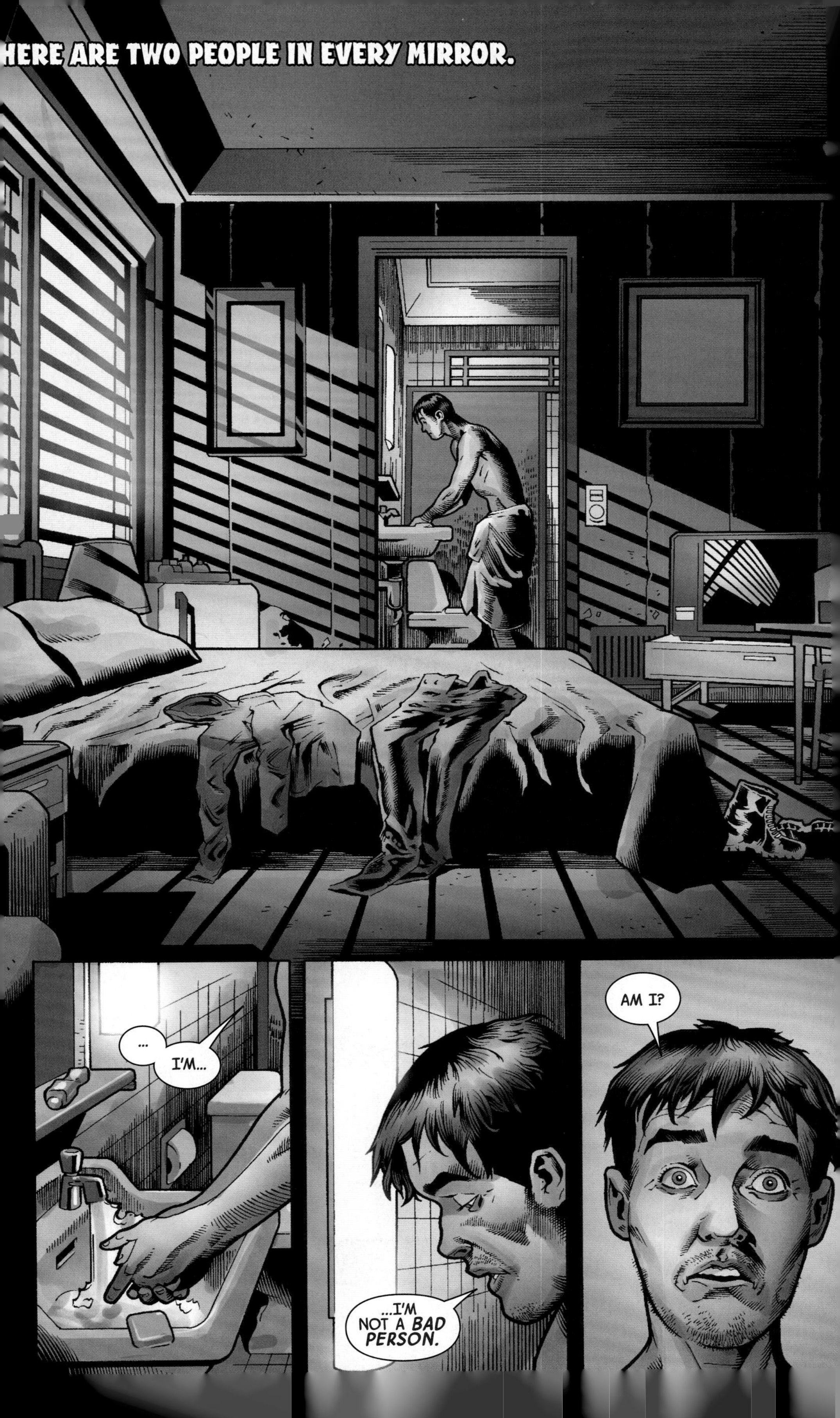
HERE ARE TWO PEOPLE IN EVERY MIRROR.
...
I'M...
...I'M NOT A BAD PERSON.
AM I?

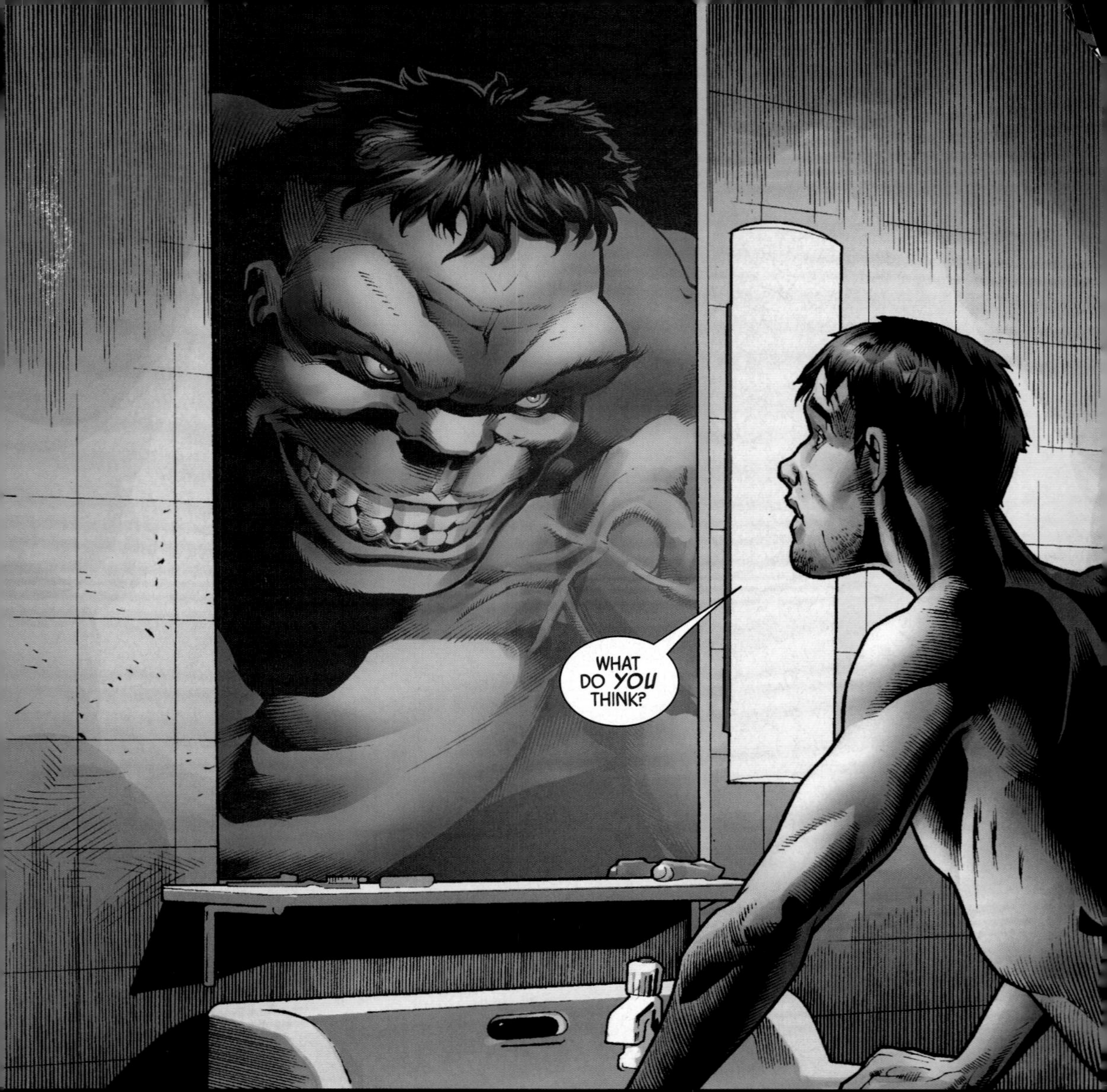
WHAT DO YOU THINK?

OR IS HE BOTH

AL EWING WRITER JOE BENNETT PENCILER RUY JOSÉ INKER
PAUL MOUNTS COLOR ARTIST VC'S CORY PETIT LETTERER ALEX ROSS COVER
CLAYTON CRAIN; KAARE ANDREWS; SAL BUSCEMA, ALFREDO ALCALA & EBER EVANGELISTA; DALE KEOWN & JASON KEITH VARIANT COVERS
ALANNA SMITH ASSOCIATE EDITOR TOM BREVOORT EDITOR C.B. CEBULSKI EDITOR IN CHIEF JOE QUESADA CHIEF CREATIVE OFFICER DAN BUCKLEY PRESIDENT ALAN FINE EXECUTIVE PROD